C000117693

THE ALTERNATIVE
PENNINE WAY

The Alternative Pennine Way

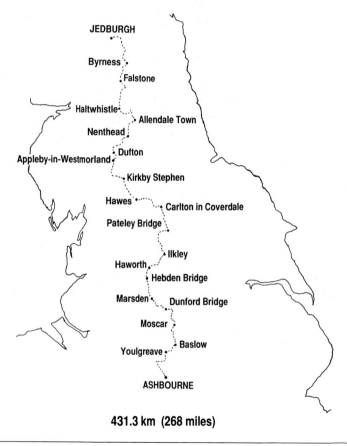

431.3 km (268 miles)

THE
ALTERNATIVE
PENNINE WAY

A Long Distance Walk from Ashbourne
in Derbyshire to Jedburgh on the
Scottish Border

by
Denis Brook & Phil Hinchliffe

CICERONE PRESS
POLICE SQUARE, MILNTHORPE

First Published 1992
© Denis Brook & Phil Hinchliffe
ISBN 1 85284 095 1

Chatsworth,
Bakewell,
Derbyshire,

Foreword

I am delighted to learn of the Alternative Pennine Way. Until recently I have been a very keen walker, counting among my proudest achievements the Lyke Wake Walk. Secondly it will pass through my family's Chatsworth and Bolton Abbey estates.

My son and I are acutely aware of how fortunate we are to have Chatsworth and Bolton Abbey and are most anxious that as many people as possible should have the opportunity to share their beauty. They are both lovely parts of the world and ideal for walking. I hope in years to come countless thousands of people will enjoy this walk with all the beauty and interest it contains.

The Duke of Devonshire
Chatsworth, 1992

Contents

Acknowledgements

Acknowledgement is due to all those who in one way or another have contributed to the compilation of this book, special appreciation going to Malcolm de Selincourt, a mutual friend of the authors, who read all the Features and corrected errors in grammar, spelling and syntax in the original text. He also walked some of the stages and his comments on the maps and map notes have proved invaluable. Particular thanks go to Walt Unsworth, for his advice and guidance on many aspects of our work, and to Brian Evans, for his many comments on legibility and layout. The Forestry Commission, and in particular Bill Burlton, have generously provided reference material and practical help on the forestry stages.

Also, we appreciate the comments made and the practical help given by Sue Arnott of the Yorkshire Dales National Park, Paul Hopkins of the Peak District National Park, Andrew Nicholson of the East Cumbria Countryside Project, David Nortcliffe of Calderdale Leisure Services, Derrick Penrose of the Chatsworth Estate, Tony Philpin of the Countryside Commission, John Sheard of the Bolton Abbey Estate and David Wilson of the National Trust.

The Department of Transport supplied information on the M62 motorway and the Scammonden Dam. Many Tourist Information Centres provided help and reference sources which have proved invaluable, and the Youth Hostels Assocation kindly assisted with information on the whereabouts of hostels.

Denis Brook & Phil Hinchliffe

Preface

We're not quite sure how and when the idea of the Alternative Pennine Way (APW) came about; perhaps it evolved on its own, until it became recognised as a species in its own right, after which it was consciously cultivated. Having lived much of our lives in the southern Pennines and walked there extensively, as well as completing the Pennine Way (PW) in 1972, we were meandering one day on a route of our own making from Holme to Hebden Bridge when it crossed our minds that this route could be extended southwards beyond the Dark Peak and northwards to Scotland. Digging out the OS maps which we had used on the PW (out of date as most of them were), we confirmed that a route could be established using existing rights of way and perhaps some permissive routes. It only remained to research it!

We deliberately designed the APW to be different in character from the PW. It does not always seek the high hills. It is not frightened of the odd kilometre or so on minor roads. It seeks out places of interest where a day could be spent on local exploration instead of forging ahead, and passes through man-made environments as well as the natural environments. In places, it crosses the PW and this extends to the walker the possibility of walking up one route and down the other, in big loops or small loops.

The route is arranged in stages so that, as far as possible (but not always), the length of each is a good day's walk finishing at a place where accommodation is possible (but not guaranteed). Such places usually have sources of provisions, which is not a minor matter on a long distance walk. We are both modest gourmets so, automatically during the research stages, we sought out good places to eat and trust that they remain so for your enjoyment. We have deliberately not listed them nor made comment on their 'gourmet rating', as their existence or rating can change overnight.

We like to think that many of your walking days on the APW will be classed as (our) ideal: a breakfast to suit your personal preference; the day's walk 'cracked' by midday, when a light lunch can be taken; an afternoon's 'stroll' to complete the day's walk in time for you to find accommodation; a hot bath, followed by a preprandial drink; an excellent dinner with a bottle of wine; then the odd drink or two whilst discussing the next day's walk and so to bed to enjoy a good night's rest.

As you can see, we are not masochists or backpackers. Nor do we subscribe to the proposition that to be a 'proper' walker you have to be covered in mud as well as being a purist. We walk to enjoy the whole journey and ourselves, and we do not set out to try to prove anything. (At one time we considered calling this walk the 'Gourmet's Pennine Way' and designing it accordingly, but we would not have got to the hills at all!)

Some readers may ask "Why another long distance route?" Our philosophy is that the more paths there are, then the more thinly will walkers be distributed along their length and the more enjoyable will be the experience. We want you to enjoy your walking and to do it your own way. Backpack if you will, there's plenty of opportunity; or gourmet like us, again there's plenty of opportunity. Above all, enjoy yourselves.

Viator's Bridge, Milldale. (First Stage)

General Notes

It is assumed that anyone attempting this walk, either all of it or in part, will have experience of hill and fell walking, so it should not be necessary for us to list the required contents of a rucksack. However, we emphasise that it is essential to wear strong, but not heavy, waterproof boots and that bivouac gear should be carried (hopefully not to be needed), for if timing goes wrong or accommodation cannot be found. Also a compass is an absolute necessity if the weather turns out to be inclement in certain sections, and for navigating through Kielder Forest.

The APW runs from south to north, only because we are resident near the south end (in SW Yorks). The germ of this idea grew there and the first sorties of research were from our own doorsteps. Besides which, the map-making can follow convention (N at the top) and still be oriented properly for the journey. Because the emphasis of description is on map representation, it should not be difficult to use them for a north to south journey (maybe after having completed the PW from south to north?)

As far as we can ascertain (Scotland excepted), the route follows rights of way (as shown on OS), permissive paths or paths over access land and in one or two places de facto rights of way. Do NOT trespass, even if you think that you ought to be able to take a short cut across a farmer's field or cross private moorland, as such action puts the walking fraternity in a bad light and may be counter-productive as far as future access is concerned. However, in places, we have shown variant routes. We have not shown these formally as definitive routes, since sections of them may not be on rights of way, but they are clearly used by custom. (Our definition of such a route is 'customary' as distinct from 'right of way' or 'permissive'.) Remember that if you choose to use a variant route, you could incur the displeasure of the landowner and/or find it blocked.

The route described is that of our personal choice for your consideration, but we would be disappointed if you followed it metre by metre without deviations. (We offer no prizes for accuracy of navigation.) If you think that a particular part is going to be boring, then find your own alternative. You will have the OS maps with you, like all self-respecting walkers.

The maps in this book must be regarded as sketch maps, but they should be accurate enough for *estimating* topography, distances, heights and directions for the whole journey; however, for precise observations the OS maps must be used. The hierarchy of the maps is as follows:

1. Frontispiece	-	which shows the whole route.
2. Stage Maps	-	Twenty in total, which show each of the stages.
3. Navigational Maps	-	These are drawn to a scale of approx 1:30,000. The National Grid is shown so that easy transfer to the OS maps can be made. Also, the one kilometre squares help in the estimation of distances.
4. Auxiliary Maps	-	At a scale of about 1:15,000 which give detail in navigationally difficult areas.
5. Addendum Map	-	Shows link between APW and Southern Upland Way.

Bearings quoted are referenced to grid north and all the information was correct in 1991, but remember that changes on the ground can occur making your own judgement necessary. The information given should be more than adequate to find your way along the APW, as the emphasis of presentation is graphical, that is by maps, and the words are merely to clarify ambiguous points. Where there is a labyrinth of routes (eg. through towns), we indicate the one we took when researching the route. Often detailed descriptions are silly, as they insult the intelligence of the walker, so we advise taking the way which you fancy, or find yourself on by chance, to reach your objective. We believe that a representation of a route, wherever it is, should be more than a description of a narrow corridor, as inevitable errors of navigation can easily be corrected if off-route information is available. Furthermore, too much detail can clutter the mind, which then has to sort out the 'wood from the trees'. The prime consideration in navigation is to know where you are and where you are aiming for, then maps can be used, together with ground information, to achieve the objective. We hope that the maps and words in this book allow this to happen, and with this in mind they are presented on the visible right-hand side of an opening with an occasional 'enlargement' on the left. Notes of historical and cultural interest are kept separate from navigational details and are always on the left. Drawings are mainly on the left, with the odd one or two on the right to assist with pagination.

Although shown on the maps, the way is not always visible on the ground. But despite this, your own initiative, coupled with the information given, should allow progress without difficulty even in stressful conditions such as when time is running out, when the weather is foul or when you're tired. It is situations like this which we feel highlight the real value of the maps; all the information can be assimilated simultaneously, as distinct from trying to form a picture from information presented serially in words. (We feel that information like "turn right at the third stile by the signpost" is of dubious value, as the stile might now be a gate and the signpost might have been removed by vandals.) In only two places do we refer to signposts - can you find them, and suggest why these two? No prizes offered. If words have to be used, then the maps have failed - usually due to limitations of scale!

We realise that some people can't come to terms with maps, but we remain adamant on this point and maintain that such people should not venture onto the hills unless accompanied by someone familiar with maps. This book is for the 'map person'.

During the shooting season (August 12 to December 10), certain open access moorland areas are closed on some days. Thus permissive paths could be closed and free access suspended. (This should not affect rights of way.) Before setting out in this period, you should check with the relevant authorities (addresses in appendix). However, in times of closure, notices giving appropriate information are usually posted at each access point, but it is better to check before attempting access to avoid disappointment. However, in the Dark Peak where closure in the shooting season could be a problem, we have shown a variant which uses a right of way.

Whilst every effort has been made to represent the route accurately on the maps and give a correct description, neither the authors nor the publisher can accept any responsibility in connection with any trespass arising from the use of the definitive route or any associated route.

Normally we walk either alone or just the two of us, as we seek the solitude of the open air and the lack of need to engage in continuous conversation. Occasionally, however, we 'allow' a party of three or four.

Consequently, we can (hopefully) move through the countryside without anyone knowing we have passed and with the minimum disturbance to wildlife. How much more you see when you are alone, or with just one or two friends! We hope that you will walk the APW, making your own modifications and in parties no greater than four. We also suggest that you do not take your dog with you, as he will need to be on a lead, most of the time, giving him no fun. He may also disturb sheep and wildlife. In addition, we request that you follow temporary diversions, arising due to countryside activities such as lambing and harvesting (either farm or forestry).

For four reasons, we suggest that the walk is not undertaken in August. Firstly, the weather is rarely good, making ground conditions atrocious and secondly, you may have problems with access (factors relevant to the whole route, not just the High Peak). Thirdly, accommodation may be difficult to find and finally, accommodation will be more expensive.

ALWAYS FOLLOW THE COUNTRY CODE

List of Symbols

▬ ▬ ▬ ▬ ▬	APW Definitive Route
▬▬▬▬▬▬	APW on road or track. Fenced, unfenced
▬▬▬▬▬	APW on fenced path
▬▬▬▬▬▬	APW on ride in Kielder Forest
▬▬ • ▬ • ▬▬ •	APW variants
....	Other paths (*)
XXXXX XXXXX	Metalled roads. Fenced, unfenced
≡≡ ≡≡≡	Tracks. Fenced, unfenced
∿∿∿	Brooks, Burns, Becks, Rivers
- - - - - - -	Contours, normally at 10-metre intervals
△ 520	Trig. Points with height in metres (*)
♨	Cairns (*)
X V	Gate or Stile (shortened form) (*)
‿	Bridge (*)
f b	Footbridge (*)
⛻	Picnic Site
🚗	Car park
☎	Public Telephone
🚻	Public Toilets
⟍⚡⟍	Electricity Transmission Line

ᘁᘁᘁ	Rock Outcrops
▬ı	Buildings
⌐┤	Fence or Wall near APW (*)
A **B** **◈**	References to Map Notes
	* Only shown when useful for navigation

Definition of Terms

Road — A way which is metalled and intended for 'normal' motor vehicles.

Lane — A way along which a motor vehicle could be driven with care, but certainly a way on which a tractor would have no difficulty.

Track — A way along which walking is easy even if the surface is rough, but along which a tractor would have difficulty.

Path — A way along which only foot passengers can pass, (could also be a bridleway).

Trod — A way made by sheep or other animals, useful for walking.

Edge — A way with steep rocks falling away on one side.

Ridge — A narrow way with steep rocks falling away on both sides.

Rigg — A broad way with land falling away on both sides.

N, SE, etc. — Approximate bearings.

25°, 217°, etc. — Reasonably accurate bearings.

S — Shops (*)

A — Accommodation (*)

F — Place which provides food, etc. inn or restaurant (*)

I — Tourist information centre (*)

* — On Stage Maps only

14

The Route

FIRST STAGE:
ASHBOURNE TO YOULGREAVE
Derbyshire Limestone Gorges and Farms
28.5 kilometres, 17.7 miles

The APW begins at Ashbourne, at the southern end of the Tissington Trail. It follows this trail, which is the course of a disused railway, for about 3.5 kilometres northwards when it leaves to go west towards Izaac Walton country. The route is then that of the tourist path up Dove Dale for about 6 kilometres and, when this swings north-west to ascend Wolfscote Dale, the APW leaves to continue northwards up Biggin Dale.

Passing through Biggin allows you to take lunch at the inn, although a shorter route is possible if this facility is not needed. Proceeding eastwards, it crosses the Tissington Trail to join the High Peak Trail for a short stretch. A 0.5 kilometre road walk takes the route to enter Gratton Dale, down which it goes for 2.0 kilometres. A walk across fields brings you into the gorge of the River Bradford, alongside disused cress beds and then up into Youlgreave.

The route is pleasant, with lots of variety; changing between limestone gorges and good agricultural land, woods and open spaces. The highest point is no more than 390 metres. In wet weather the walking will not be difficult, except for a few places which are boggy (even in dry weather).

If you take lunch at Biggin, the only provisions required will be snacks and drinks and, since the APW is never far from habitation, emergency rations need not be as plentiful as in later stages. If departure from Ashbourne is later than expected, then short cuts are available in places. Indeed, if you are one of those who wants to cover lots of miles in the shortest possible time and walk through the countryside rather than in it, then you could follow the Tissington Trail all the way from Ashbourne to Biggin and then transfer to the APW proper. But beautiful Dove Dale will be missed.

There is plenty of accommodation in Ashbourne. At Youlgreave, there is hotel and youth hostel accommodation, and B & B facilities nearby. There are shops in the village for restocking provisions.

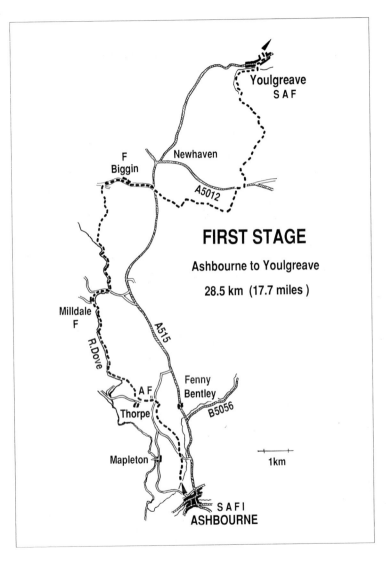

Youlgreave
S A F

F Biggin
F

Newhaven

A5012

FIRST STAGE

Ashbourne to Youlgreave

28.5 km (17.7 miles)

A515

Milldale
F

R.Dove

A F

Fenny
Bentley

Thorpe

B5056

Mapleton

1km

S A F I
ASHBOURNE

ASHBOURNE

In one of the publicity brochures Ashbourne is described as "A good centre for walking in the Derbyshire Dales and gateway to the Peak District. A market town enfolded in the hills and dales". What we would like to see added in future publications is "The start of the Alternative Pennine Way - An adventurous long distance walk"!

It is, of course, quite appropriate that the APW should start at Ashbourne as this is the true southern end of the Pennines. Twenty-one kilometres north-west of Derby, Ashbourne, nestling in the slopes of the Henmore valley, is a market town with a good selection of hotels, guest-houses, shops and many other facilities which will make your stay enjoyable. Enjoy it whilst you can as it will give you something nice to remember if you have the misfortune to be travelling in the rain across a boggy moor later on in your journey. Unfortunately Ashbourne, where in the old days six main coaching routes, including the Manchester to London route, used to meet, no longer has a railway. The northbound route of the old railway is now a nature trail and the first part of the APW. However, it is not difficult to get at, so you should have no difficulty in this respect. Also you will be able to stay at one of the old coaching inns which still remain.

In the Domesday Book Ashbourne, a medieval settlement, was called Esseburne and it is thought that this meant 'the brook of the ash tree'. If you can spare the time it is worthwhile exploring the nooks and crannies of this town. There is plenty to see in the alleys and yards behind the older premises in the main streets. The thirteenth-century parish church of St. Oswald, with its 65-metre (212-feet) slender spire celebrated the 750th anniversary of its founding in 1991. It is said that George Street is the finest street of Georgian buildings in Derbyshire, and Queen Elizabeth's Grammar School, in George Street, celebrated its quatercentenary with a visit from the Queen in 1985.

The market place used to be much more than a place where traders sold their goods, in that it was also a place of varied entertainment, including travelling shows, exhibitions of wild animals, bull baiting and travelling preachers. It also used to be the place where the Ashbourne Royal Shrovetide Football Match started. However, due to property becoming damaged during this unique event the start was moved to

Ashbourne

Shaw Croft a hundred years ago. This ancient game is played on each Shrove Tuesday and Ash Wednesday by two sides; those from the north of the River Henmore, versus those from the south. The object of the game is to get the ball (which is made of leather filled with cork shavings and weighs 1.6kg), to your own goal, where a goal is scored by tapping the ball three times against a board attached to a bridge at each end of the course. The bridges are three miles apart at Clifton and Sturston. Anyone who scores is allowed to keep the ball which becomes a treasured possession. There do not appear to be many rules governing the game but if no goal is scored by 10 o'clock at night, then the game is terminated. A curious game, its origin is unknown, but it is one for which the people of Ashbourne and many visitors still have a great deal of affection and enthusiasm.

As well as the Shrovetide Football game, there is a carnival on the second Saturday in July, the Ashbourne Show on the third Saturday in August and a Highland Gathering on the third Sunday in July. There is also a twice-weekly general market and a Thursday cattle market. Ashbourne is, without doubt, a thriving busy town with much to occupy the attention of the visitor.

Dove Dale

Ashbourne is often described as the 'Gateway to Dove Dale', so your approach to the most famous of all Derbyshire dales starts the moment you leave Ashbourne. It is also said that half the population of England lives within fifty miles of Dove Dale and indeed, if you happen to be passing through on a sunny bank holiday weekend, you may think that they have all decided to descend on this particular part of Derbyshire. You would be wrong, as there are only likely to be four or five thousand visitors to the dale! However, do not be dismayed at this prospect, as there is no road in the dale and the visitors have to park their vehicles near to the Isaac Walton Hotel, on the Staffordshire side of the river. Being motorists at heart, they are loath to step too far from the car parks and whilst many may attempt to climb up Thorpe Cloud (as the footpath erosion will testify), and others may venture up the dale over the stepping-stones and as far as Lover's Leap, you should have no problem with the rest of the journey in this picturesque part of the APW. If you are travelling during the week, you may find that there are no other visitors at all and you can enjoy

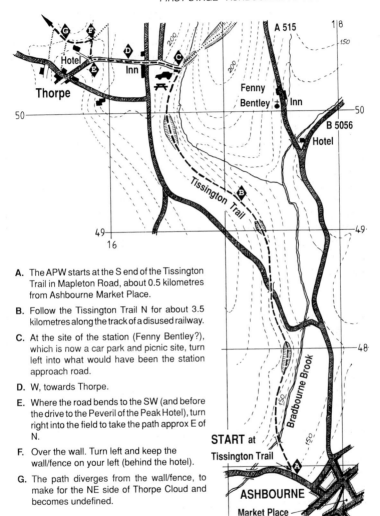

A. The APW starts at the S end of the Tissington Trail in Mapleton Road, about 0.5 kilometres from Ashbourne Market Place.

B. Follow the Tissington Trail N for about 3.5 kilometres along the track of a disused railway.

C. At the site of the station (Fenny Bentley?), which is now a car park and picnic site, turn left into what would have been the station approach road.

D. W, towards Thorpe.

E. Where the road bends to the SW (and before the drive to the Peveril of the Peak Hotel), turn right into the field to take the path approx E of N.

F. Over the wall. Turn left and keep the wall/fence on your left (behind the hotel).

G. The path diverges from the wall/fence, to make for the NE side of Thorpe Cloud and becomes undefined.

1.1

Thorpe Cloud

the delights of this walk in peace and tranquillity.

Dove Dale actually starts at the stepping-stones, just past Thorpe Cloud, 287 metres ('Cloud' is derived from the Old English 'clud', meaning a rock or hill), and extends for a distance of 5 kilometres northwards to the hamlet of Milldale. During this short walk, Dove Dale reveals itself slowly and sometimes tantalisingly to the visitor as the path through the narrow winding gorge is followed.

Dove Dale is acknowledged by most to be the finest of all the dales, and its literary associations with Izaac Walton and others only serve to enhance the beauty of its river and the gorge, and the striking limestone pinnacles which in summer may be hidden behind the lush vegetation. The path follows the river closely for most of the way, but leaves it to climb over Lover's Leap where, allegedly, about the middle of the eighteenth century a jilted damsel leaped off a cliff, determined to end her life. She was, however, unsuccessful in her attempt to end it all, as her fall was arrested by bushes and she survived to be able to walk away (we can find no record of what her subsequent fate was). From the path you will catch glimpses of Ilam Rock and Pickering Tor with its five pinnacles, on which many experienced climbers have practised their skills. The weathering of

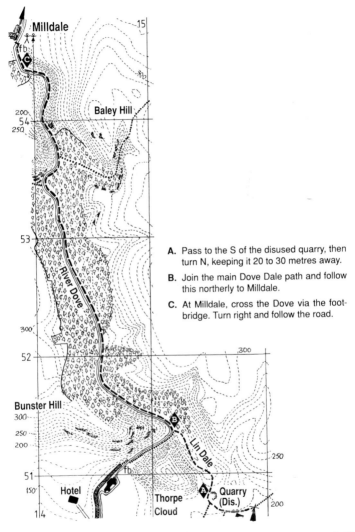

Milldale

Baley Hill

River Dove

Bunster Hill

Hotel

Thorpe Cloud

Lin Dale

Quarry (Dis.)

A. Pass to the S of the disused quarry, then turn N, keeping it 20 to 30 metres away.

B. Join the main Dove Dale path and follow this northerly to Milldale.

C. At Milldale, cross the Dove via the footbridge. Turn right and follow the road.

1.2

the limestone in the dale has produced some fascinating sculptured rocks, such as Reynard's Cave with its detached archway entrance and Lion's Rock which can clearly be seen to resemble a lion. Beware of the limestone scree which abounds in this area. Locally it is called slither-banks and you will discover why if you attempt to walk up, or down, one.

At the end of the dale you will cross the famous Viator's Bridge, a scheduled ancient monument. (See p8) It was built shortly before Izaac Walton and his friend Cotton passed over it. A passage in the *Compleat Angler* records that Walton commented "What's here? Do you use to travel in wheelbarrows in this country? This bridge certainly was made for nothing else. Why a mouse can hardly go over it; it is but two fingers broad!". The bridge was not made for wheelbarrows or mice, but for packhorses and men crossing the Dove, and the county boundary.

Izaac Walton was born in Stafford in 1593 and at the age of twenty owned a small ironmonger's shop in London's Fleet Street. He married a niece of Archbishop Cranmer in 1626 but, at the age of forty-eight, his wife and seven children died. At the age of fifty he retired and went to live in the country, still writing poetry and other articles, and in 1646 he remarried and had two further children by that marriage, one of whom died. The *Compleat Angler* was first published in 1653, when he was sixty years of age, and it was this book which ensured his rise to fame. When he was sixty-nine his second wife died and, as he had been associated with religious matters and the clergy for most of his life, he went to live at the Bishop's Palace in Winchester. It was in Winchester that he died at the age of ninety and was buried in the cathedral. His tomb can be seen in the south aisle.

When you leave the River Dove to enter Biggin Dale, you may be moved to remember Walton's farewell to this splendid river - "Well go thy way, little Dove! thou art the finest river that I ever saw and the fullest of fish."

Trailways and Railways

At the start of the APW you will find yourself walking on the Tissington Trail, one of two famous trails in Derbyshire. The Tissington Trail begins at Mapleton Road in Ashbourne and ends, 21 kilometres away, at Parsley Hey. Originally part of the London and North Western Railway's Buxton to Ashbourne branch line, built in the latter part of the last century, the trail

A. From Milldale footbridge, follow the road for about 0.8 kilometres.

B. Cross the road bridge, then left through the wicket gate to the path which follows the E side of the Dove.

C. Small stone building. This is NOT the right turn into Biggin Dale.

D. Turn right into Biggin Dale. If in doubt, check bearing; the APW goes approx 10° E of N.

E. To this point, the wall has been on the E side of the APW. Go through the gate, putting the wall on the W side.

F. Sharp left to take the northerly route to Biggin and hence via the inn.

X. Alternative route to Biggin - not via the inn.

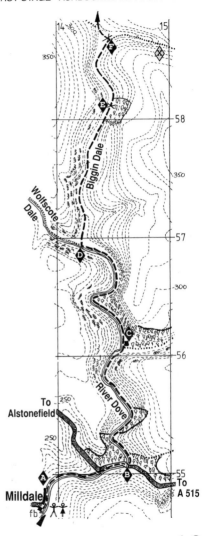

1.3

is available to walkers, cyclists and horse riders. But beware! we once met a Land-rover coming this way, which caused no little consternation amongst some inexperienced cyclists out for the day. The stations along the trail have been converted into car parks and picnic sites, some with toilet facilities and information centres.

Another famous trail which you will meet is the High Peak Trail, which perhaps has a rather more chequered history than the Tissington Trail. After the opening of the Cromford Canal, completed in 1793 and built by William Jessop and Benjamin Outram (from whose name, some Derbyshire people insist, the term 'tram', as a means of public transport, was derived), ambitious plans were drawn up to extend the canal north-westwards to join the Peak Forest canal at Whaley Bridge. However, it soon became apparent that the engineering problems would make the cost prohibitive and thoughts were turned towards a railway as an alternative. In the event, the railway proved to be a major engineering challenge, but Josias Jessop (William's son) constructed the 48-kilometre Cromford and High Peak Line in six years, at a cost of £180,000. The railway opened in 1831, using five inclined planes between Cromford and Hurdlow Summit (385 metres) and four inclines at the Whaley Bridge terminus. The main method of winching wagons up and down the inclines was to use steam engines, but a counterbalance system was used for the final incline at Whaley Bridge.

For a period of twenty years, passengers as well as goods were carried, but due to the problem of runaway wagons and consequent loss of life passenger travel was stopped in 1877. Another accident in 1878, when several wagons jumped across three set of rails, the canal and the A6, led to the construction of a 'catchpit' at the bottom of the one-in-seven Sheep Pasture Incline, near Cromford.

Towards the end of the nineteenth century it became apparent that this line was never going to make a profit and its use started to decline, sections closing down one after the other. Remnants of this remarkable engineering feat can still be seen. High Peak Wharf, the terminus, is almost intact and Middleton Top engine house still has winding equipment in working order and is sometimes opened to the public.

The High Peak Trail, opened in 1972, starts at the incline near High Peak Wharf, and continues for 27 kilometres to join the Tissington Trail at Parsley Hey. The trail includes tunnels, bridges, cuttings and embankments, the most impressive being the Minninglow Embankment. Another

A. Keep N up the dale to pass the mini sewage works.

B. Right at the road then, after a few metres, fork left to take the road to Biggin.

C. Lunch here followed by road walk.

D. Turn right to go S along the A515 for about 20 metres, then fork left into the green lane.

E. Left to go NE still on the green lane, but which has degenerated to become a rough track.

F. A stile on the left gives the clue to look out for a stile on the right, which is hidden in the trees. Through this into a large field, across whose diagonal will be seen a waymarkpost against the sky. Aim for this.

W. A short cut if you don't mind navigating across a large field with no path except for perhaps a trampled way through a standing crop.

X.Y.Z Short cut avoiding Biggin and inn.

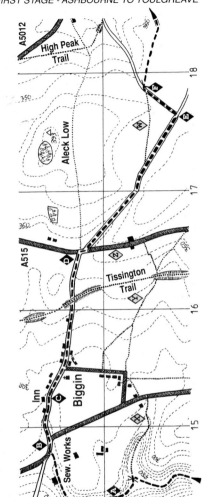

1.4

27

noteworthy feature is the famous Gotham Curve which has a radius of 50 metres (2$\frac{1}{2}$ chains), this being the smallest radius on any railway curve in the country. The APW joins the trail here.

The Peak railways, as well as their main function of carrying limestone from the many quarries in the area, also carried some passengers and general goods. The quarries show up as great scars on the face of the countryside, which in their immediate vicinity is changed from its natural green to a deathly white by a thick coating of limestone dust. The railways (which were of standard gauge) are gone, so the output from the quarries is now transported by road.

Whilst the Tissington Trail and the High Peak Trail are different in character, walking on them is a delightful experience, especially on a sunny summer day. As with many old railway lines, the flora and fauna are varied and some sections of the High Peak Trail are designated nature reserves.

Well-Dressing

There are more than a dozen villages in Derbyshire which uphold the custom of well-dressing. The village of Youlgreave (The Yellow Grove), through which you will pass and hopefully stay the night, is one that has maintained the custom over the years. In the eighteenth century it also employed a dog-whipper. He was paid the princely sum of 1s 4d (7p) per annum for discharging his duties, which were to whip the dogs out of church, so that the services could be conducted with reasonable solemnity!

Well-dressing originates way back in the middle of the twelfth century when many of the population of Derbyshire died as a result of the Black Death. In Tissington (a few kilometres north of Ashbourne) the villagers in general, and the clergy in particular, escaped the worst ravages of the plague and this was attributed to the purity of the water in the springs and five wells. The earliest reference to the religious blessing of the wells and springs, as an offering of thanks for being spared a horrendous death, goes back to 1758, although it is thought that this unique Derbyshire custom started in Tissington before this, perhaps in the fourteenth century.

As an art form, which was revived in 1951, well-dressing is now highly developed. Religious pictures embedded in clay, on a wooden backing,

A. Enter the walled track leading to the farm. On approaching which, turn right then left to pass in front of the house. Continue descending to the High Peak Trail (disused railway). Turn right on the trail.

B. At the car park and picnic site, leave the trail by turning right into the site and out into the road. Turn left and follow this road downhill until the A5012 is reached.

C. E along the A5012 (beware of traffic), for about 0.5 kilometres.

D. Turn left into the field. This entrance is easily missed.

E. Keep the wall on your left and, after about 100 metres, bend left (W) round the wall/fence to descend. Path ill-defined.

F. Keep N, then NE down Gratton Dale.

G. Left at Dale End at the road.

H. Right, to ascend the valley side.

I. Hairpin bend. Entrance to path obscured by vegetation. The path is easily missed, but is directly under the power line. Do NOT turn E with the steeply ascending narrow road. If you do, you've gone too far.

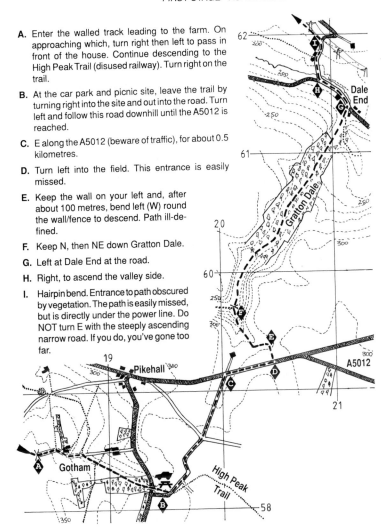

1.5

are constructed with flower petals and greenery surrounded by alder cones. The blessings used to start with the Tissington ceremony on Ascension Day, but some villages now start earlier. The dressed wells remain for seven to ten days, weather permitting, during which time events of a festive nature are held.

If you intend staying in Youlgreave at the time of well-dressing you are advised to book your accommodation early, as many visitors come to Derbyshire for these events.

Youlgreave

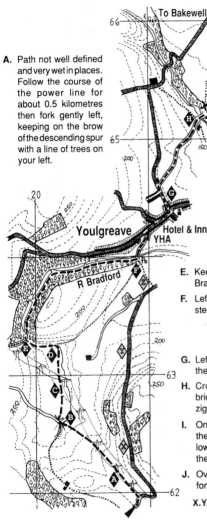

A. Path not well defined and very wet in places. Follow the course of the power line for about 0.5 kilometres then fork gently left, keeping on the brow of the descending spur with a line of trees on your left.

B. Through the stile, into the lane and cross the brook. Follow the lane for a few metres and then through the stile on the right.

C. Line of path marked by stiles.

D. Left, after crossing a 'lazy' stream.

E. Keep right, to follow the S bank of the River Bradford with its many cress beds.

F. Left over the footbridge, then ascend the steep lane into Youlgreave.

(THE FIRST STAGE ENDS AT YOULGREAVE)

G. Left at the church for about 250 metres, then fork right into narrow lane.

H. Cross the long footbridge (packhorse bridge?), over the trout pond, then make a zigzag ascent through the wood.

I. On emerging from the wood, pass through the stile and immediately turn right to follow the fence. Do NOT go ahead across the field.

J. Over the wall via the stile and straight forward, keeping the wall on your right.

X.Y.Z Short cut, if you've run out of time.

1.6

31

SECOND STAGE:
YOULGREAVE TO BASLOW

Stately Home Country
12.5 kilometres, 7.8 miles

After the long (29 kilometres), but not difficult, first stage, the second stage is short and easy. It begins with the crossing of the beautiful River Lathkill to reach higher ground which overlooks Haddon Hall and its estate. Indeed, it should be possible to visit the hall and take morning coffee (if it is the opening season). The route then climbs through the farmland and the woods, rising behind the hall, to reach Chatsworth Park. Magnificent views of Chatsworth House and gardens emerge, as a descent from the woods is made. Extraordinarily tidy Edensor is worth a few minutes of your time. The approach drive to the house is used to cross the River Derwent, before walking alongside the river in the open spaces of the park. Afternoon tea with a visit to the house is feasible because of the shortness of this stage. Leaving the park brings you to the route into Baslow.

You will need to carry lunch as there are no suitable places en route. However, an alternative to the walk through the woods of the Haddon estate is to follow the River Wye into Bakewell, where lunch can be obtained. A walk direct to Edensor is then possible. (Bakewell is well worth a visit anyway.)

Emergency rations need not be plentiful since, like the first stage, the route is never far from habitation. Hotel accommodation is available in Baslow, as are shops for provisions.

Haddon Hall

SECOND STAGE

Youlgreave to Baslow

12.5 km (7.8 miles)

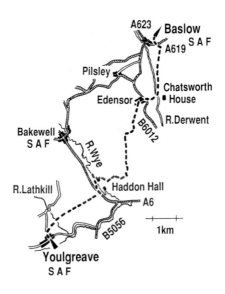

Haddon Hall

The present day external appearance of Haddon Hall is nearly the same as it was in the year 1700, at which time, after more than 600 years of development, the original hall, standing on the banks of the River Wye, had become surrounded by an impressive array of buildings and battlemented walls. The battlements, however, are decorative features and were never used for defensive purposes, as they were added at a time when private houses no longer required battlements for their true purpose, and indeed Haddon never had to be defended against 'enemy forces'.

History relates that Haddon was inhabited by many owners. Some of the most famous were William Peverel (illegitimate son of William the Conqueror), who lived there at the time the Domesday Book was being compiled in 1087 and, no doubt, the 'Peveril of the Peak' was named after him; and William Avenel, who took over in about 1150 and in 1170 gave Haddon to his two sons-in-law, Simon Basset and Richard Vernon.

Vernon soon took over sole ownership of the hall and began a 400-year term of Vernon family occupation. The last Vernon, Sir George, lived in Haddon from 1517 until 1567, at which time, as he had no male heir, Haddon passed to his daughter Dorothy and her husband Sir John Manners.

In 1641, John Manners succeeded to the title of the Ninth Earl of Rutland and went to live at Belvoir Castle in Leicestershire. The earl became the First Duke of Rutland in 1703 and continued to use Belvoir as the family residence, so Haddon gradually became uninhabited. However Haddon never be-

The Chapel, Haddon Hall

A. Cross the A6 to the causeway and turn left towards Bakewell. After about 150 metres, pass through the gap in the wall (which is easily missed, because it is small and masked by the presence of trees etc.).

B. Through the stile in the metal fence. Turn sharp right in the lane and ascend.

C. Right through the gate into the fields. The path keeps the iron fence on its right all the way to the farm.

D. Fenced track, easy to follow.

E. Leave the tracks by entering the wood between stone gate posts and ascend the well-defined path.

F. Path not defined down the large field but descend and, when Calton Houses and the wood in the valley come into view, bear left.

G. It is not apparent on the approach, but the valley bottom is crossed through a gate in a gap in the wood. Then sharp right to keep the wood on your right.

H. Do NOT descend to Calton Houses, but fork left to ascend gently keeping the wall on your right.

I. Through the wood on the track.

J. Fine view over Chatsworth Park, but paths not defined. Since the trustees of the estate invite you to walk freely in the park, you should have no difficulty in getting down to Edensor, whose houses and church (with its tall spire) are clearly visible through their surrounding trees. The right of way is as shown on the map.

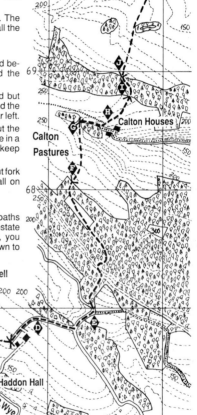

2.1

came totally abandoned or neglected, and in the early part of the twentieth century the ninth duke embarked on the long task of restoring the hall to its original splendour, using, wherever possible, original materials. This became his life's work and was completed in 1930. Most of the work was done by local craftsmen and in the banqueting hall a lead box, containing details of the restoration work, was secreted in one of the beams, so that future generations can be informed of the precise architectural history of Haddon.

If you care to spend a pleasant hour or so exploring this magnificent house, you will pass through the lower courtyard, the museum, the chapel, the kitchens, the banqueting hall, the dining room, the great chamber, the earl's bedroom, the long gallery (with its 'acoustic' roof), the state bedroom and, of course the gardens which are famous for their many roses. Lunches and teas are served in the Stables Tea Room.

Chatsworth

Chatsworth House stands out as one of the great houses of the country. The first recorded house at Chatsworth was started by William Cavendish and his wife Elizabeth Hardwick (Bess of Hardwick), in 1552 and it occupied the area of the square part of the present house. The house then faced to the east, with its back to the village.

The second son of 'Bess' was created Earl of Devonshire in 1618 and in 1686 the fourth earl, who later became the first Duke of Devonshire, began to pull the house down in order to build a much grander residence in its present Classical style. William Talman was the architect of the south and east fronts, and the new building was completed just before the duke died in 1707.

The most significant result of the first duke's work was that the back of the building became the front. The fourth duke carried out more work between 1755 and 1763, clearing the (new) front of obstructions, straightening the course of the river and removing all parts of Edensor village that could be seen from the house. Chatsworth now began to look as you see it today.

When the young sixth duke took control in 1818, he found the house too small for his liking, so he set about enlarging the place, adding many more rooms in the process and altering much of the existing structure. However, he kept the great chamber in its original state, as designed in

A. At Edensor, cross the B6012 to join the well-defined path with made-up surface.

B. Cross the River Derwent at the bridge and immediately fork left onto the path to cross the park.

C. Pass through the gate to leave the park on the fenced path. After a few metres fork left near the house on the E of the path.

(THE SECOND STAGE ENDS AT BASLOW)

D. Cross the A623, turn right for only 3 or 4 metres and then into the fenced path between residences. This path entrance is easily missed as it can be confused with a private drive entrance.

E. Leave the road at the triangle where it bends left. Ascend the lane NE. Continue to climb, leaving the houses after about 0.25 kilometre.

F. Ascend the lane, until the gate which gives access to open country is reached.

G. Many paths. Scramble to the escarpment, then NNW along its edge.

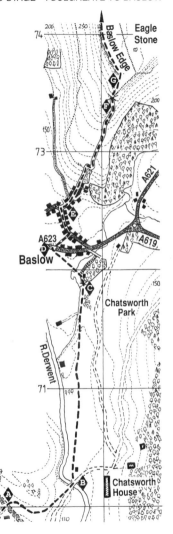

2.2

37

Chatsworth

the late sixteenth century. It is the largest room in the state apartments and contains a grand painted ceiling with a matching chimney-piece above the fireplace. During these alterations, the sixth duke also retained the chapel which, with its painted walls and ceilings, contains many fine carvings and paintings. These changes to Chatsworth became the duke's life's work and in the process he also rebuilt the village and replaced the church by the present building.

Over the years, many garden styles have been introduced at Chatsworth, including the work of perhaps the most famous 'gardener' of them all, Capability Brown. However, the gardens of Chatsworth are particularly noteworthy for their water effects, which include a canal, lakes, a grand cascade and fountains. The largest fountain of all, the Emperor Fountain, cannot easily be missed (unlike some of the paths on the APW) as, at 85 metres, it is still the highest gravity-fed fountain in the world.

Water at Chatsworth, as well as being a decorative feature, serves a useful purpose. A network of underground pipes is used to feed water to a turbo-generator, which is used to supply power to light and heat about half the estate. The water system was started in 1843 by the sixth duke's head gardener, Joseph Paxton, who later designed the Crystal Palace, and from the end of the nineteenth century, the 400 million litres of water in the lake were used to drive a turbine, until 1936, when it became more economical to be connected to the National Grid.

The present duke (the eleventh), however, restored the whole power system in 1987 and installed a new turbine with a 300kw generator and, at the same time, laid new mains cables. It is estimated that the costs of over £250,000 will have been recouped before 1995. One of the biggest problems encountered during the restoration work was the large diameter pipe which carried water down from the lake. This pipe was badly furred-up and thus wasted more than half the potential energy of the water. The engineers accepted the challenge of cleaning out the pipe, by using water pressure to force polyurethane foam 'plugs', with abrasive coatings, through the pipe. This task took five days, after which the success of the project was demonstrated by the fact that the height of the fountain was restored to its original value.

So, Chatsworth is not only a beautiful stately home, with architectural, artistic and scenic beauty, but it is also a place where the skill of engineers has contributed to the beauty and also provided a cost-effective source of power.

Black Grouse (Black Cock)

THIRD STAGE:
BASLOW TO MOSCAR

Escarpments
19.5 kilometres, 12 miles

THESE NOTES SHOULD BE READ IN CONJUNCTION WITH
THOSE OF THE FOURTH STAGE

The route climbs steeply out of Baslow onto Baslow Edge, and then follows the escarpment northwards for the rest of the way to Moscar. Except for the crossing of an intersecting valley, it keeps relatively high on Curbar Edge and Froggatt Edge reaching 458 metres at High Neb on Stanage Edge. It provides fine views from this eastern side of the Derwent Valley, particularly northwards and westwards. In the west, the Hope Valley, with Mam Tor at its head, is visible, whilst north-west the plateau of Kinder Scout can be seen. North-north-west are the high hills and peat moors of the Dark Peak. This panorama is best from Stanage Edge, which is well-known for its rock climbing. After leaving Stanage Edge the route descends to the A57, the Sheffield to Manchester road, at Moscar. This stage has less variety than the first two but it is quite different, its main features being the panoramic views - assuming the weather is clear!

In fine weather it is easy but in bad visibility some difficulty in navigation may be experienced, although the route's keeping to the escarpment helps a lot. There should be little difficulty underfoot as the way is on well-trodden paths.

The Grouse Inn may be reached a little too soon for lunch, but it is advisable to take advantage of its facilities (if you are so inclined), as it is the only possible place to stop. If you are carrying a packed lunch and hope to find shelter to 'partake' you will be unlucky, unless you find somewhere in Longshaw Country Park. As you will have deduced by now, most of this stage is very exposed, and therein lies its charm.

THERE IS NO ACCOMMODATION AT MOSCAR, so we advise you, if you are not backpacking, to leave Stanage Edge at SK238847. Follow the track downwards to meet the road and eventually into Bamford where there is accommodation and shops.

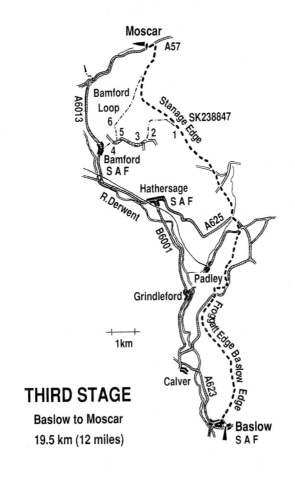

Moscar

A57

A6013

Bamford
Loop

6

5   3   2

4   1   Stanage Edge   SK238847

Bamford
S A F

Hathersage
S A F

R.Derwent

A625

B6001

Padley

Grindleford

Frogatt Edge Baslow Edge

1km

Calver   A623

THIRD STAGE

Baslow to Moscar

19.5 km (12 miles)

Baslow
S A F

(SEE MAP NOTES OF THE THIRD STAGE)

If you choose to backpack, YOU MUST GET ENOUGH PROVISIONS FOR THREE DAYS (ie. to provide for this stage, the fourth stage and the fifth stage, as the next stage where there are proper shopping facilities is Marsden, at the end of the fifth stage).

If you stay in Bamford at the end of this stage there are two alternatives on leaving:-

1. Regain Stanage Edge by partially retracing your steps. (See map notes.) or

2. Plod the 3.0 kilometres northwards on the A6013 and the A57 to the Ladybower Inn, and rejoin the definitive APW on Derwent Edge - see next stage!

If you stay in Bamford it is a long walk to Dunford Bridge where there is only one hotel but NO SHOPS, so you will require provisions for the next two stages.

Whether or not you stay in Bamford you will now need more emergency rations than previously, as this stage and the next two stages are very remote - especially the fourth. Even if you intend staying in hotel or B & B accommodation it is now that your 'emergency kit' which will, no doubt, include a 'bivi-bag', may come in useful. Be prepared!

Escarpments

The limestone part of Derbyshire is often referred to as the Limestone Dome and it is surrounded by gritstone on three sides. In the north of the Peak the gritstone moors are only about three kilometres wide but in Edale they are about 30 kilometres wide. Further south they split to the west and to the east nearly surrounding the Limestone Dome.

Due to underground movement the limestone was thrust upwards causing cracks in the gritstone and over the years this has eroded leaving edges which can clearly be seen on the western escarpment of the eastern moors, running from south of Baslow northwards to Moscar and beyond. These edges are, from south to north, Chatsworth Edge, Birchen's Edge, Gardom's Edge, Baslow Edge, Curbar Edge, Froggatt Edge, Burbage Rocks and Stanage Edge. Chatsworth, Birchen's and Gardom's Edges will be seen in front of you as you walk down through Chatsworth Park towards the house.

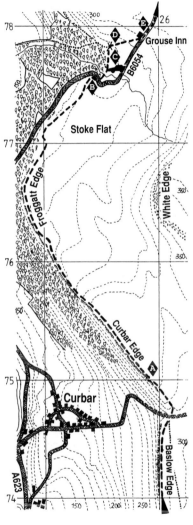

A. Easy! Follow the escarpment, either on the tourist track, or on your own route, as near to the edge as is convenient (or as near as you dare). Then proceed along Baslow Edge, Curbar Edge and Froggatt Edge.

B. Nasty crossing of the B6054. Blind bend! Up the road for a few metres, then left through stile down the bank and cross the brook to go up the opposite bank.

C. Keep the car park to the E and walk along the path, inside the wood, parallel to the wall.

D. A stile gives access to the fields, leaving the wood. The path is ill-defined, the walls are broken and the stiles are difficult to find. However, the Grouse Inn is visible ahead - make for this.

E. Refreshments at the inn, if you wish. Continue up the B6054.

3.1

43

Baslow has been described as "the gateway to some of the finest Peakland scenery", and indeed when you get up to Baslow Edge you may very well agree with this claim. On Baslow Edge may be seen a large obelisk-shaped rock which has the name Eagle Stone. It looks nothing like an eagle but we are told that the word Eagle refers to the Saxon god "Aigle", who apparently was so strong that he could pick up and throw very big rocks, ones that ordinary mortals could not even move, let alone throw. Various 'anvil' stones dotted around the countryside also owe their origin to "Aigle" - 'Anvil' merely being a corruption of "Aigle". The climbing of Eagle Stone used to be a test for the men of Baslow to prove that they were suitable for entering into the state of matrimony.

Curbar Edge is to the east of the village of Curbar, which is half-way up the side of the valley and has fine views over the Derwent. Just south of the village you can discover an unusual square 'round-house' with a circular roof built from square blocks. This was used in the nineteenth century for overnight stays by prisoners in transit. Many a rock climber has had his, or her, skills put to the test on the difficult climbs to be found

The Derwent Valley & Stanage Edge

A. After about 300 metres up the B6054, slip left into the driveway leading to the Longshaw Country Park. White gates and notices make sure that it cannot be missed.

B. Continue along the well-defined driveway.

C. At the entrance to Longshaw Lodge Gardens, a stile, on the left, takes the right of way below the gardens, some 20 metres from the building. The path then joins the other driveway from the B6521.

D. Cross the road and proceed upwards for a few metres, then left onto the path through the wood. Keep parallel with the A625, which is a few metres on the right.

E. Do not descend on the forward path. Turn right up the bank, to the stile at the A625. Then left down the road for a few metres.

F. Slip right along the track.

G. When this turns right, proceed forward down the well-defined path, to cross Burbage Brook, then upwards to the outcrop.

H. Over the outcrop, down a bit, then up to the second outcrop - Higger Tor.

X.Y.Z. If you prefer a slightly higher and longer route, this will take you over Burbage Rocks. However, you will miss the fine views up Derwent Dale, as they are obscured by the outcrops of Hathersage Moor.

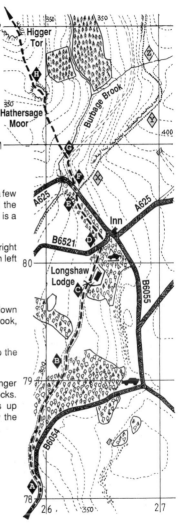

3.2

45

on the edge where some of the rocks resemble animals and birds.

Walking over Froggatt Edge and Burbage Rocks brings you to Stanage Edge which is perhaps the most famous of the edges and it is the longest edge, being about 6.5 kilometres from the Cowper Stone to Moscar Moor. You will find piles of abandoned millstones hereabouts - clearly it was more economical to shape the stones at the gritstone edges than to transport huge blocks to be shaped elsewhere. Stanage Edge is bisected by an old Roman road which goes east to west, passing Redmires Reservoir near Sheffield and continuing over the edge to Navio Roman fort which was near the town of Brough in the Hope Valley. In the past twenty years or so, rock climbing has developed to such an extent that the number of classified climbs on Stanage has increased from just over 100 to more than 500, and many national and international climbers have used these routes to improve their techniques. When you are walking along these edges beware of pitons and other equipment, especially ropes, which you may find littered around - there may be climbers on the other end!

Breaking the Journey for Bamford

1. Leave the definite route on Stanage Edge at SK238847.
2. Join the road and walk ahead to cross the cattle grid.
3. Turn right and follow the undulating road for about 1.25 kilometres.
4. Go left down the very steep track into Bamford.

Regaining Stanage Edge

If you are a 'purist', simply retrace the above. However, there is a short cut across Bamford Moor, as follows:-
Use the steep track out of Bamford to reach '4' again, then turn right up the hill, on the road for a few metres.
5. Over the stile onto the well-defined track and into the disused quarry. Through the quarry and scramble out at the opposite end.
6. No clear route. Any words of description are useless, but we suggest choosing one of the 'trods' that seem to take you over in the direction of the edge, which is visible before you. (In poor visibility, you will need a compass [30° approx]. There is a right of way shown on the map, but it could not be found on the ground when the route was researched.)

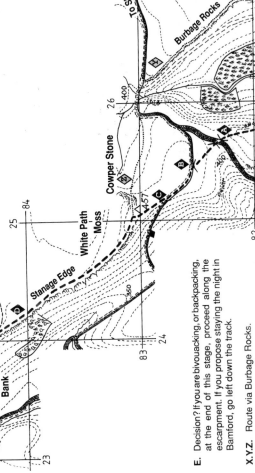

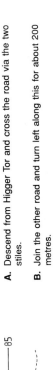

A. Descend from Higger Tor and cross the road via the two stiles.

B. Join the other road and turn left along this for about 200 metres.

C. Fork right along the path and ascend to the trig point.

D. Follow the escarpment along the well-worn path.

E. Decision? If you are bivouacking, or backpacking, at the end of this stage, proceed along the escarpment. If you propose staying the night in Bamford, go left down the track.

X.Y.Z. Route via Burbage Rocks.

3.3

47

Ladybower Inn

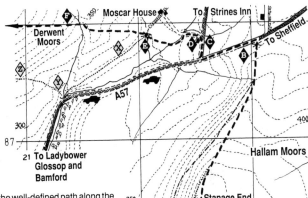

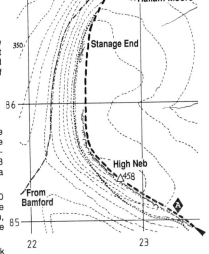

A. Follow the well-defined path along the escarpment, passing the trig point at High Neb. Pass Stanage End and then down to the A57. (Note: a right of way exists at the foot of the rocks.)

(THE END OF THE THIRD STAGE IS HERE, AT MOSCAR [NO ACCOMMODATION])

B. Left at the road for about 0.5 kilometre then right along the road leading to the Strines Inn. (Whilst this inn offers accommodation, unfortunately it is 3 kilometres along the road, which is a dreary plod!)

C. Along the Strines road for about 100 metres, then fork left to approach the cottage. Note the public footpath sign, dating from 1935 and relevant for the APW.

D. Pass the cottage and before the brook is reached turn left down its S bank, to cross it some 100 metres downstream. Follow the well-defined path.

E. Another path joins from the left (see note X.Y.Z.). Swing right through the gate and then sharp left to face a 1933 sign. Proceed in the direction of its arrow to ascend on to the Derwent Moors.

F. Cross the brook and ascend to the shooting butt. Keep to the well-defined path on the left and continue ascending to Derwent Edge.

X.Y.Z. This route brings you to Derwent Edge more southerly and at a lower level, but the reward for this slightly longer walk is a spectacular view over Ladybower Reservoir.

3.4

FOURTH STAGE:
MOSCAR TO DUNFORD BRIDGE

Peat and Heather
26.5 kilometres, 16.5 miles

There are a number of potential routes for this stage. All are excellent, each with its own characteristics. The one chosen as the definitive route takes into account the avoidance of access problems on private moorland and the minimisation of erosion problems in deep peat, but is nevertheless scenically spectacular.

On leaving Moscar, the way proceeds westwards to climb gently up the eastern slopes of Derwent Moors. On arriving at Derwent Edge it goes northwards, keeping to the escarpment as far as Back Tor on a good path, after which it descends to Derwent Reservoir. The route then proceeds up the Derwent Valley on the track along the eastern shores of the reservoirs, until it gets beyond the head of Howden Reservoir at the footbridge at Slippery Stones. At this point it leaves the main valley to enter Cranberry Clough and subsequently ascends once again to the watershed, after which it follows the bridleway along Cut Gate and goes down to the valley of the Little Don River. It then crosses into the valley of the River Don to join the course of one of the two Manchester to Sheffield railways (now dismantled), and then goes westwards into Dunford Bridge. (At the time of research, the course of the railway was not a right of way but we were assured by competent authorities, that it will be designated very soon as such, as part of a trans-Pennine trail.)

The part of the way between 203880 and Back Tor is National Trust access land, and could be closed during the shooting season. If so, take the 'Shooting Season Variant Route' which drops down to Ladybower Reservoir from 203880 and then proceeds northwards on the track/lane, which keeps on the eastern shores of the reservoirs, to join the definitive route at the head of the Derwent Reservoir.

Because of the difficulty, length and remoteness of this stage, proper emergency rations and emergency overnight equipment should be carried, together with normal provisions for two days. REMEMBER - there are no shops in Dunford Bridge and only one hotel. You have been

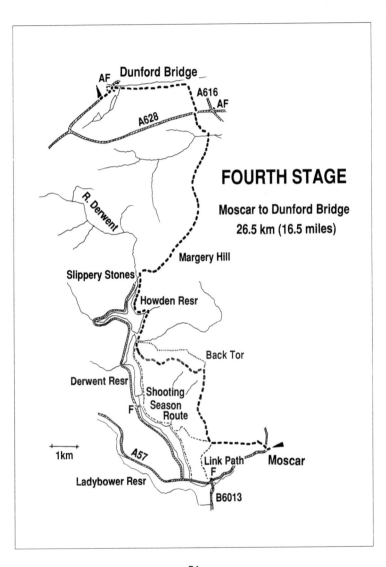

FOURTH STAGE

Moscar to Dunford Bridge
26.5 km (16.5 miles)

Dunford Bridge
AF
A616
AF
A628
R. Derwent
Margery Hill
Slippery Stones
Howden Resr
Back Tor
Derwent Resr
Shooting
Season
Route
F
1km
A57
Link Path
Moscar
F
Ladybower Resr
B6013

warned before, but we warn you again! However, there is accommodation at The Flouch Inn where the A616 crosses the A628.

THIS STAGE IS ONE OF THE MOST DIFFICULT ON THE WHOLE OF THE APW

Northwards over Derwent Dale

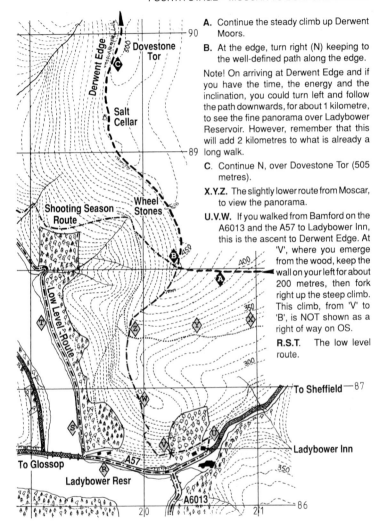

A. Continue the steady climb up Derwent Moors.

B. At the edge, turn right (N) keeping to the well-defined path along the edge.

Note! On arriving at Derwent Edge and if you have the time, the energy and the inclination, you could turn left and follow the path downwards, for about 1 kilometre, to see the fine panorama over Ladybower Reservoir. However, remember that this will add 2 kilometres to what is already a long walk.

C. Continue N, over Dovestone Tor (505 metres).

X.Y.Z. The slightly lower route from Moscar, to view the panorama.

U.V.W. If you walked from Bamford on the A6013 and the A57 to Ladybower Inn, this is the ascent to Derwent Edge. At 'V', where you emerge from the wood, keep the wall on your left for about 200 metres, then fork right up the steep climb. This climb, from 'V' to 'B', is NOT shown as a right of way on OS.

R.S.T. The low level route.

4.1

Gritstone Moors

The upper Derwent Valley sits in classic millstone grit country, characterised by sculptured outcrops and peat-heather-grass vegetation. The gritstone is impervious to water and the peat retains it like a sponge, yielding it slowly to the brooks which rarely run dry even in times of drought. There is surely more water stored in the peat than in the reservoirs! In contrast to the White Peak in Derbyshire, the gritstone moorlands with their sombre appearance can present a very gloomy aspect to the visitor, especially if the cloud is low and it is raining, as it usually is.

In West Yorkshire, the millstone grit, so called because it was used to make millstones, can be several thousands of metres thick and the geologists record that the original deposits were laid down under shallow water which was subjected to strong currents. This action caused pebbles, some quite large, to become embedded in the grit which is sometimes mistaken for granite. Due to the beds and shales, gritstone escarpments are susceptible to landslips and Mam Tor (dubbed the 'Shivering Mountain'), in north Derbyshire, has had many landslips over the years resulting in the closing of the motor road, which became unfit for traffic.

The escarpments form gently sloping plateaux which are sandy and dry when the drainage is good, and wet and peaty when the drainage is

poor and the rainfall heavy. The vegetation will give you an indication of altitude and dryness. For instance, heather grows best on fairly dry gritstone moors up to about 600 metres, and above this more bilberry will be seen than heather. If you are lucky you may also see cloudberries, which are small moorland plants with white flowers and a delicious orange-coloured fruit which is shaped like a small strawberry. However, if

Saltcellar

54

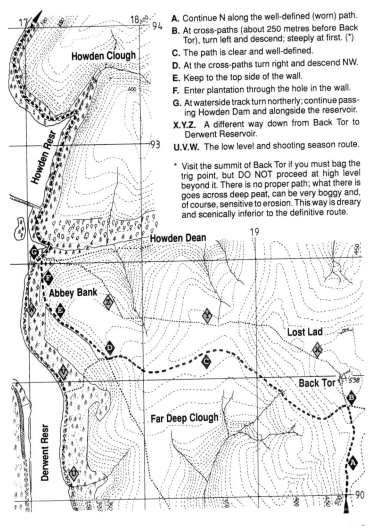

A. Continue N along the well-defined (worn) path.

B. At cross-paths (about 250 metres before Back Tor), turn left and descend; steeply at first. (*)

C. The path is clear and well-defined.

D. At the cross-paths turn right and descend NW.

E. Keep to the top side of the wall.

F. Enter plantation through the hole in the wall.

G. At waterside track turn northerly; continue passing Howden Dam and alongside the reservoir.

X.Y.Z. A different way down from Back Tor to Derwent Reservoir.

U.V.W. The low level and shooting season route.

* Visit the summit of Back Tor if you must bag the trig point, but DO NOT proceed at high level beyond it. There is no proper path; what there is goes across deep peat, can be very boggy and, of course, sensitive to erosion. This way is dreary and scenically inferior to the definitive route.

4.2

the ground is wet, then cotton grass will be predominant, especially on thick, poorly drained peat. When you see cotton grass be warned, the peat on which it grows can be dangerous to walk on!

Over the centuries, peat has been used as a source of fuel and to this day certain villagers around this area have the right to cut peat and some even exercise this right. In the Yorkshire Dales, peat was used on a large scale for domestic heating and the saying was "It costs nowt but work." Peat was used by blacksmiths, lead miners and also for burning in limekilns. The demise of these trades and the availability of alternative fuels led to the end of peat cutting in general.

The gritstone moors provide excellent water collecting areas and during the first part of this stage you will see the Derwent reservoirs below you. These reservoirs provided the training ground for the 'Dam Busters' in World War II, and in commemoration of this a Lancaster bomber is portrayed on the sign of the Ladybower Inn. Ladybower Reservoir submerged the villages of Ashopton and Derwent, and up to some years ago the top of the spire of Derwent church was visible when the water level was low. During the drought of 1976, it was possible to wander in the streets of Derwent village, the water level was so low. The reservoir has a perimeter of 21 kilometres and a maximum depth of 41 metres.

From Cut Gate, if visibility is good, you will see to the north-west a high mast with white flashing aircraft hazard warning lights. The mast marks the site of the BBC's Holme Moss Transmitting Station. Opened in October 1951, it was the highest powered television transmitter in the world and was designed to serve the whole of the north of England. Holme Moss is at a height of 524 metres, and the original mast was 228 metres high. Due to north-east winds blowing in from the North Sea, substantial accumulations of ice occur on the mast structure and supports and horizontal icicles are quite common in severe winter weather. In very bad winters, some difficulty has been experienced in gaining access to this remote site and in 1963, following heavy snow on the last day of February, explosives were used to blast away five-metre-high snow drifts. The present mast is relatively new, having recently replaced the old one, and it carries aerials to radiate BBC VHF Radio transmissions, but no television.

Away to the north-north-east, you may see the concrete tower of the Emley Moor Television Transmitting Station. The original steel mast,

A. Continue N along the track.

B. Pass (do NOT cross) the packhorse bridge at Slippery Stones. (*)

C. Leave the main Derwent Valley and enter Cranberry Clough.

D. Ascend on the well-defined bridleway.

E. The route is still well-defined and crosses the deep peat in a wide cutting.

F. Begin the descent.

* This bridge was removed from Derwent Village and rebuilt here when Ladybower Reservoir was constructed.

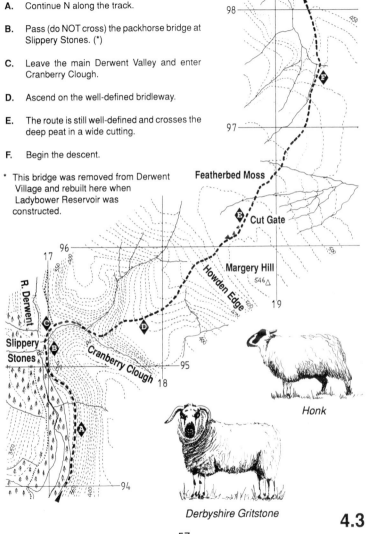

Honk

Derbyshire Gritstone

4.3

380 metres high, collapsed in March 1969 due to ice loading, after three days of freezing mist. Amazingly there were no injuries and only slight damage to a nearby chapel. The new tower originally caused an outcry from some members of the public, but most are now proud of the 'highest lighthouse in the north', also known as the Shelley Christmas Tree.

Gritstone moors, as well as being places to put towers and masts, provide a wide variety of walking conditions. We have been subjected to all these conditions during our many years of walking. The sight, the sound, the smell and the 'feel' of the moors provide a source of infinite enjoyment, and the occasional soggy boots or wet socks pale into insignificance when compared with the pleasure received from walking in such magnificent countryside.

Upper Windleden Reservoir

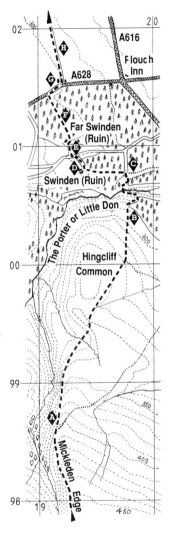

A. Continue northerly on the well-defined path.

B. Zigzag down to the R. Little Don and cross.

C. After ascending the N bank of the river for about 150 metres, turn left (due W) along the path through the forest.

D. At the ruins of Swinden, turn to the NW along the track for about 150 metres.

E. Left, then right through a gate to cross the middle of a field to re-enter the forest at the ruins of Far Swinden.

F. Clear route through the forest.

G. Turn right at the A628, for about 150 metres, then left at the house into the bridleway.

H. Keep the wall on your right all the way.

4.4

DUNFORD BRIDGE

Be careful as you cross the A628, as this is one of the main Sheffield to Manchester roads and it is a very busy highway. The 'transport lobby' wants a motorway (naturally), across here and down Longdendale, so that the ever increasing numbers of vehicles can make their way to join the traffic jams in Sheffield and Manchester.

In Dunford Bridge there is one hotel (a remnant of the railway age), a few houses, a public telephone, a letterbox, *but no shops.* Dunford Bridge is at the east end of the Woodhead railway tunnel, which carried one of the Manchester to Sheffield railways. The railway is now dismantled, and one of the pair of tunnels carries the electricity transmission line, so as to avoid the need for towers marching over the hills. It re-emerges in the Longdendale valley, about five kilometres to the south-west. This railway was one of the first (the first?) intercity routes to be electrified, and was intended to carry coal from the Yorkshire coalfield to Manchester. It was designed to be regenerative, in that the fully loaded coal trains coasting down Longdendale generated electricity, which was fed back into the system to augment the supply for the trains climbing up the eastern side into Dunford Bridge. Regrettably World War II and subsequent economies prevented the system becoming properly developed.

As you leave Dunford Bridge you cross the dam of Winscar Reservoir, which is relatively new. It was opened in the seventies and unlike most reservoirs in this area it does not have a clay-cored dam. It has a plastic membrane instead, which when installed was considered somewhat of an innovation and, as with conventionally constructed reservoirs, the earthworks are there to support and protect the core.

Swaledales

Blackface

A. Continue on the path, keeping the wall on your right.

B. Cross the railway bridge, then through the stile to descend the bank to the dismantled railway.

C. Keep along the course of the railway to Dunford Bridge.

(THE FOURTH STAGE
ENDS AT
DUNFORD BRIDGE)

D. Ascend the road, and after about 0.6 kilometre turn right at the picnic site to follow the lane to the dam at Winscar Reservoir. Cross the dam and follow the access road.

E. Join the main road and proceed NNW. Pass the track leading to the dam of Harden Reservoir. Beyond the houses on the right, the footpath goes off the road to the left. The road walk to here is about 0.6 kilometre.

F. Into disused stone quarries.

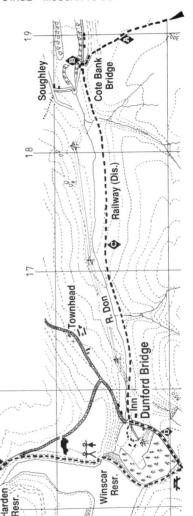

4.5

FIFTH STAGE:
DUNFORD BRIDGE TO MARSDEN

Reservoir Country
21.5 kilometres, 13.3 miles

This stage begins by crossing the dam of Winscar Reservoir. The route then ascends gently by road and through old quarry workings to reach the head of a tributary valley of the River Holme, from where fine views down the Holme Valley can be seen. It then descends into the great basin, which forms the head of the Holme Valley, at Yateholme and skirts the lower slopes of Black Hill. After climbing to the head of the Wessenden Valley, it follows this valley down to Marsden on a high path again giving fine views. There are also one or two interesting variants to the route.

There is no really difficult walking as you will be on well-used paths and tracks. The highest point is 450 metres on the A635 at Wessenden Head, which is exposed and could be unpleasant in bad weather conditions. The scene is varied; hill farms, open moorland, forest, a moorland village and plenty of reservoirs.

There is an inn which provides food and a hotel in Holme. There are no other possible places to get food or provisions en route, but as the route is never far from habitation only modest emergency rations need be carried.

There are plenty of shops and inns in Marsden, but curiously the accommodation is out of the village. The bunkhouse/guesthouse is to the south, about 1 kilometre out of the centre, and can be reached from the APW without entering Marsden itself (see Accommodation List).

Remains of Hades

FIFTH STAGE

Dunford Bridge to Marsden

21.5 km (13.3 miles)

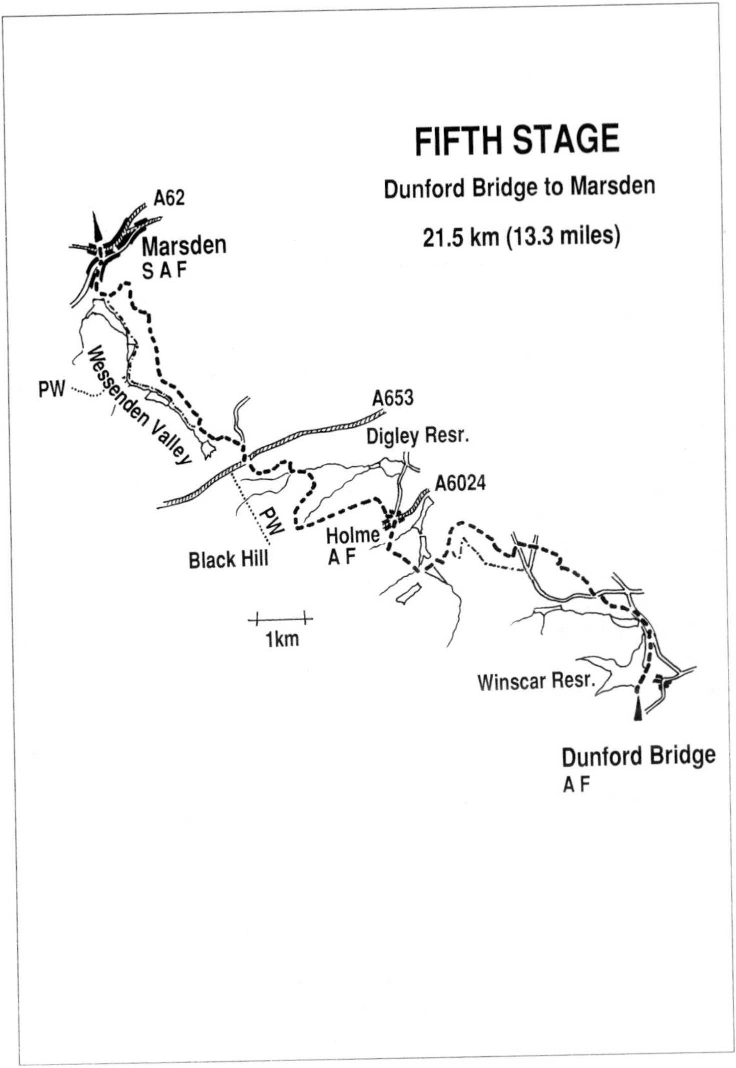

A62

Marsden
S A F

PW

Wessenden Valley

A653

Digley Resr.

A6024

PW

Black Hill

Holme
A F

1km

Winscar Resr.

Dunford Bridge
A F

Elysium

A. Labyrinth of paths and tracks in old quarry workings. Right of way not clear, but use compass to keep NW. Old quarry track might be useful until it turns W.

B. Right through the stile onto descending path through plantation.

C. Follow well-defined path through remains of farmstead at Hades. This then becomes a rough track to cross a deep clough and joins a better track 300 metres E of Elysium. Pass Elysium and cross the unmade road.

D. Left at road for a few metres, then right through gate into fields. Keep wall on your right until path becomes defined, then follow the contour (more or less) around the spur.

E. Through stile, then left to ascend a few metres on the track. Then fork right to descend walled path through the forest.

F. Left into the walled track (house opposite), then right over the reservoir dam.

G. Right over the stile, descend and emerge from plantation. Then steep descent to brook and footbridge.

H. Through stile. Short, steep ascent, then left in NW direction and gentle ascent over moorland. Do NOT follow the main path forward in a NE direction.

I. Paths confusing. Compass bearing (approx N) will be useful.

J. Short, steep descent (steps) over footbridge, then ascend.

K. Through the garden gate and across the lawn. Keep the house on your right.

L. Cross the A6024 into Fleece Inn car park entrance. Follow walled track to meet the road. Then turn left and follow the road upwards.

X.Y.Z. High level route with good views (until the trees grow up). Hard underfoot on a metalled road for 2 kilometres, then pleasant walled track.

W. Walled unmade road which can be used to link the definitive route with the high level route.

To Holmfirth

Hades

Elysium

To Holmbridge

Holme

A6024

Inn

Hot.

Ramsden Resr.

Yateholme Resr.

Riding Wood Resr.

5.1

Reservoirs

On your journey north you will see many reservoirs, especially on the Dunford Bridge to Marsden section.

In the eighteenth century reservoirs were being built to keep the water-wheels turning in the industrial valleys. Later, in the early part of the nineteenth century, more reservoirs were needed to feed water to the canals then being built, and of course, water flowed away each time the locks were used for a craft to gain or lose height. In the latter part of the nineteenth century and the early part of the twentieth century, industrial towns began to spring up and the old streams, wells and cisterns could not be relied upon to provide adequate supplies of water for domestic and industrial uses. Reservoirs were the answer to this problem. The Colne Valley (which runs roughly north-east from Marsden), was at one time a major centre of the wool industry and, as such, relied on water as a means of providing power and transport. Water was also required in quantity for many other industrial processes and domestic use.

It is clearly advantageous if reservoirs can be built in areas of high rainfall and Wessenden is just such a place, as indeed you may discover. Prevailing winds from the south-west, coming from the Atlantic and

Holme

A. Steady climb up lane which turns into a walled track. Fine views.

B. Remember to close the gates after you!

C. On emerging from the walled track onto the open moor begin counting paces.

D. After about 500 paces, the way forks right onto a poorly defined path. An orange-roofed post, marking the course of a gas pipeline should be visible as a guide.

E. Path becomes well-defined.

F. After crossing the footbridge, zigzag up, keeping NW, to stile giving entry to enclosed land.

G. Ascend the field, then through the stile to enter the walled track. Turn left.

H. At the corner where the track turns sharp right, keep ahead through the gate/stile and follow the defined path.

I. Pair of old gateposts and remains of walls. Turn right to ascend to the A635.

J. Cross the A635 and follow the road to Meltham for about 0.25 kilometre.

K. Left through gate into descending, unfenced track.

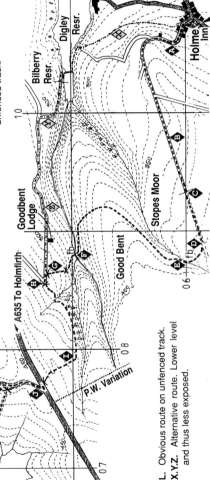

L. Obvious route on unfenced track.

X.Y.Z. Alternative route. Lower level and thus less exposed.

5.2

67

saturated with moisture, ascend the Pennine slopes and deposit that moisture as rain on the high ground. Rainfall, in the Wessenden area, in excess of 130 centimetres per annum used to be quite common, although in the last few years amounts much less than this have fallen.

Not only is high rainfall helpful, but ground conditions must be such as to channel as much water as possible into the collecting basins of the reservoirs. The area around Wessenden is ideal in this respect as the high rainfall on the ridges results in a saturated subsoil and this allows the water to find its way to streams feeding the reservoirs. Also run-off is helped by the steep clough slopes which run back to the high plateaux. Furthermore, water percolating through the surface beds of grit, on reaching the lower impermeable shales, follows the incline of the beds and appears as springs issuing from the clough sides.

Around Marsden, there are some ten or eleven reservoirs, originally built for power, canal and domestic use, but let us confine ourselves to the four reservoirs in the Wessenden Valley. From the top, they are named Wessenden Head, Wessenden Old, Blakeley and Butterley.

The first to be constructed was, as its name implies, Wessenden Old, built in 1790 to keep the Colne Valley water-wheels turning. It was enlarged in 1842 to have a capacity of 487 million litres, with a surface area of 7.7 hectares. The next to be built was the Wessenden Head Reservoir which was completed in 1881 at a cost of £57,510.00 and contains 373 million litres. The third reservoir down the valley was the third to be completed, in 1903, at a cost of £102,279.23 (£102,279 4s 8d). Blakeley, considered by some to be the most beautiful of the Wessenden series, nestles in a narrow deep part of the valley and bracken-clad hills rise from the dark waters (the waters are really dark due to the high peat content). On the south side is a rocky promontory, covered with bracken, heather and bilberry (have you ever tasted wild bilberry pie?) on top of which is a 'rocking stone'. Containing some 360 million litres Blakeley covers an area of 3.85 hectares. Butterley, the last reservoir in the valley, was started in 1891 but major difficulties encountered during its construction delayed completion until 1906. As the reservoir was filling, leaks began to appear when it was only half full and water poured from the face and sides of the embankment. An additional £79,670.25 (£79,670 5s 0d) was required to inject cement grouting into the fissures of the rocks to ensure a watertight embankment. The total cost of this reservoir was

Issues Road, Holme

£369,164.00, the capacity is 1,834 million litres, the embankment is 33.8 metres high, the surface area is 17.5 hectares, the greatest depth of water is 28.6 metres and the top water is 235 metres above sea level.

We were brought up on water running from these hills. It is soft water, which means that when you have your bath in Marsden you will require very little soap. Settling tanks are required to filter out the peat - sometimes before the reservoir, sometimes after and sometimes both. It is delightful to drink and its slightly peaty taste goes well with a tot of whisky.

Cloudberry

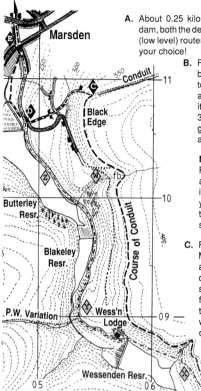

A. About 0.25 kilometre after having passed the first dam, both the definitive (high level) and the alternative (low level) routes are visible across the clough. Make your choice!

B. For the definitive route cross the footbridge, then scramble up the hillside to gain the path. Follow the course of a water conduit which is almost level; it falls only about 15 metres in just over 3 kilometres, and thus keeps high, giving good views over the valleys and hills.

NOTE!

From **B** to **C**, is NOT shown on OS as a right of way. However, we know that it has been walked for well over 50 years and therefore we assume that there will be no problems. Indeed, the southern half is on National Trust land.

C. From here, the object is to drop into Marsden and the multitude of paths and tracks makes clear description difficult for a single route. Suffice it to say, keep descending and have no fear of passing through what appears to be 'back yards'. The map shows what is probably the simplest way down, but not the shortest. If in doubt, get to the lane at SE053107 and follow it down.

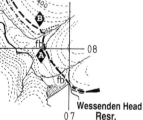

D. A few metres below the junction of the lane and the track, fork left to descend steps to the valley bottom. Proceed to Marsden through the mill yard.

E. The road ahead both joins and passes under the A62. You should pass under.

W. Link to the road and short cut, if desired, but views less spectacular.

X.Y.Z. Low level alternative. Clear path/track all the way to Marsden. Picturesque.

(THE FIFTH STAGE ENDS AT MARSDEN)

5.3

SIXTH STAGE:
MARSDEN TO HEBDEN BRIDGE
Pennine Crossings
22 kilometres, 13.7 miles

A characteristic of this stage is the number of ascents and descents. This is due to the crossing of five valleys, and it highlights the difference between the PW and the APW in this area. Whereas the PW keeps, more or less, to the watershed, the APW crosses the drainage valleys whose rivers flow eastwards. From the energy point of view, this stage will consume more than the PW, but our route provides better going underfoot. Also the APW crosses six trans-Pennine roads, if you include the A62 at Marsden, one of which is the M62. Further, it crosses two trans-Pennine railways and two (former) trans-Pennine canals, again including that at Marsden.

The nature of the landscape is characterised by hill farms, mostly derelict or converted into 'desirable dwellings', and it is clear that in former days there would have been more economic activity on the land. The route uses tracks, paths and lanes which would have been well-trodden by the local inhabitants as they went about their daily business. Gritstone is the main geological feature, and there is another batch of reservoirs. Walking and navigation will not be difficult even in poor weather, although be prepared for plenty of wind and rain because the route is quite exposed.

In contrast to the two previous stages, there is plenty of opportunity for buying lunch, and which hostelry you use will depend on timing. There is the Turnpike Inn on the A672, the New Inn on the A58 and the Blue Ball Inn nearby. If you are ahead of time, there is still another in Cragg Vale - the Hinchliffe Arms. Only modest emergency rations will be needed.

Hebden Bridge has many shops and there is plenty of accommodation. You might find it worthwhile staying a couple of nights to provide a day to look around and a climb up to historic Heptonstall is interesting.

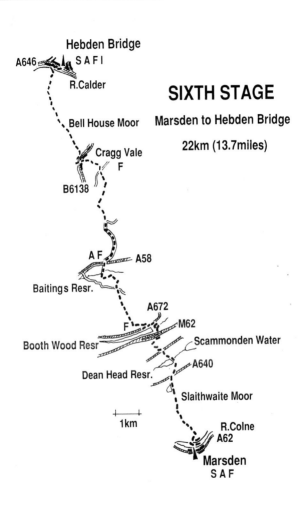

Hebden Bridge
S A F I
A646
R.Calder

SIXTH STAGE

Marsden to Hebden Bridge

22km (13.7miles)

Bell House Moor

Cragg Vale
F

B6138

A F   A58

Baitings Resr.

A672

F   M62

Booth Wood Resr

Scammonden Water

Dean Head Resr.   A640

Slaithwaite Moor

1km

R.Colne
A62

Marsden
S A F

MARSDEN

When you enter Marsden from the Wessenden Valley you will meet the Colne Valley which runs north-east towards Huddersfield. Marsden is 11.7 kilometres from Huddersfield and 29 kilometres from Manchester and has several claims to fame.

Way back in the eleventh century, about the time of William the Conqueror, Marsden was known as Marchdene (from two words March, or Marsh - a swampy place and Dene - a valley). About 1350, we find that Marsden was a hunting ground for the Lord of Pontefract (where the cakes come from), and was a forest 4 kilometres long by 3.25 kilometres wide. In the middle of the fifteenth century the Prior of Nostell Priory (near Wakefield) leased Marsden from Henry VI and around this time a chapel of ease was built. It was built so that the 300 worshippers of Marsden need not make the difficult journey to Almondbury (the other side of Huddersfield), to visit their parish church. The records show very few references to Marsden in the fifteen hundreds, but in the sixteen hundreds when a tax of 2s (10p) was levied on every hearth in every dwelling, we discover that there were about 550 inhabitants living in 82 homes. At the beginning of the eighteenth century the land around Marsden was divided into enclosures of about one to three hectares, and on each block of three or four enclosures stood a house in which the occupants were mainly engaged in carding, spinning, dying and weaving. In 1710 a certain Robert France, who lived in Holmfirth, built a mill for scouring and fulling the cloth produced by the weavers and forty-five weavers signed a legal agreement to use this (the first) mill.

The first road joining Huddersfield with Manchester was constructed by 'Blind Jack of Knaresborough' in 1760 and it was said to be his most magnificent achievement. The eighteenth century also saw the development of the Huddersfield Narrow Canal (q.v.) which led to the building of the Standedge (pronounced "Stanedge") canal tunnel. However, in the middle of the nineteenth century another tunnel was built, this time for the railway. Having taken three years to construct, this first railway tunnel was opened in 1848, but it was not long before the increase in traffic led to a second tunnel being built. Work began in 1868 and finished two years later at a cost of £121,500. This tunnel is 6.6 metres shorter than the other one. In 1890 the L&NW Railway Co. started work on yet another (double) tunnel, which was completed in 1894. Standedge is

A. Pass under the A62. Turn left at the N side of the churchyard and, after about 100 metres, cross the river by the packhorse bridge. Turn left and ascend the walled path, keeping the junk yard on your left.

B. Use the road bridge to cross the Huddersfield Narrow Canal and the trans-Pennine railway, then turn right. After about 40 metres, turn left into Spring Head Lane to begin the ascent of the valley side passing in front of Ingle Nook.

C. Turn left to ascend in the walled path, following the Colne Valley Circular Walk (waymarked).

D. Cross the track and continue the ascent via the walled path. (Wet in places.)

E. Cross the open moor on a well-defined path and go across the dam of Cupwith Reservoir.

F. Right at the A640 for about 50 metres, then left into the fenced track.

G. Beyond the house (more junk), pass through the stile and turn left into the fields to descend the valley (very steep).

H. Cross the dam of Deanhead Reservoir. Ascend, making for the wall which runs straight up the valley side, then climb upwards keeping to the E of the wall.

I. Cross the stile in the fence. Keep climbing, now on the W side of the fence, diverging slightly to get to the gate at the road.

J. Cross the B6114, then follow the well-defined path to the brow and descend. The M62 is stretched out before you.

X.Y.Z. Variation, to take in Tunnel End of the canal. Follow the tow path under the railway and over the canal to get to Tunnel End. Leave via access lane, cross the road keeping the inn on the left and ascend the steep path. Use tracks to rejoin the definitive route.

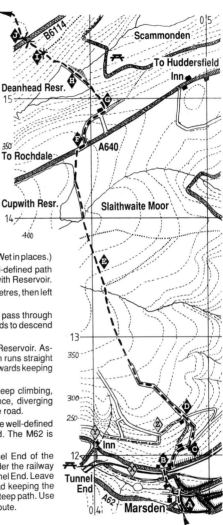

6.1

75

unique in having four tunnels through the hills over such a great length; another splendid example of Victorian engineering resourcefulness.

The early seventeenth century saw the development in Marsden, by Enoch and James Taylor of a shear frame, which was designed to cut the nap of the cloth to a uniform level, this work formerly being done by hand by croppers. The machine produced better results more quickly, but it was seen to be putting the croppers out of business. It so happened that at about that time a Nottinghamshire man, named Ludlam, had caused a bit of a fuss by breaking machines which had taken over from hand knitting and lacemaking. The Luddite Movement spread to the West Riding of Yorkshire and in particular to the Colne Valley. A great hammer was used by the Luddites to smash the machines; it was called Enoch and the saying was - "Enoch has made them and Enoch shall smash them." The Luddites caused much disruption and many of the mills built fortifications and used troops to repel the rioters. The riots ended abruptly, with the hanging of the ringleader in York on January 8, 1813. Enoch and James Taylor then started the first (and the last, as far as we know) iron foundry in Marsden. When the brothers retired from the business, a nephew and the son of a partner took over and developed the business even more, to include the manufacture of boilers and steam engines. The highly skilled workers were the talk of the town and had the best of everything to eat and drink, in contrast to the poor mill-workers who were on a subsistence diet of porridge, barley bread, potatoes, oatcake and occasionally some bacon.

A glance at various lists of tenants in those days reveals that many families had the same, or similar sounding names. With so many Haigs, Mellors, Marsdens and Shaws it became necessary to define, for instance, which Jim Shaw one was talking about. Thus, it came about that someone might have been referred to as 'Jim o' Jud's' - Jim of Jud's (Shaw). This by-naming used to be extended to as many as four first names and the one that sticks in our mind is Jim o' Jud o' Ned o' Vic's. A variation is a by-name based on a family tradition, for example one of our grandfathers was known as Jim o' Drummers. Legend has it that one of his ancestors was a drummer at the battle of Waterloo.

As with many towns and villages, Marsden has its own legend - that of the cuckoo. It appears that way back in history the good people of Marsden decided that if they could persuade a cuckoo to be a permanent

Marsden Cuckoos

resident near the village, then maybe because of its association with favourable weather the rigours of winter could be avoided and they would be blessed with a permanent summer. When the cuckoo next visited Marsden the inhabitants quickly erected a tower to imprison the bird. However, they omitted to put a roof on the tower and, much to their astonishment the bird flew away! A similar tale is told of many localities in the North! A few kilometres down the road towards Huddersfield, is a small town called Slaithwaite, pronounced "Slathwaite", or "Slawit" by the locals. Rumour has it that the people of Slawit had been involved in contraband running and hearing that the duty men were around decided to hide the goods by sealing them in a container and submerging it in the canal. One bright moonlit night they decided to recover their goods by raking the container out, but they were surprised by the duty men. On being challenged they replied that they were raking out that 'big white cheese', as they chose to call the reflection of the moon.

Ever since, the residents of Slawit have been known as the "Slawit Moon Rakers".

Marsden nowadays is mainly a dormitory town, having lost most of its textile mills. A few trains a day convey passengers to and from Huddersfield or Manchester and there are three or four buses each hour to Huddersfield. The town centre is designated as a conservation area and the old stocks have been preserved. The grave of Enoch Taylor can be seen in the churchyard.

The Huddersfield Narrow Canal

During your journey you will cross three canals. If you are going south to north, the first is the Huddersfield Narrow Canal at Marsden, the second is the Rochdale Canal at Hebden Bridge and the last is the Leeds and Liverpool Canal which you will cross at Bingley. Each of these canals has a fascinating history.

The Huddersfield Narrow Canal (sometimes referred to as the Huddersfield Ashton Canal), was constructed around 1774. It was in two parts, in that narrow boats from Huddersfield terminated at the Marsden wharf. Here, all the goods were unloaded from the boats and taken by carts and packhorse over Standedge (pronounced "Stanedge") to Diggle. The goods were then loaded into boats for the forward journey towards Ashton-under-Lyme. Marsden and Diggle thus became thriving dockyards, with many warehouses and all the supporting services.

By the end of the century, traffic jams were the order of the day in Diggle and Marsden, and considerable congestion was to be found on the moorland routes between the two towns - the pedestrians didn't stand a chance! It was decided, therefore, to built a tunnel through the hills. The necessary Act of Parliament being passed in 1794, work started in 1798. However, two further Acts were required and these were passed in 1800 and 1804. Work was completed and the tunnel opened in 1811 at a cost of about £200,000. There were, of course, no mechanical borers or even diggers in those days, so the whole length of the tunnel, 4.99 kilometres was built, starting at both ends, using only gunpowder, picks and shovels.

The tunnel entrances are arched for some distance before giving way to bare rock. Up to the tunnel entrances, boats were towed by horses walking along the tow-paths, but in the tunnel, 'leggers' were employed. 'Leggers' lay on the boat and pushed with their feet along the roof of the

*Tunnel end,
Marsden*

tunnel. At the wide parts which are, in places, quite cavernous with enough room to allow boats to turn around or pass each other, poles or boat-hooks were employed to keep the boats moving. The journey usually took 3½ to 4 hours.

The Marsden entrance is 133 metres above the water level at Huddersfield and 200 metres above sea level. The height difference required many locks, (74 between Huddersfield and Ashton) and six reservoirs were constructed to feed the canal. Due to the cost of maintenance being so high and income so low, and the fact that railways had taken most of the trade, few boats used the tunnel after 1905 and traffic stopped entirely during World War II, the canal becoming abandoned in 1944. The tunnels were barred at each end in 1951, although the odd boat is driven through the tunnel every two years or so to carry out an inspection. Some of the locks have been 'cascaded' and some have been filled in, as indeed have parts of the canal itself. Currently, moves are afoot to redevelop the canal for tourist and pleasure traffic and much work has been done in this respect, especially at Marsden.

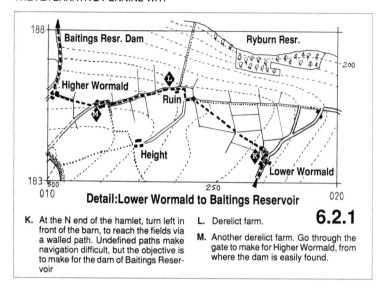

Detail:Lower Wormald to Baitings Reservoir

K. At the N end of the hamlet, turn left in front of the barn, to reach the fields via a walled path. Undefined paths make navigation difficult, but the objective is to make for the dam of Baitings Reservoir

L. Derelict farm.

M. Another derelict farm. Go through the gate to make for Higher Wormald, from where the dam is easily found.

6.2.1

M62 - Motorway Across the Pennines

We remember times not so long ago when the 160-kilometre road journey from Liverpool to Hull was made very difficult, due to the roads over the Pennines being made impassable by snow and ice. The building of the M62 has changed all that, and reduced the journey time from a tortuous five hours to a relatively easy two hours.

The idea of a fast road across the Pennines was first discussed in 1930, but preliminary work on the trans-Pennine Motorway was not started until the spring of 1961, when the then Minister of Transport asked the county councils of Lancashire and the West Riding of Yorkshire to devise a suitable route. In 1964, the line of the motorway had been fixed and work started in May 1966. The building of a new reservoir at Scammonden (see "Scammonden Dam" Feature), close to the proposed route of the motorway led to a re-siting of the proposed dam with the motorway running across the embankment.

The Pennine Way footbridge, at Windy Hill on the county boundary, marks the highest elevation of the M62 at 400 metres and from here the

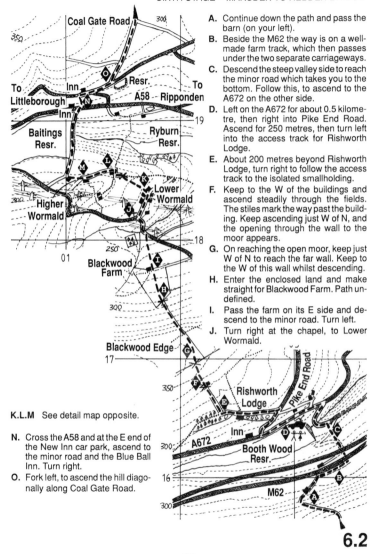

A. Continue down the path and pass the barn (on your left).

B. Beside the M62 the way is on a well-made farm track, which then passes under the two separate carriageways.

C. Descend the steep valley side to reach the minor road which takes you to the bottom. Follow this, to ascend to the A672 on the other side.

D. Left on the A672 for about 0.5 kilometre, then right into Pike End Road. Ascend for 250 metres, then turn left into the access track for Rishworth Lodge.

E. About 200 metres beyond Rishworth Lodge, turn right to follow the access track to the isolated smallholding.

F. Keep to the W of the buildings and ascend steadily through the fields. The stiles mark the way past the building. Keep ascending just W of N, and the opening through the wall to the moor appears.

G. On reaching the open moor, keep just W of N to reach the far wall. Keep to the W of this wall whilst descending.

H. Enter the enclosed land and make straight for Blackwood Farm. Path undefined.

I. Pass the farm on its E side and descend to the minor road. Turn left.

J. Turn right at the chapel, to Lower Wormald.

K.L.M See detail map opposite.

N. Cross the A58 and at the E end of the New Inn car park, ascend to the minor road and the Blue Ball Inn. Turn right.

O. Fork left, to ascend the hill diagonally along Coal Gate Road.

6.2

81

next 11 kilometres eastwards across the moors to the outskirts of Huddersfield presented the motorway builders with their greatest challenge. This area is one of the wettest in the country, and for two of the three summers worked on the contract the Pennines received some of the highest recorded rainfalls, with 168 centimetres falling during the first year. This made the peat bogs impassable and special vehicles with a very low ground pressure had to be utilised. The peat varied in depth from 1.5 metres to 6 metres and a unique method of excavation was devised. This involved cutting straight down through the peat and then excavating the peat from the exposed vertical edge, using vehicles operating on the more solid strata under the peat. The peat was useless, and heated dump-trucks were used to transfer the glutinous mass to the surrounding hillsides. Blind Jack of Knaresborough didn't have this problem in the sixteenth century.

The heavy rainfall in this area meant that special consideration had to be given, not only to dispersing water from the motorway itself, but also to preventing water running off the hillsides and onto the carriageways. An intricate system of drainage channels has been installed, which takes care of these problems, and in addition ensures that the catchment systems for the Yorkshire Water Authority are not denied water. The design of the deep cuttings and embankments is such as to minimise the risk of snow drifts and the National Physical Laboratory's wind tunnel was used to achieve the best possible characteristics. Even the safety barriers have, in places, been built using tensioned steel wire ropes instead of the usual barriers in an effort to reduce the likelihood of snow build-up.

You will have noticed that sheep abound in this area, and precautions had to be taken to prevent strays on the carriageways. A special 1.5-metre-high fencing with a low wind resistance to eliminate snow drifts was designed. The apertures at the bottom are smaller to prevent lambs getting through and the whole fence is plastic coated in a grey colour which merges with the surrounding landscape.

The material from the cuttings was used to build the embankments and special blasting techniques were employed to produce the correct grade of material. At various times during the work more than 2,000 machines were employed and vast amounts of material were shifted.

A comprehensive communication system has been provided so that the computers in the Wakefield control centre have access to a wide variety of information about conditions on the motorway. The equipment on the motorway includes wind speed and direction indicators, road surface temperature and humidity indicators, salinity indicators, visibility indicators and the provision of television cameras giving views of the mountain areas. Using these monitoring systems, the computers can analyse the information received and the operators can take action to give appropriate warnings to traffic.

The APW passes under the M62 near Stott Hall Farm where the carriageways diverge to pass around the farm. If it is a nice day when you journey through this area, just pause to reflect what it must have been like working on the construction, and the battle against the elements that was fought on the route of the M62 - Motorway Across The Pennines. If it is not a nice day, you will get an impression of what it might have been like anyway!

The Wars of the Roses? The hard shoulders in Lancashire were dressed with RED schlamme, whereas in Yorkshire they were surface dressed with a WHITE balliden chipping!

Lower Wormald

Scammonden Dam

At the time the West Riding route of the M62 was finally being settled (see "M62 - Motorway Across The Pennines" Feature), Huddersfield's water authorities were deciding on the site of a new dam. After talks with the motorway authorities, a co-operative was embarked upon, which at the time was unique in this country and possibly the world. The M62 crosses the Deanhead Valley on the embankment of Scammonden Dam, and as a result, Huddersfield benefits from a bigger reservoir than would otherwise have been possible.

The engineers at Scammonden embarked on a comprehensive grouting programme before building the dam. This was done to seal the foundations and prevent leakage under and around the dam. The massive task of constructing the dam embankment took just over three years.

The total catchment area for Scammonden is 523 hectares with an additional 1,619 hectares in the Colne Valley, this being linked to the reservoir by the Bradshaw Tunnel which is nearly three kilometres long. In addition there

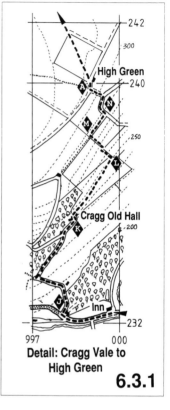

Detail: Cragg Vale to High Green

6.3.1

is a further 150-hectare catchment area downstream of the dam. The average annual rainfall in this area is 1,321 millimetres (52 inches) - you have been warned!

Buried in the massive dam structure is a comprehensive array of instruments including twenty-two piezometers (to measure the height of the water table in the underlying shales and sandstone), and three inverted pendulums (to indicate relative movement). The rockfill contains thirty-five piezometers, four horizontal movement gauges and three vertical movement gauges. The clay core contains a bewildering variety of instruments to

A. Continue on Coal Gate Road for about 1.5 kilometres.

B. Fork left through the gate, into the well-defined track. Open moorland to the W.

C. (From here to the inn and church at Cragg Vale the APW is the same as the way-marked Calderdale Way.) At the highest point, near to the derelict bunker, turn right (approx NE), to keep on the high ground. Follow the well-defined track.

D. This fork left is easily missed, so monitor your position carefully.

E. At the road junction, proceed on the road ahead for about 200 metres, then turn left to descend the track.

F. Turn right (still with the Calderdale Way), for approx 100 metres, then left.

G. Zigzag right then left, at the house. Through stile and follow the paved way downwards.

H. Another stile. Left and level for 100 metres, or so. Continue with the paved way downwards, until the house access track is reached. Down to the B6138.

I. At the B6138, sharp right then sharp left, to gain the church and the inn.

J. Right, up the very steep lane. NOT ahead along the road and NOT through the ornate gatehouse.

K. In front of Cragg Old Hall, left and right to pass on the NW side of the outbuildings. Enter the field through the gate and follow the middle path to ascend diagonally to the rough steps at the corner of the field. See across for details.

L. Over the steps and wire fence (stile). Ascend the field for a few metres (wall on right), then over the stiles to the other side. Continue with the wall on your left.

M. Where a broken wall crosses your path and a path comes in from the left through a gate, turn right and walk on the level.

N. Turn left to join the path ascending the valley, to the farm buildings of High Green. Details across.

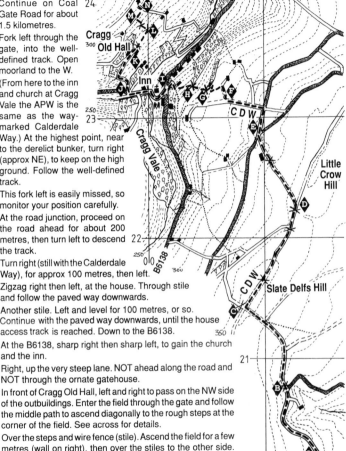

6.3

85

measure the magnitude and direction of stresses, to detect arching effect and to measure pore pressure ratios across the core. In addition, there are other gauges measuring settlement and overflow. The gauge houses are located at the downstream toe of the dam. A 'Mekometer Station' has been built 150 metres downstream which measures the distance between two points to an accuracy of one part in a million, so that all horizontal movements of the dam and the ground under it can be directly related to this point. This must surely be the most instrumented dam in the country?

The completed scheme provides a pleasant recreational area. Trees have been planted and picnic areas with car parks and other facilities have been provided. A sailing club uses the water and the success of the whole enterprise can be gauged by the number of visitors on a sunny summer weekend.

Cragg Vale Coiners

A way of overcoming poverty in the late eighteenth century was to make your own money, and this 'art' thrived especially in the more remote parts of Calderdale. The most notorious gang operated in Cragg Vale, at a time when the road up the valley was little more than a track. Most of the coiners were weavers and farmers, living in isolated farmsteads where they could not easily be surprised by the revenue men.

The coiners' leader, self-styled 'King' David Hartley, lived at Bell House (the APW passes within 100 metres) and his partner-in-crime David Greenwood lived at Hill Top, both at the top of steep hills. By the time the officers of the law had toiled their way up the hills, the coining equipment was safely hidden away. Gold for counterfeit coins was obtained by shaving the edges of guineas and filling new edges on. The shavings were melted down and made into blanks which were used to make replicas of Portuguese coins, then in wide circulation.

The coiners of Cragg Vale are seen nowadays in a romantic light, but in reality they were selfish, cowardly and brutal. On one occasion they murdered an excise man and on another they heard a man in an inn talking too freely about their exploits, so they pushed him into the fire and burnt him to death.

The murder of the excise man proved to be their undoing. Several were executed for counterfeiting, and the body of 'King' David Hartley was brought back to the Calder Valley after his execution at York. His grave can be seen in the churchyard at Heptonstall. You will find a display of coining equipment if you visit Heptonstall Museum.

A. At High Green, right on the access track, then enter the rectangular enclosure at its S corner (gate and stile). Proceed diagonally to its N corner, then onto the open moor making towards the chimney and roof just visible on the skyline 1.5 kilometres away.

B. Keep NW on the paved path (NOT to the house). Path becomes wet and boggy. A gap in the wall with a gate can be seen on the skyline. Make for this.

C. At the head of the valley, keep approx NNW, path undefined. NOT along the line of a broken wall.

D. Enter walled lane ahead through gate.

E. Turn right on the track (NOT down the metalled road), then turn left.

F. Under the lane and enter the wood.

G. Zigzag down, path defined.

H. The first objective is to get to the centre of Hebden Bridge, but there is a railway, a canal and a river to cross. Use your initiative, there is no problem. The definitive route is shown on the map.

(THE SIXTH STAGE ENDS AT
HEBDEN BRIDGE)

The second objective is to get to the N end of the town beside Hebden Water. Again, use your initiative. The APW crosses the A646 at traffic lights, into Bridge Gate. After a few hundred metres, it crosses Hebden Water at St. George's Street. It then goes NE, following Valley Road, and recrosses Hebden Water on the road bridge into Victoria Road. It passes through a developing housing estate to cross Hebden Water once again via Foster Lane Bridge, which is a packhorse bridge.

I. Ascend the walled path for a few metres, then turn right (N) along the branch walled path.

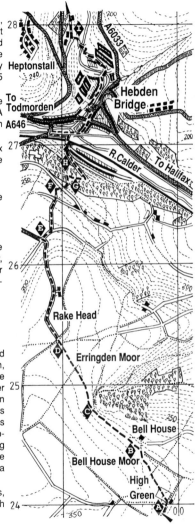

6.4

SEVENTH STAGE:
HEBDEN BRIDGE TO HAWORTH

Brontë Country
12.5 kilometres, 7.8 miles

This is a very short stage, and it can be completed in a morning if you make an early start. After a little local difficulty getting through the maze of streets in Hebden Bridge, navigation is very straightforward. The route follows Hebden Dale northwards for about 1.5 kilometres. The dale then turns westwards to Hardcastle Crags, but the APW continues northwards up Crimsworth Dean (a deviation to Hardcastle Crags is possible if there is time). After climbing out of the dean the route passes over moors which the Brontë family must have known well, and then descends into Haworth. The highest point is about 425 metres and most of the way is on well-defined tracks which would have seen more traffic in earlier days. The only traffic now will be walkers and the occasional Land-Rover, or similar, getting access to a remote dwelling.

If you choose to make Haworth for lunchtime, only a morning drink/snack need be carried, together with the minimum of emergency rations.

Cragg Old Hall

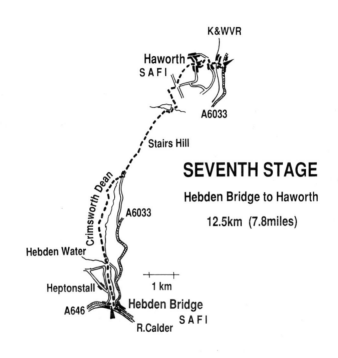

K&WVR

Haworth
S A F I

A6033

Stairs Hill

Crimsworth Dean

A6033

SEVENTH STAGE

Hebden Bridge to Haworth

12.5km (7.8miles)

Hebden Water

Heptonstall

A646

1 km

Hebden Bridge
S A F I

R.Calder

If the day is pleasant and you want to dawdle, you will need to carry lunch as there is nowhere to buy anything between start and finish.

There is plenty of accommodation in Haworth although, because of its popularity, lodgings may be difficult to find in the tourist season. There are, of course, plenty of shops and if you do arrive by lunchtime there is plenty to do and see in the afternoon. Besides visiting the Parsonage Museum, you could visit the Keighley & Worth Valley Railway at Haworth Station.

HEBDEN BRIDGE

There are several buildings and features of interest in Hebden Bridge and many of these are included in a 'history trail', a self-guided walk around the town. A booklet describing the route is available from local shops and the tourist information centre. Having chosen your accommodation from the wide selection of hotels, pubs, guest-houses and bed & breakfasts, you may care to spend an extra day exploring the town and the surrounding countryside.

The old packhorse bridge built in the town centre about 1510 to replace the fourteenth-century wooden bridge from which the town got its name, and repaired several times since, carries a stone-setted packhorse track across Hebden Water. The steep track goes up the hillside from the bridge towards Heptonstall, and is known as the Buttress. The White Lion Hotel, dated 1657, was one of the first buildings in Hebden Bridge and was once a farmhouse (the old barn can be seen opposite). The inn was later a stagecoach halt on one of the Halifax to Rochdale routes.

Bridge Mill, between Old Bridge and the White Lion, was built on the site of the manorial corn-mill of Wadsworth and the building dates back more than five centuries. The weir, across the adjacent Hebden Water diverted the river to the mill's former water-wheel. Nutclough Mill, a five-storey factory alongside Keighley Road, was one of the cornerstones of the early co-operative movement in the nineteenth century. The Antiques Centre in Market Street, dated 1777, was once a Baptist chapel and among the gravestones to be seen outside is one which records that the man buried there was murdered "because he became poor"!

Another town centre feature is the Black Pit Aqueduct, built in 1797, on the Rochdale Canal (q.v.). Various toll-houses existed in the town during the eighteenth and nineteenth centuries, but the only one remaining

Yorkshire Roofs & Lancashire Roofs

can be seen in Commercial Street - it is now a newsagency. The original dry dock on the canal, filled in and built on after the canal ceased to be a commercial proposition thirty years ago, has been excavated and converted into a marina.

In Hebden Bridge there is so little flat land that some houses are built on top of others. What appear to be four-storey buildings are actually two dwellings built into the steep hillside so that the ground floor of the lower one has an entrance on one street, and the ground floor of the higher one has an entrance on another street further up the hillside. Some of the top houses are also built as 'back-to-backs', with a balcony between the second and third storeys to enable residents to have independent access to their homes. This type of housing can also be found in other parts of Yorkshire.

Whilst in Hebden Bridge, a visit to Heptonstall is well worthwhile, as it is one of the most historic villages in the Pennines. As in Hebden Bridge, there is a 'history trail', which will guide you around many of the interesting features. At the centre of the village are the ruins of the Church of St. Thomas à Becket, founded between 1256 and 1260. It was damaged by a severe storm in 1857 and never fully repaired, but the bulk of the ruin is from the fifteenth century, though some of the original building remains.

The eleven-sided font from the old church can be seen in the adjacent Victorian parish church, built in 1854. Off Northgate is the octagonal Methodist church, built in 1764 and claimed to be the oldest continuously used Methodist church in the world. The old grammar school at Churchyard Bottom, founded in 1642, was developed as a museum in the early 1970s, and nearby the old Cloth Hall is now a private residence. Throughout the village and the district, there are many old weavers' cottages, with their long rows of mullioned windows which were designed to let in as much light as possible to the looms. Some of these buildings were demolished a few years ago and a 'Weavers' Square' was developed on the site using many different types of Yorkshire paving, including cobbles, pebbles, setts, flagstones and concrete. There are many other features and buildings of interest for those who wish to spend more time in the village.

The only crop that could be grown effectively in such a wet area as Hebden Bridge was oats, which unfortunately is a low-yielding crop. The locals supplemented their diet with a pudding made from dock leaves. These were not the large cow docks used by walkers to ease the pain of nettle stings, but the smaller sweet dock. This was boiled up with nettles, oatmeal, onions and salt, and the result was 'dock pudding'. Dock pudding is still made and 'exported' in jars to Calder Valley exiles, and recipes can be obtained in Hebden Bridge which boasts that it had the first 'World Dock Pudding Champion' in 1971. The pudding should be served fried in bacon fat, with bacon and fried potatoes seasoned with salt, pepper and vinegar.

The Rochdale Canal

When you arrive at the Rochdale Canal, you will immediately realise that it is different from the Huddersfield Narrow. It is considerably wider and each of the ninety-two locks, with one exception, can take one barge or two narrow boats, whereas the Huddersfield Narrow locks can only take one narrow boat. Built by William Jessop, a colleague of the famous Thomas Telford, the Rochdale was completed in 1804 and its 53-kilometre route linked the canals at Sowerby Bridge and Manchester, to complete a coast-to-coast waterway. It was one of three canal routes over the Pennines, the other two being the Huddersfield Narrow and the Leeds and Liverpool. The Huddersfield Narrow is the only one having a long tunnel on its route through the Pennines. The Rochdale climbs over 92

A. Pass the cottages (on your right) and enter the wood. Paths diverge, but keep left to ascend gently through the wood to reach the lane at B.

B. North along this lane.

C. Calderdale Way crosses lane here. Right, off the lane and follow the Calderdale Way beside Hebden Water.

D. Over Hebden Water and ascend to the road. Cross this road and enter the path, keeping the car park on your left.

E. Join lane and ascend ahead.

F. Route easy to follow - wet in places.

CDW - Calderdale Way.

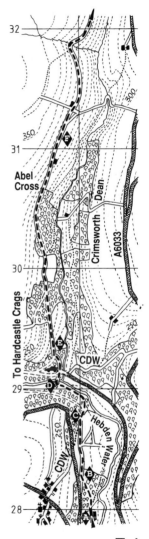

7.1

metres on the Yorkshire side, by means of thirty-six locks, and the horse-drawn barges carried vast quantities of wool, cotton, finished cloth and, more importantly, coal to fire the hungry furnaces of the new 'steam-age'. It is recorded that, at its peak, over 295,000 tonnes of goods were carried each year. As well as the many locks, there were four aqueducts and one of these, the Black Pit Aqueduct, built in 1797, was the biggest single structure in the canal's length. The four arches over the River Calder can be seen at the end of Holme Street (near the post office), in Hebden Bridge.

Unfortunately, the canal went out of commercial use over 30 years ago and parts of it, as with the Huddersfield Narrow, have fallen into disuse. At Sowerby Bridge the canal disappears altogether, the water being piped underground through the town. However, an active restoration group is in existence and attempts are being made to revitalise the canal for pleasure trips. It seems that the local councils are beginning to realise that a canal can be an asset to the community and efforts are being made to prevent further deterioration in the fabric of the waterways.

Hebden Bridge

A. Continue on the clearly defined track to Grain Water Bridge.

B. Join the metalled road and ascend to Lane Head, where the way degenerates to a track.

C. Over the watershed at Top of Stairs.

D. Descend via Stairs Lane and Bodkin Lane to Leeshaw Reservoir.

E. The track is now a lane which passes on the low side of the dam.

F. Turn left to ascend the access track to Westfield Farm.

G. Keep the farm on your left and enter the fields. Keep the wall on your right.

H. Enter the open moor. The APW keeps to the wall side.

I. Join the road and turn left.

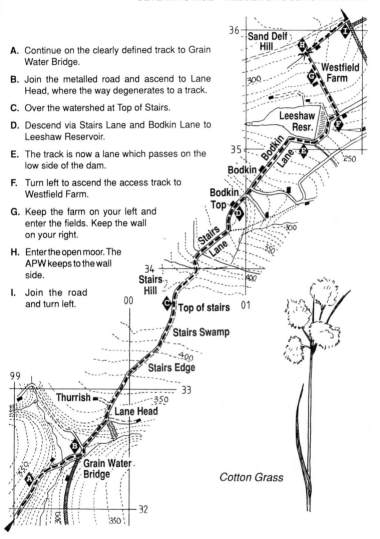

Cotton Grass

7.2

HAWORTH

Almost all walkers approaching Haworth will be aware of its literary association with the Brontës (q.v.), though few will realise that had it not been for a certain William Grimshaw the story of the Brontës might have been very different indeed.

Haworth was not recorded in the famous 1086 Domesday Book, but it is mentioned in records during the fourteenth century when the village had forty inhabitants in 1380. Details of marriages and deaths have been kept in the church parish registers since 1645, and throughout the history of Haworth the Church has played a prominent role. Since Elizabethan times the parish clergymen of Haworth have been chosen by agreement between the Bishop of Bradford and a group of local worthies and in May 1742 William Grimshaw was appointed curate.

When Grimshaw was appointed (for life) the parish church was a chapel of ease, provided so that the parishioners did not have to walk all the way to Bradford to take part in services. Grimshaw's arrival on the scene was at a time when the Church was not very well thought of by the local inhabitants. However, by sheer hard work and by demonstrating that he cared for his flock, he was able to win his parishioners over to his way of thinking. During his early years at Haworth he was converted from Anglicanism to Methodism by the famous John Wesley who visited Haworth many times. In August 1784 after preaching in the church at 5.00am, Wesley later preached to a congregation of over 4,000 in the churchyard, where, incidentally, it is reputed that over 40,000 lie buried. The trees in the churchyard were planted in the mid-eighteenth century by the Board of Health to prevent the water supplies being contaminated by 'graveyard waste'.

Returning to Grimshaw, his popularity as a minister was such that in 1755 it became necessary to enlarge the church. Even then he preached to capacity congregations and many still had to worship outside. Grimshaw died in 1763, but by that time he had put the Church on a firm and popular footing in Haworth and it was from this base that Patrick Brontë was able to be successful when he took over as rector, fifty years later in 1820.

Main Street, Haworth is made from stone setts, clearly designed for horses, not motor cars. At the turn of the nineteenth century there were several stone quarries being worked in the vicinity and when a wagon, with as heavy a load as ten tonnes of stone, descended Main Street the

Haworth

wheels were fastened, a 'slipper brake' was put under the wheels and the horses then pulled the wagon downhill. The jumbled confusion of houses in Main Street was mainly built in the late eighteenth and early nineteenth centuries, when hand-loom weaving was a major industry. Some of the three-storey buildings have long rows of mullioned windows, behind which two or three looms used to be situated. At the top of Main Street is the Black Bull Inn, once the 'watering place' of the famous (or infamous?) Branwell Brontë. At one time three other inns, the White Lion, the White Cross and the King's Arms, were all nearby. Hand-loom weaving and sandstone quarrying must both have been very thirst-provoking trades as there were so many inns in Haworth!

The neat, clean and tidy streets of Haworth today are very different from what would have been seen in the times of the Brontës. Open sewers were commonplace and the drinking water was polluted. This resulted in diseases such as typhoid and cholera being prevalent at a time when the population of Haworth was at its highest, and, no doubt, explains why people died at such an early age. In 1850 people died at an average age of twenty-six and more than 40 per cent of children died before reaching the age of six.

Both Haworth Parsonage and Haworth parish church are not as you would have seen them at the time the Brontës were around. The parsonage, now a museum, was altered by one of Brontë's successors who added a north and west wing as well as making other alterations. However, by standing in the graveyard and viewing the rather sombre sandstone Georgian exterior, one can get a good impression of what the building would have looked like when originally completed in 1779. The parsonage was owned by the Church until 1928 when it was bought and presented by the Brontë Society to be used as a Brontë museum. On display in the museum are many items actually used by the Brontës, and every effort has been made to furnish and decorate the rooms to replicate the style of living of the Brontë family. The church standing adjacent to the parsonage is a 'new' church built in 1875 by Patrick Brontë's successor John Wade, who wanted a new church partly because the old one was rather dilapidated and partly because the Brontë image was a 'hard act to follow' and he wanted to start afresh. There are, of course, many items of interest for Brontë devotees in the church which is open to the public.

Railway enthusiasts will find it difficult to pass through Haworth without visiting the railway station, as this has now become the HQ of the Keighley and Worth Valley Railway Preservation Society. The society runs an all-year-round service (usually steam-hauled), on an eight-kilometre stretch of line between Oxenhope and Keighley and at Haworth Station can be found the locomotive works yard, bookshop, souvenir and transport relic shop. *The Railway Children* was filmed in the Worth Valley twenty years ago and this event promoted the popularity and brought back many memories of the 'golden age of steam'.

The Brontë Family

Brontë-philes will already be aware of the significance of the name Brontë. However, for those who may wonder what effect the Brontës had on the literary world a few words of explanation are given below.

Three sisters, Anne, Charlotte and Emily Jane were born to Maria, the Cornish wife of Patrick Brunty (or Prunty) of Irish descent. The Bruntys also had a son, Branwell, and two other daughters, Maria and Elizabeth. The family moved to Haworth in 1820 when Brunty, who by now had changed his name to Brontë, was appointed rector, but his wife Maria died of cancer in 1821 at the age of thirty-eight and Brontë's sister 'Aunt

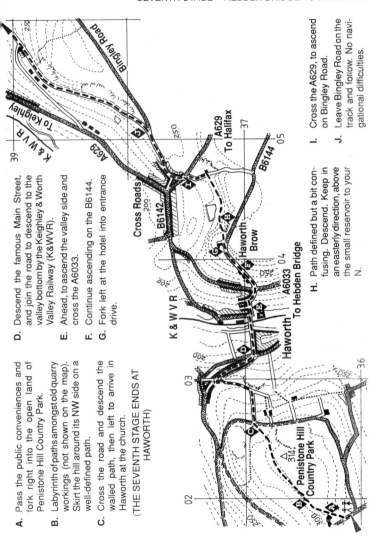

A. Pass the public conveniences and fork right into the open land of Penistone Hill Country Park.

B. Labyrinth of paths amongst old quarry workings (not shown on the map). Skirt the hill around its NW side on a well-defined path.

C. Cross the road and descend the walled path, then left to arrive in Haworth at the church.

(THE SEVENTH STAGE ENDS AT HAWORTH)

D. Descend the famous Main Street, and join the road to descend to the valley bottom by the Keighley & Worth Valley Railway (K&WVR).

E. Ahead, to ascend the valley side and cross the A6033.

F. Continue ascending on the B6144.

G. Fork left at the hotel into entrance drive.

H. Path defined but a bit confusing. Descend. Keep in an easterly direction, above the small reservoir to your N.

I. Cross the A629, to ascend on Bingley Road.

J. Leave Bingley Road on the track and follow. No navigational difficulties.

7.3

Branwell' stayed to look after the rector, the five sisters and their brother. The children apparently led a lonely though happy life and in 1824, with the exception of Anne and Branwell, were sent off to a school for daughters of the clergy. However, harsh schooling and poor conditions were said to have helped Maria and Elizabeth on their way to an early death, after which Charlotte and Emily speedily returned home where their father and aunt became their tutors.

The literary talents of the children were already becoming apparent. Drawing on their childhood imagination, the children wrote in verse and prose about the mythical countries of Gondal and Angria, using minuscule handwriting in tiny books. These countries of their fantasies encompassed many exotic places and were inhabited by many famous people.

Branwell, although a reasonable artist, was a failure when it came to earning a living. He half-heartedly tried various jobs, then took to drink and eventually opium, allegedly to counteract the pain of consumption. Branwell died in 1848 at the age of thirty-one.

The three girls, after leaving school, decided to go and work as governesses in various private households, but they universally disliked the job and decided to set up a school of their own. Charlotte and Emily went off to a school in Brussels in 1842 to augment their qualifications. Unfortunately Charlotte formed a hopeless and unreciprocated attachment to the married proprietor, a Monsieur Hager. Disillusioned in love, Charlotte returned to Haworth. The three sisters decided to abandon the idea of forming a school and put their literary talents to work.

Initially, using the pseudonyms of Acton Bell (Anne), Currer Bell (Charlotte) and Ellis Bell (Emily Jane), the initials of the pseudonyms corresponding with their own initials, the girls started to write books for publication. Their first joint effort, *Poems,* in 1846, proved to be a disaster with only two copies being sold, so they decided to concentrate on prose.

Anne wrote two novels, *Agnes Grey* and *The Tenant of Wildfell Hall* - she died of consumption in 1849 at the age of twenty-nine. Charlotte wrote *The Professor, Jane Eyre, Shirley* and *Villette.* She married her father's curate in 1854 and died in pregnancy during the following year at the age of thirty-eight, leaving a part-finished novel *Emma.* Emily Jane wrote a single novel *Wuthering Heights,* which together with Charlotte's *Jane Eyre* are perhaps the best known of the Brontë writings. Emily died of consumption in 1848 at the age of twenty-nine.

Patrick Brontë outlived them all and died in 1861 at the ripe old age of eighty-one. His legacy was the writings of the Brontë sisters - surely one of the most remarkable literary families that ever lived. Their influence is felt not only in Haworth and its immediate surroundings, but also in the many towns and villages in northern England where they lived or visited. Their books will remain for ever amongst the greatest in the English language.

Brontë Parsonage, Haworth

EIGHTH STAGE:
HAWORTH TO ILKLEY

Industry and Moors
18.5 kilometres, 11.5 miles

A characteristic of the towns in West Yorkshire is that they sit in valleys keeping their industrial activity localised, whilst only a few kilometres away there are open hills and moors. This stage glimpses this characteristic. The first few kilometres skirt Keighley, whilst lunchtime sees you in Bingley. A highlight is the one-kilometre walk on the tow path of the Leeds and Liverpool Canal, passing both the three-rise and the five-rise lock systems. The second highlight, especially if you're a Yorkshireman, is the walk over Ilkley Moor (more correctly Rombalds Moor, since Ilkley Moor is merely a localised part of the whole massif). Whatever the weather this part must be done baht 'at, whether you're with Mary Jane or not!

This stage clearly brings out the contrast between the initial part, industrial towns, and the subsequent part, open moors (highest point about 385 metres). The latter is exposed and could be onerous in bad weather, especially over one section which is quite boggy. Only modest

Wuthering Heights

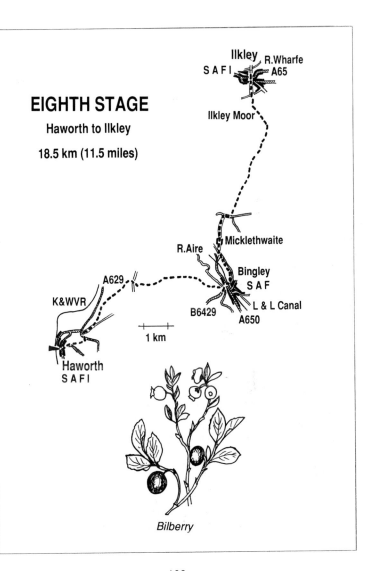

EIGHTH STAGE

Haworth to Ilkley

18.5 km (11.5 miles)

Ilkley
S A F I
R.Wharfe
A65

Ilkley Moor

Micklethwaite

R.Aire

Bingley
S A F

A629

L & L Canal

K&WVR

B6429

A650

1 km

Haworth
S A F I

Bilberry

emergency rations will be required, as you're never more than three kilometres away from 'civilisation'.

There are plenty of shops and inns etc in Bingley and, of course, Ilkley has, as well as shops and inns, plenty of accommodation.

'Brownie points' will not be lost if you choose to use the Keighley & Worth Valley Railway to get from Haworth to Keighley, and then use the tow path of the Leeds and Liverpool Canal to get to Micklethwaite. However, you will miss the three-rise and the five-rise lock systems.

The Leeds and Liverpool Canal

The Leeds and Liverpool Canal is said by canal cruising enthusiasts to be the most magnificent of all the Pennine crossings, and the only one currently navigable throughout its whole length. Indeed, the canal winds through the moorlands of Yorkshire and Lancashire, amongst the most beautiful scenery. An Act of Parliament in 1770 allowed building to commence and 45 kilometres had been completed from Liverpool by 1775. By 1777, from the eastern end, 54 kilometres were completed , but it was not until 1816 that the central section between Blackburn and Wigan

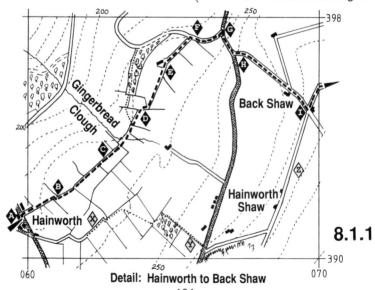

Detail: Hainworth to Back Shaw

8.1.1

A. Left at the lane for a few metres, then right to enter the track giving access to fields and stiles.

B. Initially keep the wall on your right. Ensure that you use the stile to transfer to the other side of the wall, so as to put it on your left. (See across for details.)

C. More fields and stiles.

D. Right then left (stiles).

E. Wall on your right. Pass in front of the house and down the access track.

F. Right at the lane.

G. Right at the road, to ascend steeply for 100 metres.

H. Left into the lane.

I. Sharp left where lanes cross.

J. Right and left.

K. Follow the tracks and lanes.

X.Y.Z. Slightly shorter alternative.

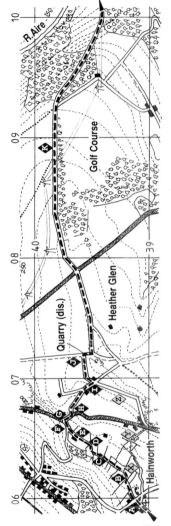

8.1

was completed. The total length from the Aire and Calder Navigation at Leeds to the River Mersey at Liverpool is nearly 205 kilometres and ninety-one locks are necessary to deal with the gradients.

One of the most distinctive features of this canal is its wide locks, which will take craft up to 18.9 metres long by 4.4 metres wide (with a 1.2 metres draught, a 2.7 metres headroom and barges of this size used to carry loads of up to 46 tonnes). Another distinctive feature, which is on the APW route, is the five-rise staircase locks at Bingley, which, together with the Standedge Tunnel on the Huddersfield Narrow Canal, share the distinction of being two of the Seven Wonders of the Canal World. Staircase locks share gates at the centre, instead of having top and bottom gates for each chamber. There is also a three-rise staircase at Bingley with a rise of just over 9 metres, but the Five Rise is the more magnificent with a lift of just over 18 metres. Stand at the bottom of the rise and try to work out what happens if boats are going up and down at the same time. Apparently, even most experienced canal users are daunted at the prospect of attempting the rise. However, complicated instructions are displayed and the resident lock-keeper is available for detailed advice.

Near Bingley there is also a swing bridge, still in good condition, as indeed is the canal generally. The traffic nowadays is for pleasure only and in times of drought sections may have to be closed, due to the storage

Descending the Five Rise

reservoirs becoming exhausted as pleasure craft use the locks. A wide-beam lock contains 250,000-273,000 litres of water, compared with a narrow canal lock, which contains 114,000-137,000 litres. No prizes are offered for working out how much water flows down Five Rise when a boat goes up or down!

On Ilkla Moor Baht 'at

$\frac{4}{4}$

C   G7   C   F   D
/Weer 'as t' bin sin' ah saw /thee?   On /Il-kla ___ Moor ___ baht ___ /at.

G7   C   G   D7   G
/Weer 'as t' bin sin' ah saw /thee?   /Weer 'as t' bin sin' ah saw /thee?

CHORUS

G7 C   F G7   C
On /Ilkla Moor baht 'at, On /Ilkla Moor baht 'at, On/Ilkla Moor baht /'at.

2. Tha's bin a coortin' Mary Jane,
      On Ilkla Moor baht 'at.
  Tha's bin a coortin' Mary Jane.
  Tha's bin a coortin' Mary Jane.
      CHORUS

3. Tha'll goo an' get thi deeath o' cowd,
      On Ilkla Moor baht 'at.
  Tha'll goo an' get thi deeath o'cowd.
  Tha'll goo an' get thi deeath o' cowd.
      CHORUS

4. Then we shall 'a' t' bury thee,
      On Ilkla Moor baht 'at.
  Then we shall 'a' t' bury thee.
  Then we shall 'a' t' bury thee.
      CHORUS

5. Then t' worms 'll come an' eight thee up,
      On Ilkla Moor baht 'at.
  Then t' worms 'll come an' eight thee up,
  Then t' worms 'll come an' eight thee up,
      CHORUS

6. Then t' ducks 'll cum an' eight up
      t' worms,On Ilkla Moor baht 'at.
  Then t' ducks 'll cum an' eight up t' worms,
  Then t' ducks 'll cum an' eight up t' worms,
      CHORUS

7. Then we shall go an' eight up t' ducks,
      On Ilkla Moor baht 'at.
  Then we shall go an' eight up t' ducks,
  Then we shall go an' eight up t' ducks,
      CHORUS

8. Then we shall all 'ave etton thee,
      On Ilkla Moor baht 'at.
  Then we shall all 'ave etton thee,
  Then we shall all 'ave etton thee,
      CHORUS

Ilkley Moor

As you walk over Rombalds Moor, you ought to be aware that you are crossing a stretch of moorland which has a particular significance for Yorkshiremen. Ilkley Moor became the birthplace of the national anthem of Yorkshire, "On Ilka Moor Baht 'at" (q.v.) when, according to popular belief, a visiting church choir from Halifax composed the song during a picnic near the famous Cow and Calf Rocks.

About 10,000 years ago the glacier of the last ice age melted, the valleys became heavily wooded and man returned to set up camps near the rivers. Hunting game on the hills, they left pieces of flint used as parts of weapons and these can still be found on the higher parts of Rombalds Moor. Clearings were made by the Mesolithic people and their way of life continued for thousands of years. In 2000 BC, the Neolithic people built burial cairns and the Twelve Apostles Stone Circle on Baildon Moor. Bronze Age man produced the cup and ring marks on many rocks in the area, these being circular hollows three to ten centimetres across surrounded by a circle of rings. The Swastika Stone, another relic of the Bronze Age, about 2,800 years old near Hebers Ghyll, is thought to be Yorkshire's oldest rock carving. The curved swastika resembles others found in Sweden but, like the cup and ring marks, its purpose is not known. No metal relics of the Bronze Age are left on the moor as the acidic peat and soils are corrosive. There are, however, several Bronze Age enclosures with hut circles.

Ilkley Moor is one of fourteen moors making up Rombalds Moor The higher parts were used for grazing in the thirteenth and fourteenth centuries, thus removing every vestige of woodland and turning the moor into heathland and bogs. In the nineteenth century the expansion of Ilkley and other nearby towns required vast quantities of stone for building and Hangingstones Quarry, near the Cow and Calf Rocks, was one of the prime sources of this stone.

The Cow Rock, a 15-metre high crag, is one of Ilkley's most famous landmarks and is often used as a training ground by rock climbers. From the top of the Cow one can see a marvellous panoramic view of Wharfedale. The Calf is a huge boulder at the base of the Cow and local legend has it that there was once a Bull Rock, standing at the entrance to the quarry, but the 'Bull' was cut up to provide stone for the Crescent Hotel in Ilkley. The Cow and Calf Rocks remain, however, a monument for those who cross Ilkla Moor, Baht 'at or otherwise.

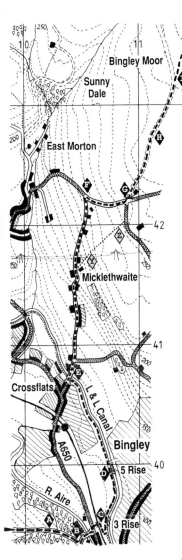

A. Continue the descent on the track.

B. At the road turn left and down into Bingley. Lunch?

C. Cross the A650 (busy; be careful), then left towards Keighley for 50 metres, or so. Right into the pathway with high walls on either side, pass under the railway, right to emerge duly on to the tow path of the Leeds and Liverpool Canal at the three-rise locks. Left, northwards.

D. Follow the tow path for about 1.5 kilometres passing the five-rise locks.

E. Over the road bridge (swing) and northwards through Micklethwaite, ascending.

F. At the T-junction, sharp right to ascend the steep hill.

G. Leave the road at the clearly defined gate/stile to enter Bingley Moor. (Do NOT mistake the gate giving entrance to the quarry some few metres before the proper entrance.)

H. Follow the track.

I. Fork right to leave the track at the sign, path well-defined.

Y.Z. Short cut if you don't mind the hassle of finding it and then the floundering about.

8.2

ILKLEY

Ilkley is described as the 'Gateway to Wharfedale'. The Romans built the fort Olicana in 79 AD and took advantage of the curative effects of the medicinal springs. It was not until the mid-eighteenth century, however, that Ilkley rediscovered 'the waters', when Squire Middleton started to promote the newly fashionable cold water bath cure at White Wells on the edge of Ilkley Moor (q.v.). He opened his outdoor spa baths consisting of deep circular plunge baths hollowed out of the solid rock and fed by icy green mineral spring water at the rate of 450 litres per minute. It was said that a plunge into the waters produced 'tingling sensations' which could cure many Victorian maladies from gout to melancholia. The Wells House Hydropathic Company added roofs and extensions in 1865, and White Wells is now a museum where, amongst other exhibits, a stone plunge pool can be seen. Outside White Wells are the steps from which ladies used to mount donkeys for the journey back to town.

In the mid-nineteenth century, Ilkley took advantage of the Victorian fashion and became a spa town with many large hydros being built. About this time, coinciding with the opening of the railway system, the rich wool men from Bradford and Leeds decided that Ilkley was a pleasant place to live. They built elegant Victorian mansions with spacious formal gardens laid out with rhododendrons and other evergreens. By 1895 Ilkley was a flourishing spa town with fifteen hydros.

At the turn of the century the fashion changed, the requirement for hydropathic treatment declined, the days of the Heather Spa were numbered and Ilkley became a holiday town. There is now ample accommodation to suit all tastes and many inns and shops to cater for your every demand. Before you leave Ilkley, a quick look around the town is recommended as there are many items to attract your attention.

These include:-

Riverside Gardens, with its old packhorse bridge.

Mill Ghyll, a landscaped Victorian gill.

The Victorian Arcade, - now a shopping centre.

All Saints' Parish Church, with its thirteenth-century south doorway and sixteenth-century nave and aisles housing Ilkley's famous Saxon crosses.

The Manor House, standing on the site of the Roman fort, dating from the sixteenth century with a seventeenth-century king-post roof.

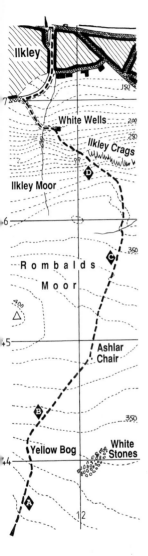

Old Bridge, Ilkley

A. Follow the defined path.

B. Path less defined due to bogs.

C. Path defined.

D. Various paths descend into Ilkley, one is as good as another. (Only the definitive APW shown.)

(AT ILKLEY THE EIGHTH STAGE ENDS)

White Wells

8.3

NINTH STAGE:
ILKLEY TO PATELEY BRIDGE

Wharfedale
30 kilometres, 18.6 miles

The authors assert that you have been in the Yorkshire Dales since you crossed from Derbyshire into Yorkshire proper in stage four. However in this, the ninth, stage you enter the Yorkshire Dales as defined by tourist organisations. On leaving Ilkley, the APW and the Dales Way follow the same route for a few kilometres beside the River Wharfe. Both ways have to leave the river near Addingham, as there is no riverside path from here to Bolton Priory. The APW ascends the eastern side of the dale to pass just below Beamsley Beacon, then descends to the river via Storiths at Bolton Priory which is well worth a visit. The riverside path is followed (beware when the river is in flood) past the Cavendish Pavilion and Barden Tower, and on to Howgill. Here the APW leaves Wharfedale, which stretches north-west, and follows the minor dale of Fir Beck north-eastwards, through High Skyreholme, to ascend onto the moors separating Wharfedale from Nidderdale. The descent into Pateley Bridge passes Greenhow Hill noted for quarrying and mining as far back as Roman times.

If you feel energetic, if the weather is fine and it's not the shooting season, a variant route can be taken from the Cavendish Pavilion over Simon's Seat to rejoin the definitive route at High Skyreholme. If the weather is bad, this alternative is not recommended unless you are used to navigating in cloud. Except for the moorland crossing the way follows well-defined paths, but even the crossing is not difficult to navigate although a compass will be required if cloud is down. Here it could be wet underfoot, but not boggy. Please note that no dogs are permitted on this variant route.

This part of Wharfedale is classic Dales country with farms, very green fields, dry stone walls, meandering lanes, woods and places of historical interest. The highest point on the definitive route is 410 metres on High Crag, from which point there are no grand views. You reach 486 metres if you go over Simon's Seat and the views from the top are spectacular. Indeed, on a clear day, looking southwards you can see the tower of Emley Moor TV Transmitter 50 kilometres away, whilst 60 kilometres to the south

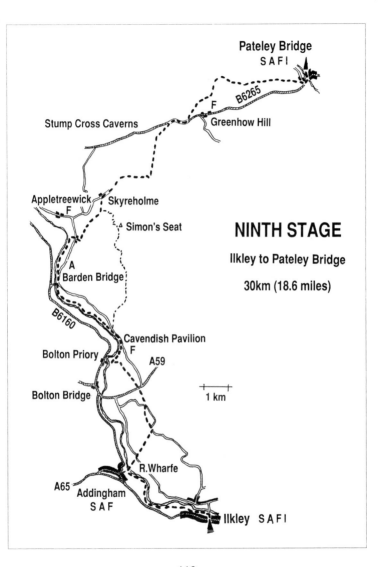

Pateley Bridge
S A F I

B6265

Stump Cross Caverns

F
Greenhow Hill

Appletreewick
F
Skyreholme

△ Simon's Seat

NINTH STAGE

Ilkley to Pateley Bridge

30km (18.6 miles)

A
Barden Bridge

B6160

Cavendish Pavilion
F

Bolton Priory
A59

Bolton Bridge

1 km

R.Wharfe

A65
Addingham
S A F

Ilkley S A F I

Bolton Priory

you will see the cooling towers of the power stations in the Vale of York.

Addingham is probably too early for lunch, but the Cavendish Pavilion may be just right. However it is advisable to take provisions in case the pavilion is closed, and it is also advisable to take modest emergency rations in case things go wrong when going over the moors between the dales.

There is plenty of accommodation at Pateley Bridge and there are bunkhouses at Barden Tower and Howgill if you choose to make this stage into two stages. There is a shop at Addingham and a small shop-cum-cafe at Howgill and, of course, there are plenty of shops at Pateley Bridge.

Bolton Abbey

Bolton Abbey and Bolton Priory have been centres of attraction for visitors for many years and, in the heyday of Victorian Ilkley, travellers in their thousands used the railway to sample the delight of Bolton. Girton, Landseer and Turner all painted in these magnificent surroundings with backdrops of heather-covered moorlands, whilst Wordsworth and Grey were moved to write in romantic terms about this part of Wharfedale.

Most people in Yorkshire know about 'Bolton Abbey' and, by long usage, the village is called Bolton Abbey. However, the ecclesiastical ruin is properly the Priory of St Mary at Bolton and is not an abbey. Bolton, by

114

A. Descend the main shopping street, crossing the A65 at the traffic lights.

B. Just before the bridge over the River Wharfe, enter the municipal park down the steps to the left.

C. Follow the S bank of the river, passing the old bridge and join the Dales Way (DW).

D. Enter the track and follow it to its end at the sports centre.

E. Cross the meadows on the well-defined path.

F. Follow the S bank upstream and join the course of the old A65.

G. Turn right along the access lane to the site of the mill which is now a housing complex.

H. Ahead through the housing complex.

I. Follow the lane into Addingham.

J. Turn right into the path leading to the church (over small footbridge).

K. Keep to the well-defined path, S of the church. Cross its approach lane.

L. Turn right at the main road.

M. Cross the suspension bridge over the Wharfe and follow the path to West Hall. Right then left.

N. Along the access lane to the road.

O. Join the road and proceed ahead for about 120 metres.

P. Through the gate and follow the bridleway ascending.

9.1

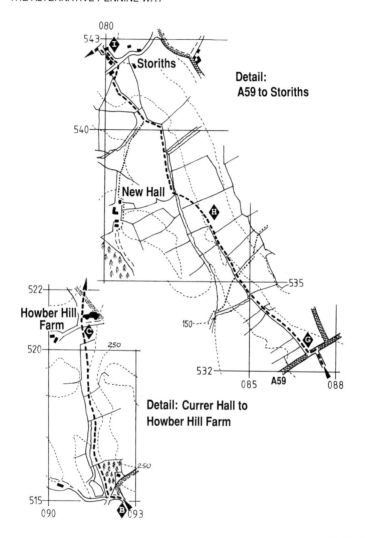

Detail:
A59 to Storiths

Storiths

New Hall

Howber Hill
Farm

Detail: Currer Hall to
Howber Hill Farm

A59

9.2.1

A. Ascend the bridleway and enter the walled track. Continue to the farm and turn right to reach the road.

B. Join the road and turn left for 200 metres or so. Then descend left, as if going to Currer Hall, but take the footpath on the right (N) between the small lake and the wood. (See across for details.)

C. Leave the fields. Cross the farm access track and then cross the road.

D. Descend towards Ling Chapel Farm.

E. Cross the access track and enter the enclosed field for Deerstones. (The descent through this field is not shown on OS maps.)

F. Cross Kex Beck via the footbridge, and climb steeply into Deerstones (zigzag).

G. Left then right at the A59 crossing. (See across for details.)

H. Fields and stiles etc into Storiths.

I. Leave Storiths westwards on the walled path.

J. Descend through the trees to the grounds beside the River Wharfe and Bolton Priory. (You must cross the river if you wish to visit the priory.)

K. There are two paths along the E bank of the river. If the Wharfe is in flood take the high level route, as the riverside route will be impassable.

L. Join the road and proceed N.

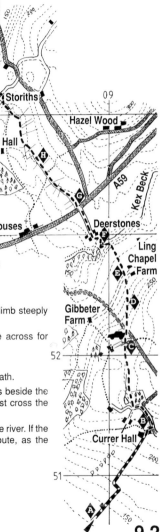

9.2

the way, means 'an enclosure with a house'. The priory was founded at Embsay in 1120 by Cecily Romilly, who was the daughter of the first Norman lord, Robert de Romille. Cecily's daughter, Alice, granted the manor of Bolton to the Augustine cannons thirty-five years later, and the Prior and the canons moved into these idyllic surroundings in 1155.

As time went by the priory developed, with the church being built first, and in 1310 it came under the patronage of the famous, powerful and wealthy Cliffords of Skipton. In the fourteenth century, the Scots saw fit to raid the priory and some damage was sustained. The last Prior, Richard Moone, started work on the West Tower in 1520, but the Dissolution of the Monasteries in the sixteenth century saw an end to his work and to the power and wealth of the monasteries.

The estate was sold by the Crown to the Earl of Cumberland in 1542, later passing by marriage to the Earl of Burlington and subsequently, again by marriage, to the Dukes of Devonshire who currently own the estate. Before handing over the priory to the crown in 1539, Prior Richard Moone walled off the nave of the priory church so that it could be retained as a parish church, and it is interesting to note that services have been conducted here for some 850 years. Today, apart from the church, few ruins of interest remain, although by walking through the remnants, one can gain an impression of what life must have been like when the priory was inhabited by a prior and fifteen canons, together with supporting staff.

The APW uses the east bank of the River Wharfe, but it is well worthwhile crossing the river to explore the ruins. There is a bridge, but you may wish to risk getting wet by using the stepping-stones. The Dukes of Devonshire, as well as owning the Bolton Estate, own the Chatsworth (q.v.) Estate and you may detect a certain similarity in the way these two picturesque areas have been developed. The present (eleventh) duke has created a trust under the name of 'The Trustees of the Chatsworth Settlement' and the trust owns, with a few exceptions, Bolton Abbey village and the surrounding countryside for several miles around. The village and most of the estate are included within the Yorkshire Dales National Park as a designated area of outstanding natural beauty.

As on the Chatsworth Estate, it is the trust's policy to allow walkers to use Bolton Abbey Estate's many permissive paths at all times, and freedom of access is permitted over all parts of Barden Moor and Barden Fell. In fact the whole estate is well-maintained, particularly the areas frequented by the public. However, it should be noted that the trust may close off these

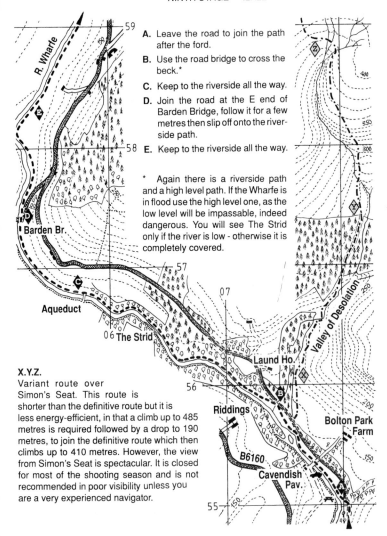

A. Leave the road to join the path after the ford.

B. Use the road bridge to cross the beck.*

C. Keep to the riverside all the way.

D. Join the road at the E end of Barden Bridge, follow it for a few metres then slip off onto the riverside path.

E. Keep to the riverside all the way.

* Again there is a riverside path and a high level path. If the Wharfe is in flood use the high level one, as the low level will be impassable, indeed dangerous. You will see The Strid only if the river is low - otherwise it is completely covered.

X.Y.Z.
Variant route over Simon's Seat. This route is shorter than the definitive route but it is less energy-efficient, in that a climb up to 485 metres is required followed by a drop to 190 metres, to join the definitive route which then climbs up to 410 metres. However, the view from Simon's Seat is spectacular. It is closed for most of the shooting season and is not recommended in poor visibility unless you are a very experienced navigator.

9.3

access areas at certain times during the shooting season (from August 12), and also in times of drought when there may be a high fire risk. Notices will be posted at all access points giving details of closures. Also the permissive paths may be closed, or diverted, at times for 'management purposes'.

Barden Tower

The route of the APW is on the east bank of the River Wharfe, so, if you have visited the priory, it will be necessary for you to recross the river before continuing on your way. Just over one kilometre from the priory, you will arrive at Cavendish Pavilion, built in 1880, on the opposite side of the river to our walk. A newly rebuilt bridge takes the Dales Way over the river at this point, and if you require refreshments or a meal, you too should cross to the Pavilion.

You may now care to decide which route you intend to use to get to Pateley Bridge - it is decision time! The definitive route of the APW stays with the east bank of the river, allowing you to see the Strid and Barden Tower. The variant route takes you through the Valley of Desolation (so called because a storm caused desolation there 150 years ago), and over the magnificent viewpoint, Simon's Seat. If you opt for the alternative, your mind might be changed for you by a closure notice (for shooting?) at the access point at Waterfall Cottage. Whether using the definitive or alternative routes, it's back to the east bank, hopefully suitably refreshed.

About one-and-a-half kilometres from the Pavilion, you will notice the river narrowing. At its narrowest point is the Strid and it seems almost possible to stride over (is this where the name Strid originates?) Do NOT attempt to stride or jump over the Wharfe at this point, as many drownings testify to its danger. Remember the depth and the width of the Wharfe at the priory, requiring fifty-seven stepping-stones at the crossing point. The same amount of water is flowing at the Strid! Recent underwater research has revealed that whilst the Strid is only one-and-a-half to two metres across, it is up to nine metres deep, the water swirling through a series of deep and dangerous potholes. If you fall in, you may not surface for several days and your journey to Pateley Bridge will be abruptly curtailed.

Continuing along the east bank, you will pass a rather delightful stone bridge crossing the river just less than one kilometre from the Strid. The bridge is an aqueduct, carrying a Bradford Corporation water pipeline from Nidderdale (q.v.), but it may be used as a footbridge. About a kilometre further on you will arrive at what has been described as the 'loveliest bridge

A. The path leaves the riverside to join the road.

B. Cross the road into the walled track and ascend.

C. Turn left into Howgill lane and ahead for about 1.5 kilometres.

D. Through the gate to the low side of the ruined outbarn (stile).

E. Fields and stiles and over the footbridge.

F. Between the cottages and turn right at the lane.

G. Do not miss the turn to the right.

X.Y. Descent off Simon's Seat.

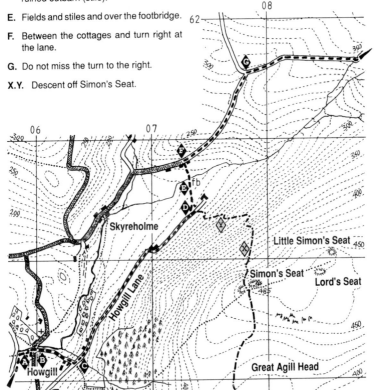

9.4

Barden Tower

in Wharfedale', Barden Bridge. The way continues northwards, but if you wish to visit Barden Tower cross the bridge; the tower is about 300 metres up the hill on the left. A gate, about 150 metres up the hill, gives access to this old hunting lodge in the Forest of Barden.

The name Barden means 'the valley of the wild boar' and the Forest of Barden covered much of Wharfedale from Bolton Priory to Appletreewick (pronounced Ap'tr'ick), it being a forest in the historical sense of a woodland district kept for hunting. The tower was one of several lodges, built to house the men who looked after the forest.

In the eleventh and twelfth centuries, whilst it would have been more primitive than in later years, it became the most important lodge as the forest courts were held there. It seems that the forest officials ruled the area and were able to punish offenders if found guilty of misconduct. The officers of the Forest of Barden were the agister, who looked after the cattle and the pigs grazing in the forest; the forester; the regarder, who surveyed the forest; the verderer, who looked after the game and the timber and was thus in an important position; and the woodward, who was in charge of the timber.

Barden later became a defensible stronghold, built to withstand attacks from the marauding Scots, and in 1310 the Cliffords came into possession of Barden, but it was not until 1484 that the tenth Lord Clifford (The Shepherd Lord), came to live at the lodge, preferring this to the grandeur of his seat at Skipton castle. After his death in 1523, Barden fell into disrepair and his son used it only as a hunting lodge.

However, that was not the end of the lodge, as in 1658 and 1659 along came Lady Anne Clifford who restored the buildings even though she did not actually own them.

When Lady Anne died in 1676, Barden reverted to its rightful owners and gradually fell into disuse. In 1774, the roof was removed and sold and the tower eventually became the ruin it is today. Now owned by the Dukes of Devonshire as part of the Bolton Abbey Estate, Barden Tower is well worth visiting, if only to take refreshments in the oak-panelled Priest's House next to the tower. Situated alongside is a barn, some 200 years old, built on two levels and which has recently been converted to provide hostel-type accommodation for twenty people in four bedrooms.

A Shepherd's Work is Never Done

You will see many species of fauna whilst walking, but the one you will see most is the sheep. There are many breeds of sheep and as a result of careful breeding, sheep have been developed to suit the climate, differing types of ground, available pasture and, of course, the purpose for which they are bred. Some of the Yorkshire Dales have sheep named after them. The Wensleydales are large, hornless, blue-faced, long-coated sheep which tend to live on the lower ground, as they are not particularly robust animals. The Swaledales, on the other hand, are far more hardy and able to live on exposed ground in most weathers. However, even they can have problems in extended periods of snow. Horned, and recognisable by their black faces with grey muzzles, often white around the nose, with grey mottled legs and fine, thick, shaggy fleeces, Swaledales can be seen along most of the Pennines from south-west Yorkshire to Northumbria. Other breeds to be found in the Dales include the Dalesbred and the Rough Fell.

Further north, in the Border country, you will see Scottish Blackface sheep as well as the Swaledale. Slightly heavier than the Swaledale, the horned Blackface has a predominantly black face with white patches, and a tendency to white hair towards the muzzle. On some of the grassier Border foothills the local Cheviot breed may be seen. With white faces and no horns, they are sometimes called Border Cheviots to distinguish them from the North Country Cheviot, a heavier breed now found in north Scotland, imported from the Borders at the time of the Highland clearances.

Each flock of sheep has its own patch of land known as a 'heaf' in west Yorkshire, a 'heugh' in north Yorkshire and a 'heft' in the Borders; each of these words derives from the Icelandic 'hefta' meaning 'to hold in'. Each farm will have three of four hefts where the lambs have grown up with their mothers. Each ewe knows where the best grazing is at different seasons and the safe places in a storm; she never leaves her ground. Even families of ewes within each heft have their own special corners and favourite ground. So, when you look across the areas of grazing during your walk, the eye will scan across a number of hefts, each with its attendant grazing and shelter. The sheep do not mix, but stay close to their territories, even though they may belong to different farmers and are using common grazing.

Sheep farming is a hard life and there is something to occupy the shepherd throughout the year. The shepherd's year starts in autumn when the shortening hours of daylight in October and November trigger ovulation and so start the breeding cycle of the ewes. Where possible, the ewes are brought down to fenced and sheltered ground in the valleys, but often the tups (rams) are turned out to the ewes on the open hills.

Winter brings problems to the hill farmers, who do their best to bring the ewes from open ground to safe places in the valleys when snow is imminent. The ewes seem to have a sixth sense and will avoid hollows and keep away from shelter, thus minimising the risk of being buried in snow drifts. However, you may still see a few purpose-built snow shelters on the hills, consisting of high stone walls, usually circular and about twelve metres in diameter. Feeding the ewes in bad weather is another problem faced by the farmer. Fodder is often left in strategic places (sometimes stored in old railway box-trucks), or it can be taken out to the hills using four-wheel drive vehicles or specialised snow vehicles. It used to be frowned upon to feed hill sheep in winter, as it was believed that hand feeding reduced the capacity of the stock to survive the bad weather. Nowadays, many farmers feed hay and a few concentrates to ewes as lambing time approaches. Hard, brown, circular, stone-like blocks, fortified with treacle and nitrogenous chemicals, are licked by the ewes to help them better digest the dead grass and forage on the moors.

Spring comes late to the hills and lambing is normally around April time. If possible, the ewes are brought down to fenced and sheltered areas where grazing is better and supervision easier. Some farmers have erected buildings in which to house the ewes at lambing time. With 600 ewes a shepherd might manage alone, but with 800 to 1,000 ewes an extra man will be hired for lambing. A ewe recognises her lamb by its smell, but it may take 24 hours for her to do this with certainty. It is most important that you

A. Through the gate and left, to turn back on yourself and pass through the stile behind the wall. Make for the stone building (to do with water?).

B. Path undefined. Walk on 25° approx.

C. Path vague along the line of rushes. Head for the stile over the wall, when visible.

D. Descend on indifferent path towards the ruin.

E. NE on the green track.

F. Walk about 0.7 kilometre eastwards on the B6265.

G. Left into the walled path at the NE end of Prim Gap Farm.

H. At Far Side, left then right to pass the house on its NW.

I. Pass Low Far Side and descend to the old mine workings.

J. Very confusing on the ground amongst the old mine workings. Over the ford on the track to make NE (the track can be seen ahead).

K. Through the gate and after about 300 metres turn right, opposite the site of a building (trees grow from the remains).

L. Half way down the approach to the empty house, turn left into walled track.

9.5

should not touch lambs, however forlorn and abandoned they may look. The human scent on a lamb may mean that its mother fails to recognise it on its return to the flock, sometimes with dire consequences.

It has been said that a shepherd can recognise each individual sheep in his flock by its gait, looks and marking. However, the traditional and official markings are published in various 'shepherd's guides', and the one for the northern Pennines contains identifications for over 1,500 marks. The marks (horn burns, wool and ear marks), belong to the farm and the initials burnt onto a sheep's horn are often those of a farmer who lived there many years ago.

As spring turns into summer, the fleeces of the ewes 'rise', as the new wool lifts the fleece from the skin of the sheep; this is the time for clipping. Nowadays the whole flock is sheared at one time and machine clipping, often by contract, has taken over from the old-fashioned sheep shears, the pattern of which has remained largely unaltered since its introduction in Roman times. After shearing, the fleeces must be kept clean, carefully 'wrapped' or 'rolled', and packed into huge rectangular bales for subsequent collection by the buyer, perhaps the Wool Marketing Board.

Autumn is the climax of the year, when the sheep sales are held. It is also a period of intense, sometimes competitive, social activity. Farmers, families and friends from the surrounding countryside descend on the local market town where, as well as the locals, the town fills with buyers, who may be dealers or farmers, from all over the country.

Gone are the days when sheep used to be 'salved'. This consisted of smearing the sheep all over with a mixture of tar, oil and fat (sometimes, butter made from ewes' milk was used). The purpose of salving was to prevent scab, but it took a man up to one hour to salve one sheep. And as for the smell - well! Also gone are the days when sheep used to be washed in order to get rid of the salve and make the fleece 'rise'. Washing used to employ two or three men working up to their armpits in water, and an hour and a half was about as long as they could stand before being replaced by another team. The occasion was used as a social event after the work had been completed. Drinking and music went on far into the night at the washings and a good time was had by all. Whilst salving and washing are no longer practised, 'dipping' and 'mouth-drenching' (administering drugs orally) are used as methods of attempting to control the many parasites that threaten the health of the sheep.

A shepherd's work is never done!

A. Turn right at the Nidderdale Way (NDW).

B. Follow the track, which becomes a lane.

C. On entering the trees, turn left off the lane to reach a stile (not obvious from the lane). Enter the fields.

D. Fields and stiles. Simply keep the wall on your right.

E. Turn right at the lane, then left at the B6265. Enter Pateley Bridge.

(THE NINTH STAGE ENDS AT PATELEY BRIDGE)

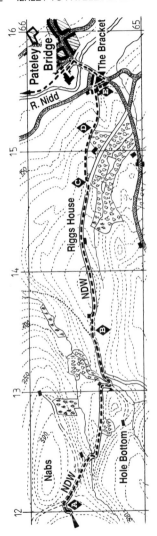

9.6

The APW leaves Pateley Bridge along the east bank of the River Nidd, on the same path as the Nidderdale Way. It continues northwards on the east bank of Gouthwaite Reservoir to Bouthwaite, where it crosses the Nidd to Ramsgill. It then joins the other leg of the Nidderdale Way, but now high in the fields away from the river so as to get views of the dale. It crosses How Stean Beck and, if you are interested in geology and/or the unusual, a visit to How Stean Gorge can be made. It is about 0.5 kilometre off route and about 1 kilometre west of Lofthouse, but remember that this adds 1 kilometre to the day's walk. However, you could break this stage into two by staying at Lofthouse - there is an inn. Passing through Lofthouse (lunch?), the way is back to the east bank of the Nidd, but then climbs the steep valley side to reach a track on the rim of the dale. After following the rim for four kilometres or so, the route crosses the moor to reach Great Haw and then descends into Coverdale at West Scrafton. Two kilometres across the dale is Carlton.

Nidderdale and Coverdale are smaller and quieter than the well-known tourist dales, probably because neither has a main through motor-road. Indeed upper Nidderdale is a dead end for motors. The countryside is characterised by a typical Yorkshire Dales landscape of farms, woods and places of historical interest; but this dale is different from most in having several reservoirs like the dales of South Yorkshire. The highest point is Great Haw at 544 metres and, except for the moorland crossing at Great Haw (beware in the shooting season), the tracks and paths used are well-defined and are unlikely to be troublesome in wet weather. The moorland stretch could be difficult in cloud and wet, so the use of a compass is advised.

Food is available at Wath and Ramsgill (hotels), and Lofthouse is well positioned for lunch (bar meal) which can be obtained at the inn. There are no shops en route, but emergency rations need only be minimal as the exposed moorland crossing is quite short and not particularly hazardous.

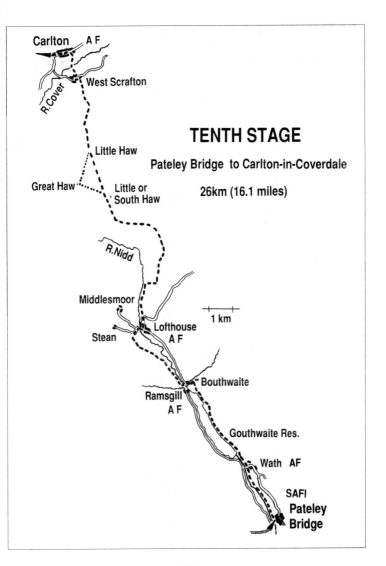

Carlton A F

West Scrafton

R.Cover

TENTH STAGE

Little Haw

Pateley Bridge to Carlton-in-Coverdale

Great Haw

Little or
South Haw

26km (16.1 miles)

R.Nidd

Middlesmoor

1 km

Lofthouse
A F

Stean

Bouthwaite

Ramsgill
A F

Gouthwaite Res.

Wath AF

SAFI
**Pateley
Bridge**

As there is little opportunity to get provisions until you get to Aysgarth, it is suggested that provisions for two days are obtained in Pateley Bridge.

Whilst there is accommodation in Carlton it is limited to an inn and one or two B & B places, so it is wise to book before leaving Pateley Bridge.

PATELEY BRIDGE

As you cross the Grassington to Pateley Bridge road (B6265), the village of Greenhow is a few hundred metres to the east. Greenhow at 396 metres, is one of England's highest villages and evidence of a past history of lead mining is to be seen hereabouts, the Romans having started this activity during their occupation of this area. About three kilometres to the west of Greenhow are the famous Stump Cross Caverns situated in desolate boggy moorland on the edge of the B6265, with the entrance 335 metres above sea level. The limestone caverns provide an illuminated glittering spectacle of stalactite and stalagmite formations. Easy access, good headroom and surprisingly dry floors all contribute to the fascination of this show-piece.

On entering Pateley Bridge, and before you arrive at the bridge, keep an eye open for The Bracket. This will be found jutting out from a baker's shop, on the left side of the road, towards the adjoining premises. Enquiries reveal that a one-time occupant wanted to extend his premises, but was prevented from doing so by the objections of his neighbour. His reaction was to erect The Bracket, a huge metal construction still in excellent condition, on which to build an overhead extension. It seems as though the extension never got built and The Bracket remains a feature of the town.

Continuing towards the bridge, you will pass the recreation ground on your left, with swings and slides in a fenced dog-free area. The bridge from which Pateley Bridge takes its name is probably eighteenth century, standing on the site of the original wooden bridge first recorded in 1320. The first half of the name derives from Patleia meaning 'the path through the glade' and dating back to the twelfth century. The original Patleia was almost certainly situated up the hill, near the fourteenth-century church of St Mary (now in ruins), originally a chapel of ease to save the long journey to Ripon.

In 1320, Pateley received its charter to hold markets and fairs, and this helped to develop the road system. In the mid-nineteenth century, before the Nidd Valley railway was built, a horse omnibus met passengers and transferred them to and from Nidd Bridge Station, which was on the now

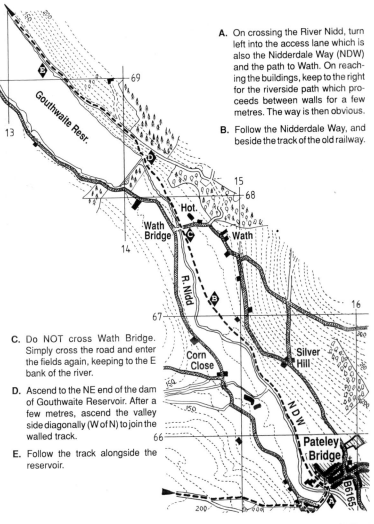

A. On crossing the River Nidd, turn left into the access lane which is also the Nidderdale Way (NDW) and the path to Wath. On reaching the buildings, keep to the right for the riverside path which proceeds between walls for a few metres. The way is then obvious.

B. Follow the Nidderdale Way, and beside the track of the old railway.

C. Do NOT cross Wath Bridge. Simply cross the road and enter the fields again, keeping to the E bank of the river.

D. Ascend to the NE end of the dam of Gouthwaite Reservoir. After a few metres, ascend the valley side diagonally (W of N) to join the walled track.

E. Follow the track alongside the reservoir.

10.1

defunct Harrogate to Ripon line, and Pateley Bridge. Clearly the town was already becoming the gateway to the 'best end of Nidderdale' and was developing as a focal point of life. At the end of the eighteenth century, Nidderdale, a part of the parish of Kirkby Malzeard and having connections with Fountains and Byland abbeys, was noted for its production of butter and bacon. Also, several water-powered mills were processing flax and hemp. Later, in the nineteenth century, Pateley became a centre for the production of large slabs of millstone grit for railway platforms, public buildings and dock quays. The old Scot Gate Ash Quarries are up the hill to the north-east, and remains of the workings are still apparent, including 'the incline' which was used to facilitate the transport of stone down to Pateley Bridge sidings.

From the main street, you may see silhouetted on the skyline towards the south-west a structure resembling two 'stone men' - not an uncommon

sight on the fells. However, this is Yorke's Folly which in reality is a mock ruin, allegedly built by the Yorke family of Bewerley at a time when work was scarce in the district. From this vantage point there are excellent views over the dale, including the famous Brimham Rocks. It is said that, on a fine day, York Minister can be seen, 48 kilometres away.

Visitors who take an interest in matters theatrical should not leave Pateley Bridge without visiting Pateley Playhouse in Church Street. Originally a Primitive Methodist chapel, built in 1856, it became a Salvation Army citadel from 1936 to 1959, and Pateley Bridge Dramatic Society acquired the building in 1963, converting it into a theatre which was opened in 1969. The

The Bracket, Pateley Bridge

Playhouse is a cosy, intimate theatre seating seventy-two in comfort, and the society produces and presents three or four shows a year.

Pateley Bridge is a happy, friendly place with a good range of hotels, inns, restaurants and shops including one which repairs walking boots, although it is hoped that you will not have to take advantage of this facility.

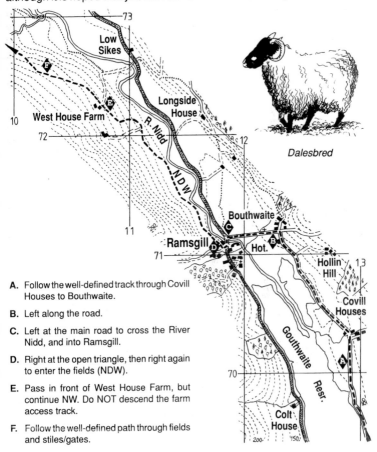

Dalesbred

A. Follow the well-defined track through Covill Houses to Bouthwaite.

B. Left along the road.

C. Left at the main road to cross the River Nidd, and into Ramsgill.

D. Right at the open triangle, then right again to enter the fields (NDW).

E. Pass in front of West House Farm, but continue NW. Do NOT descend the farm access track.

F. Follow the well-defined path through fields and stiles/gates.

10.2

133

You have a long way to go yet! There are banks, churches and chapels, a health centre, a police station and a bus station.

Upper Nidderdale

On leaving Pateley Bridge you will find yourself sometimes walking along the route of the old Nidd Valley Light Railway (NVLR). This line was built in the early part of the present century to transport men and materials to the reservoir workings at the head of the valley. It was also used as a means of public transport and at one time it was possible to have a day's excursion from Leeds all the way to Lofthouse. The old station at Wath, now a private house, is still recognisable and it is recorded that in 1922 there were five trains in each direction daily, the single fare from Pateley Bridge to Wath being 2½d (1p). The NVLR closed in 1936, and the Nidderdale Line between Harrogate and Pateley Bridge, which was opened in 1862, closed in 1951.

The city of Bradford developed greatly in the nineteenth century, and the demand for water was met by building reservoirs in upper Nidderdale. Gouthwaite was the first to be completed in 1901. Just over three kilometres long, with a dam 152 metres long and 24 metres high, Gouthwaite holds 7,280 million litres and has become the habitat for about forty species of water fowl. Also, numerous other varieties of birds are to be seen in this idyllic area.

At the head of Gouthwaite reservoir stands Ramsgill, described as 'the most attractive of all Nidderdale villages', it even has peacocks on the village green. Behind the present church, built in 1842, is to be found the gable end of the chapel built in the twelfth century by the monks of Byland Abbey for their grange. This 'most attractive of villages', however, conceals a murky past, as it was the birthplace of the notorious and scholarly Eugene Aram. Born in 1704, this talented schoolmaster was alleged to have been involved in the murder of a certain Daniel Clarke at Knaresborough in 1745. Aram and an accomplice, Houseman, were said to have hidden the body in Saint Robert's Cave where it was discovered, fourteen years later. The motive for the alleged murder is not clear, but despite putting up a magnificent, self-conducted defence, Aram was found guilty and hanged in York in 1759. The trial caused immense public interest at the time, with many famous public figures being involved, including Sir Henry Irving and Lord Lytton.

The village of Lofthouse, where you may consider having lunch, or

A. Join the walled track and follow it to the right over the brook, and hence down to the valley floor.

B. Join the road and turn right to go over the bridge. (About 0.5 kilometre up this minor valley, off route, there is How Stean Gorge which is well worth a visit if you've time.)

C. Where the road bends right, leave it left-wards to join the path, and after 200 metres cross the private road and then cross the Nidd.

D. Sharp right and into Lofthouse. (Lunch at the hotel?)

E. Left to leave the village northwards.

F. Leave the road and continue northwards on the track.

G. Just beyond the out-barn on the right at Thrope Farm, leave the track to ascend the valley side. Keep to the wall side.

H. Leave the enclosed land and keep ascending up the valley side, following the path which turns left in the wood.

I. You reach Thrope Edge by the shooting house and turn left (northwards) on the track. Follow this.

J. Keep ahead on the edge.

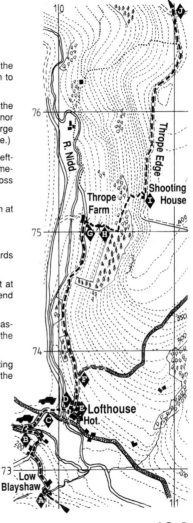

10.3

135

even staying the night if you are having an 'easy' day, is usually considered to be the head of Nidderdale, although it is possible to go further by road. As the name implies, Lofthouse means 'houses with lofts or upper storeys', and it has been in existence since the Norse people came from the Lake District to settle in the dale. Some lead mining was carried out in the late nineteenth century, but it has largely been sheep farming country since the time of monastic occupation. The nearby How Stean Gorge is well worth a visit if you have the time. On the payment of a fee the gorge, in places only two to three metres wide, can be viewed from the wooden bridges which cross and recross the stream flowing 20 to 25 metres below. This wooded gorge is a splendid sight, especially when the stream is in spate at which times the water level has been known to rise ten metres. (Refreshments available.)

The APW leaves Lofthouse to climb over the hill to Carlton, but on the opposite side of the valley will be seen the tiny village of Middlesmoor, clinging to the hillside, 294 metres above sea level. It has a small church, built in 1865 replacing the former church on the same site. Dedicated to Saint Chad, it is the oldest church in upper Nidderdale to be still in use, having been licensed for baptisms, marriages and burials in 1484, as a chapel of ease for Kirkby Malzeard.

Beyond Middlesmoor, visibility permitting, you will see Scar House and Angram reservoirs, nestling under the bulk of Great Whernside (704 metres). The highest reservoir, Angram, was completed in 1914, and Scar House below it was completed in 1936. Scar House dam is claimed to be the largest masonry dam in Europe, with some of the stones being 4.5 metres long! To get water from these two reservoirs to Bradford, a 58-kilometre conduit was built, including a 6.5-kilometre tunnel beneath Greenhow Hill. Between the two reservoirs lies the deserted hamlet of Lodge, and a story centres on the old inn which was frequented by travellers using the packhorse way into Coverdale. The story goes that the inn, kept by a woman and her daughter, was used regularly by a group of Scots pedlars who apparently disappeared one day after a visit to the inn. Years later three headless bodies were discovered in the peat, and it was assumed that these were the missing pedlars, murdered by the innkeeper and her daughter. The hill where the inn stood was named Dead Man's Hill, and is known as such to this day.

The River Nidd rises on Great Whernside where it feeds Angram and Scar House reservoirs, before disappearing down a pothole, named

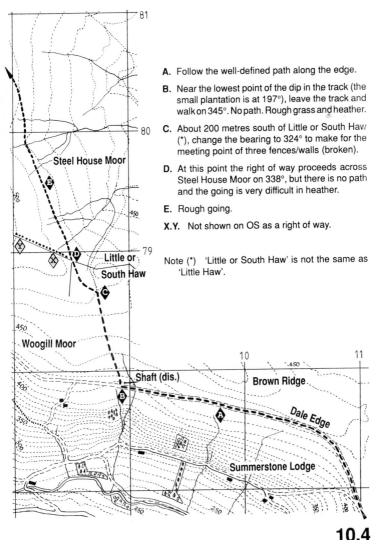

A. Follow the well-defined path along the edge.

B. Near the lowest point of the dip in the track (the small plantation is at 197°), leave the track and walk on 345°. No path. Rough grass and heather.

C. About 200 metres south of Little or South Haw (*), change the bearing to 324° to make for the meeting point of three fences/walls (broken).

D. At this point the right of way proceeds across Steel House Moor on 338°, but there is no path and the going is very difficult in heather.

E. Rough going.

X.Y. Not shown on OS as a right of way.

Note (*) 'Little or South Haw' is not the same as 'Little Haw'.

10.4

Near Low Blayshaw, Nidderdale

Manchester Hole, and reappearing below Lofthouse. The river bed, dry except in times of flood, can be seen alongside the road. The river passes through Ramsgill and into Gouthwaite Reservoir, through Wath to Pateley Bridge and on through lower Nidderdale to Ripley and Knaresborough, finally crossing the Vale of York to join the River Ouse at Nun Monkton.

Upper Nidderdale certainly lives up to its reputation. It has beautiful scenery, a 'Colorado Canyon', reservoirs, potholes, flora and fauna, romantic villages, an old railway and historical intrigue, all packed into a small valley of perfect proportions. Whether the weather is fine or dull, upper Nidderdale is a delightful part of the country and one of the highlights of the APW.

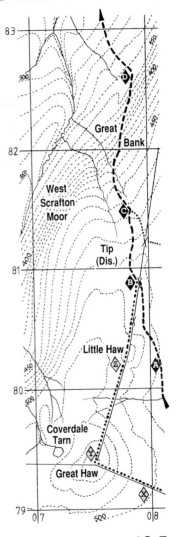

A. Rough and undefined.

B. Cross the fence through the stile and descend on 334° for about 150 metres, then turn N. Path not clear.

C. The way becomes clearer as you descend, and the path becomes well defined in due course.

D. Continue down the well-defined path.

X.Y.Z. Not shown on OS as a right of way.

10.5

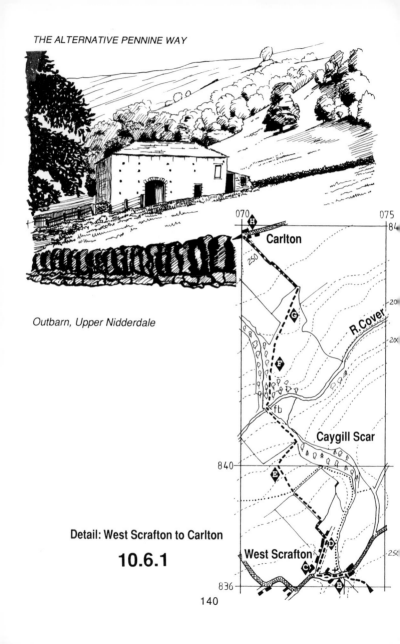

Outbarn, Upper Nidderdale

Detail: West Scrafton to Carlton

10.6.1

070   075
                                                    84

Carlton

250

R. Cover

20

200

fb

Caygill Scar

840

West Scrafton

250

836

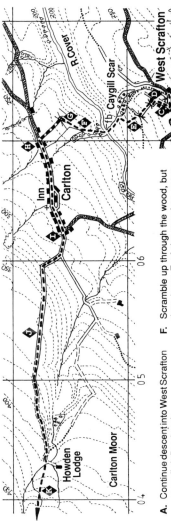

A. Continue descent into West Scrafton on well-defined path.

B. Enter road and turn left, pass chapel and cross the bridge.

C. Turn right off the road onto open 'green'.

D. 150 metres from the road, turn left into walled pathway. Follow path with right turn within the walls, then enter fields. Turn left and keep the field wall on your left. (See across for details.)

E. Descend steep field. River comes into view. Get to the footbridge.

F. Scramble up through the wood, but then keep E of the wood to enter large field. Do NOT follow the gill into the wood.

G. Aim for the NE corner of the field (no path), to enter fenced path.

H. Left at the road to get to the centre of Carlton.

(THE TENTH STAGE ENDS AT CARLTON)

I. At the W end of the village the road turns south. Keep westwards on the lane which degenerates into a track.

J. Follow the well-defined path.

K. Ascend on the well-defined path.

141

10.6

ELEVENTH STAGE:
CARLTON-IN-COVERDALE TO HAWES
Wensleydale - The Big Dale
24 kilometres, 15 miles

On leaving Carlton, the APW departs Coverdale and climbs over Carlton Moor and then descends into Waldendale to reach West Burton. Walden Beck joins Bishopdale Beck within one kilometre of the latter's joining the River Ure near West Burton, so the APW crosses Bishopdale before entering Wensleydale at Aysgarth. It crosses the Ure at the Upper Falls and then continues on the north side of the river to reach Hawes, passing through Askrigg and Sedbusk on the way.

The character of the route is pleasant dales scenery - fields, walls, outbarns, farms and watercourses. Except for the crossing over Carlton Moor, at 485 metres, the way is low level, but all the route is on well-defined paths with short sections on minor roads. From the dale side, just west of Askrigg, there is a fine view of Raydale, although Semer Water is not visible. The Roman Road out of Bainbridge, leading over Cam Fell, is very clear. From West Burton to Hawes you are never far from habitation, so if you have traversed Carlton Moor safely you will need no emergency rations. However, Carlton Moor can be tricky in low cloud, so set out prepared.

There is accommodation as well as shops at Aysgarth, Askrigg and, of course, at Hawes. There will also be accommodation in the villages off route, so this stage should not be at all hazardous.

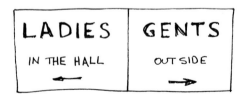

Sign in pub, Lofthouse

142

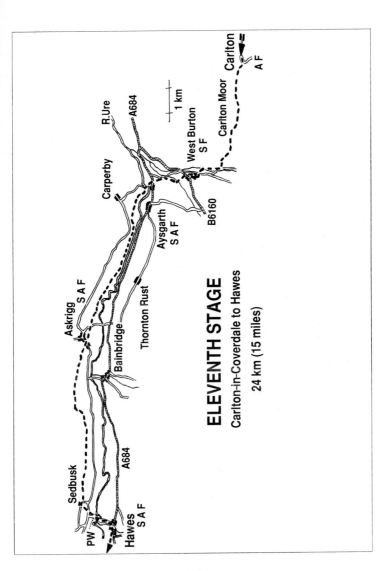

ELEVENTH STAGE

Carlton-in-Coverdale to Hawes

24 km (15 miles)

1 km

Carlton
A F

Carlton Moor

West Burton
S F

B6160

R.Ure

A684

Carperby

Aysgarth
S A F

Askrigg
S A F

Thornton Rust

Bainbridge

Sedbusk

A684

PW

Hawes
S A F

CARLTON-IN-COVERDALE

A glance at a map of the Wensleydale area of the Yorkshire Dales will show three dales almost parallel to one another, running in a north-easterly direction. These are Bishopdale, Waldendale and Coverdale. The longest of the three, Coverdale, is attractive, secluded and little-known, but that was not always the case. In bygone times, Coverdale was a much-used Pennine crossing. Armies and abbots, packhorses and peasants, Bronze Age man and bootmakers all used the route through the dale, and for centuries the way over Dead Man's Hill (see Feature "Upper Nidderdale") was used as a means of access into Nidderdale and beyond.

Industries in Coverdale have included coal mining, lead mining, quarrying for roof stones and flagstones, the manufacture of cheese and racehorse breeding and training. Only the latter two remain, as will be witnessed by anyone spending a little time in the dale.

The dale even boasts its own abbey, dating back to the twelfth century. The few remains of Coverham Abbey, now in private grounds, may be viewed by application. Nearby is the old abbey mill, Coverham church and Coverham bridge. This small village, in splendid surroundings, presents a living picture of times past. Further up the dale at Caldbergh is the alleged birthplace of Miles Coverdale, born in 1488, who was the first to produce a complete translation into English of the Holy Bible and other religious documents.

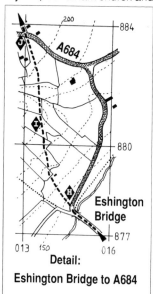

On your journey from Pateley Bridge, having passed the Haws, you will start your descent into Coverdale, first making your way through the remains and spoil of lead mines. As you approach West Scrafton you will see much evidence of quarrying; Gilbert Scar and other quarries in this area were worked until the turn of the century. Wagons on rails were used to recover the stone from underground levels. The slabs of stone were then split into roof slates and flagstones, which were considered to be of a very high quality and

Detail:
Eshington Bridge to A684

11.1.1

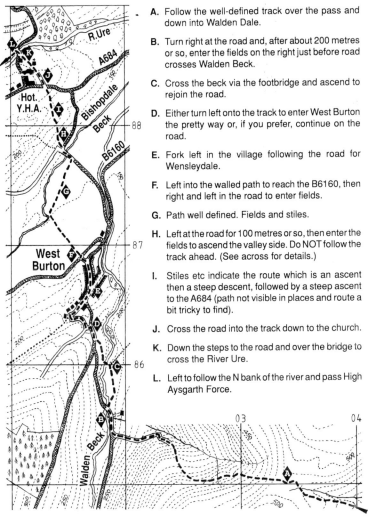

A. Follow the well-defined track over the pass and down into Walden Dale.

B. Turn right at the road and, after about 200 metres or so, enter the fields on the right just before road crosses Walden Beck.

C. Cross the beck via the footbridge and ascend to rejoin the road.

D. Either turn left onto the track to enter West Burton the pretty way or, if you prefer, continue on the road.

E. Fork left in the village following the road for Wensleydale.

F. Left into the walled path to reach the B6160, then right and left in the road to enter fields.

G. Path well defined. Fields and stiles.

H. Left at the road for 100 metres or so, then enter the fields to ascend the valley side. Do NOT follow the track ahead. (See across for details.)

I. Stiles etc indicate the route which is an ascent then a steep descent, followed by a steep ascent to the A684 (path not visible in places and route a bit tricky to find).

J. Cross the road into the track down to the church.

K. Down the steps to the road and over the bridge to cross the River Ure.

L. Left to follow the N bank of the river and pass High Aysgarth Force.

11.1

were widely used in the surrounding areas and elsewhere. As you pass through West Scrafton you will cross a stream flowing between limestone banks; nearby is Tom Hunter's Parlour, a cave in which a highwayman of that name is supposed to have been captured.

Carlton was at one time inhabited by Bronze Age man, as is evidenced by the existence of three Bronze Age tumuli just off the road which runs through the village. There is one in the garden of Manor House Farm, another in the field at Town Head and a third, the largest, behind the Forester's Arms Inn. Houses line each side of the main street for a distance of about one-and-a-half kilometres and a small church, adjacent to the school, was built as a chapel of ease for Coverham. The oldest building in the village is thought to be the barn of Old Hall Farm, with an inscription "WFS 1659" on the door-head. There were two village inns at one time, the Forester's Arms and the Moorcock. The Moorcock was previously called the Hare and Hounds, and before that it was known as the XYZ. This was not a route indication on the APW, but the inn was thus named in commemoration of a famous racehorse which scored a hat-trick by winning the Richmond Gold Cup three times in succession. Sadly, the Moorcock no longer exists, but happily the Forester's remains for your enjoyment.

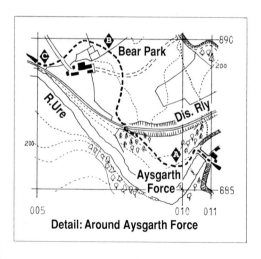

Detail: Around Aysgarth Force

11.2.1

A. Do not be tempted to wander along the bank of the Ure. Keep to the path which leaves the river and ascends into the trees to cross the dismantled railway. (See across for details.)

B. The route passes around the N side of the farm. Stiles etc guide the way.

C. Reach the railway boundary and follow it through the fields.

D. Join the course of the railway where a path comes in from the right.

E. Follow the railway track for about 200 metres, then leave it to cut off the field corner.

F. Join the track and follow it to the river. At the river turn right and keep on its N bank.

G. Pleasant walk but difficult in places where there is a likelihood of flooding.

H. Keep to the fields on the S side of the railway.

11.2

147

Askrigg

A. Transfer to the N side of the course of the railway. Precise point of transfer is not easy to locate, but the small beck gives a clue. Cross 100 metres beyond it.

B. The way seems blocked by the barn. Pass around the N side then through gate or stile to enter the walled lane.

C. Cross the road and enter the fields through gate or stile.

D. Enter walled path leading into Askrigg.

E. Cross the high street and into the lane on the N side of the church.

F. Two gates. Pass into the fields through the right-hand one.

G. Through the buildings to the bank of the beck, keeping it on the left. Cross the footbridge.

H. Ascend the well-defined path in the trees which surround the beck.

I. Emerge from the wood via the stile into open fields. (There are two parallel paths here, each with a stile. It does not matter which is used although the APW uses the higher one. The waterfall at Mill Gill can be visited, if desired, by a short detour up the gill before emerging into the fields.)

J. Path not defined, but keep beside the wall on your right.

K. Leave the fields, then ahead on the metalled lane.

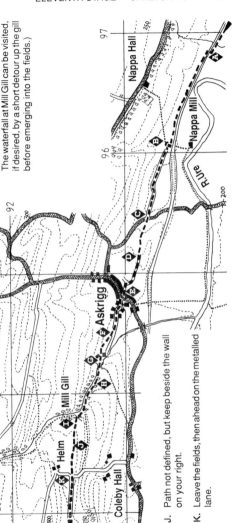

11.3

149

HAWES IN WENSLEYDALE

Wensleydale is one of the best known dales in Yorkshire. Unlike most of the dales, it does not take its name from the river which runs through it, but from the village of Wensley, which at one time was the market town of Wensleydale, having been granted its market charter in 1202. In those days Wensley, a town of some importance, was called Wensela and formally the dale was known as Yoredale, but it has had its present name since about the middle of the twelfth century. The River Ure, which runs through the dale, rises on Abbotside Common.

At the mention of the name Wensleydale, most people's thoughts turn to cheese, and before the advent of factory-produced cheese, almost every farmhouse in the dale was engaged in cheese-making. It is believed that the original cheese-making recipes of Jervaulx Abbey have been passed down through the ages and form the basis of the present Wensleydale cheeses, which are thought by some gourmets to be the superlative cheeses. In the days of Jervaulx, the cheese was made from ewes' milk.

Jervaulx Abbey, situated a few kilometres east of the APW in the grounds of Jervaulx Hall, was founded in 1115 in upper Wensleydale, but in 1150 the monastery removed to its present site because upper Wensleydale was thought to be rather inhospitable. The Cistercians, from Citeaux in Burgundy, founded many abbeys in Yorkshire during the twelfth century and many of the fells and dales were granted to the abbeys. Jervaulx was granted most of upper Wensleydale and part of upper Ribblesdale. In addition to rearing sheep, the monks developed great skill in breeding and rearing horses and many of the granges had wheat and fulling mills. The abbey was a big landowner employing many workers and was responsible for the development of the land and establishment of farms. However, all was not 'sweetness and light', as some of the dalesfolk resented the monasteries taking over their land, grazing rights, fishing rights, hunting rights and mills. Today, the extensive ruins of Jervaulx are open to the public, but it is suspected that few visitors will realise what a profound effect the abbey had on the dale.

Middleham, situated further up the dale from Jervaulx, is an Anglian settlement being the middle village between East and West Witton. It has had a fortress since a motte and bailey was built on William's Hill in Norman times by Ribald, the brother of Alan the Red of Richmond. Nothing is left of the original wooden structure, but the motte and bailey remains for all to see. About 1190 the present stone castle was built. It became the

A. Follow the lane to Skell Gill.

B. Over the bridge and through the hamlet to enter the walled track.

C. Turn left. Do NOT go forward to ford the beck.

D. Keep SW along the unfenced green track over the brow.

E. The path is reasonably defined. Keep the wall on your left all the way. Also pass the barns, houses etc keeping them on your left.

F. Into the walled track.

G. When the track bends left (S) enter the fields through gate, then keep the wall on your left.

H. Through fields. Stiles in the walls direct the way.

I. At Litherskew, leave the field via the stile and cross the track to enter the buildings complex. Make sure that you leave in a westerly direction.

J. Fields and stiles again.

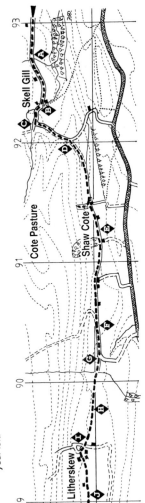

11.4

stronghold of the Nevilles and was called 'the Windsor of the North' when Richard, Earl of Warwick, took it over. Following the death of Warwick at Barnet in 1471 Edward IV gave the estate to the Duke of Gloucester, who became Richard III. In 1646, after the Civil War, much of the castle was pulled down and the stone used for buildings in Middleham, many of which still remain. However, enough of the castle still exists to this day for one to get an impression of its original glory.

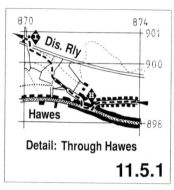

Detail: Through Hawes

11.5.1

Aysgarth Falls, in Wensleydale, have long been popular and much visited. Originally the parish of Aysgarth, covering the whole of upper Wensleydale, was the largest parish in England. It was on the coach route through the dale and several coaches a day, travelling between York and Lancaster, changed horses in this small village. The name Aysgarth means 'an open space with conspicuous oaks', many of which still remain. In 1784 a cotton spinning mill was built here, but it was not very successful and having been allowed almost to fall down, it was burnt down in 1852 and a more successful woollen mill, which later became a flour mill, was built on the site. However, it is the falls (or force) that have remained a constant attraction. You will see the Horseshoe (or Upper) Falls as you cross the Elizabethan bridge over the Ure, and from the north bank as you walk upstream. You may see the Middle Falls by taking a short walk downstream on the north bank of the river. Further downstream still, the Lower Falls, a series of splendid cataracts, are seen at their best when the river is in spate. The falls were so famous that when, in the late nineteenth century, a proposal was made to erect an immense iron railway bridge over the falls, a public outcry ensued. Eminent public figures such as William Morris and John Ruskin set up a defence association with Lord Wharncliffe as its president. The project, however, turned out to be financially unsound and was abandoned, so the falls were preserved in their original beauty.

At the head of Wensleydale, Hawes (spelt 'Hause' in the Lake District), meaning 'a pass between the hills', obtained its market charter in 1700. In 1795 the turnpike to Lancaster was constructed, and in 1898 the first cheese factory in the dale was built in the town. The railway from Leyburn,

A. Fields and stiles.

B. Enter the small wood through a stile and emerge from the wood, using a second stile, after about 100 metres.

C. Pass through Sedbusk on the road and, after about 100 metres, turn left through a stile into fields. Descend.

D. Ascend over spur. Stiles give directions.

E. Cross the road (right and left) through stiles.

F. Descend to beck and stone bridge.

G. Join the road (and PW) for Hawes. (You are travelling the APW S to N,

but your 'opposite number', travelling the PW S to N, will be walking in the opposite direction.)
(THE ELEVENTH STAGE ENDS AT HAWES)

H. In the main street, some 50 metres W of the 'one-way system', a 'back lane' goes off N and, after a few metres, turns approx NW. This leads to a few shops and the rear car park of the Fountain Hotel. Beyond the car park, the path goes between buildings on the left and a wall on the right, emerging into open fields. (May be difficult to identify at first, but soon becomes clear.) See across for details.

I. Cross the dismantled railway and turn left. Path reasonably defined.

J. Join the A684 and walk NW along it to Appersett.

K. Cross Widdale Beck with the road and, N of the track leading to Widdale, a stile gives access to fields. The path against the wall is then parallel with the road.

L. Left to the River Ure, to follow it NW (upstream).

M. Keep to the S of the trees, which are between the path and the river.

N. Where the river comes in from the N and turns sharply ESE, enter the wood through the stile.

11.5

constructed in 1877, enhanced the success of the market and brought increased trade and prosperity to the town. Today, Hawes is a thriving, bustling community which provides a full range of services for the traveller, including hotels, inns, restaurants, shops and banks. The nooks and alleyways are well worth exploring as is Gayle, an adjacent village about one kilometre to the south, with geese and waterfalls in Duerley Beck.

If you stay two nights in Hawes, you may care to visit the village of Hardraw which is situated about two kilometres to the north. Hardraw Force, with its entrance via the Green Dragon Inn, is the main attraction of this tiny village, once famous for its stone Hardraw 'flags'. Hardraw Force, a waterfall 30 metres high, has been the scene of several public 'spectaculars' over the years, as well as being a fascination in its own right. In Victorian times, because of the acoustic properties of the wooded ravine leading to the 'scar', it became a well-known venue for brass band contests, the first being held in 1885. Many bands from Wensleydale, Swaledale and elsewhere performed in this natural amphitheatre. Thousands of people came to hear the music and the contests became an annual event, and this has recently been revived. Choir contests also took place and these became equally popular. As a novelty, the famous Blondin walked across the gorge on a tightrope, pausing in the middle to cook an omelette. If you are feeling adventurous you can walk behind the waterfall and see the view from a most unusual vantage point.

The dale is also famous for the Wensleydale long-case clock, the manufacture of which goes back to the seventeenth century. It used to be the custom to keep the clock half an hour fast so as never to be late, and it still is the custom in parts of the dale.

Dogs

There are several places on the APW where dogs are kept, either for guarding property or as working dogs. We do not mind being escorted through farm premises by a watchful and quiet dog, but what remains a constant source of amazement is the antics of some dogs which appear to be permanently secured, usually by chains or ropes. On sensing an approaching visitor, such dogs will project themselves forward, barking and snarling, until the strangulation effect of the chain or rope prevents any further progress. One might imagine that 'lessons would be learned' by these dogs - but no! Are these examples of stupid dogs, or are they aggressive because they are chained?

Entirely different are the working dogs, and the ones most frequently encountered are the Border Collies. Usually quiet, invariably obedient, these dogs are without doubt an essential part of the team on all farms engaged in rearing sheep. The intelligence, instinct, staying power and ability of the Collie to control sheep is often demonstrated on many of the hills and dales along the route of the APW.

Nowadays, sheepdogs are almost entirely controlled by whistled commands, this method replacing the old-fashioned shouted commands. Commands such as 'way here' (go left), 'come by' (go right) and 'stay here' (lie down) are heard when the shepherd is near to the dog, but whistles are used at greater distances and can be heard up to a mile away on the moors.

The television programme *One Man and His Dog* has brought home to millions of viewers the amazing abilities of these animals. Usually included were 'the fetch', the dog's (wide) approach to the sheep; 'the gather', getting the sheep together; 'the drive', the ability to take the sheep away from the shepherd'; 'the shed', singling out one sheep from the flock and 'penning', getting the half-dozen or so sheep into a pen. In all these exercises, and of crucial importance, is the ability of the dog to control the sheep by 'eyeing' them.

The 1981 Countryside Act requires that dogs, other than working dogs, should be on a lead in fields containing sheep. A strange dog, even in the next field, whether on a lead or not, can make ewes and lambs run or gather, creating a risk of mis-mothering. Sheepdogs are usually very quiet with ewes and lambs and there seems to be a quite unusual understanding between them. Even so, many shepherds leave their dogs at home during the lambing season, something which visitors may care to consider during this critical period.

Wensleydale

TWELFTH STAGE:
HAWES TO KIRKBY STEPHEN

The High Point - Metaphorically
24.8 kilometres, 15.4 miles

You will leave Hawes on a back lane, but you will enter Appersett on the main road. The River Ure is followed by path and by road to reach the lane into Cotterdale. The next 10 kilometres or so is along The High Way, or Lady Anne Clifford's Way, which climbs Cotter Riggs to Cotter End. The High Way keeps high on the north-east side of upper Wensleydale, until it crosses the watershed just before Hell Gill Bridge. The bridge spans Hell Gill Beck, which is the principal headwater of the River Eden. The route then descends with The High Way to the B6259 at The Thrang, after which it continues on paths and bridleways beside the River Eden into Kirkby Stephen.

In the opinion of one author, the walk from Cotter End to Hell Gill Bridge is the most spectacular point of the whole APW (the other thinks that this 'honour' is shared with another section further on in the walk). To the south-west one can see Widdale Fell, Whernside and Barbon High Fell. To the west are Baugh Fell and Wild Boar Fell. To the north-west one sees the Vale of Eden with Cross Fell and the northern Pennines beyond. The highest point is 500 metres at Cotter End.

The way from Hawes to The Thrang is on a well-defined track, but the route between The Thrang and Pendragon Castle is a bit tedious in farmers' fields. The route on to Kirkby Stephen is on bridleways.

Whilst you are never far from habitation you are for the most part high, and access could be difficult in an emergency, so appropriate rations and kit should be carried.

A very spectacular alternative walk goes over Mallerstang Edge, Nine Standards Rigg and through Hartley to Kirkby Stephen. However, the route from Hell Gill Bridge to the B6270 is NOT shown as a right of way on OS, nor is it on access land, so bear in mind our warning in the General Notes.

Except for The Thrang, there are no shops or places offering accommodation en route, but you will be well provided for in Kirkby Stephen.

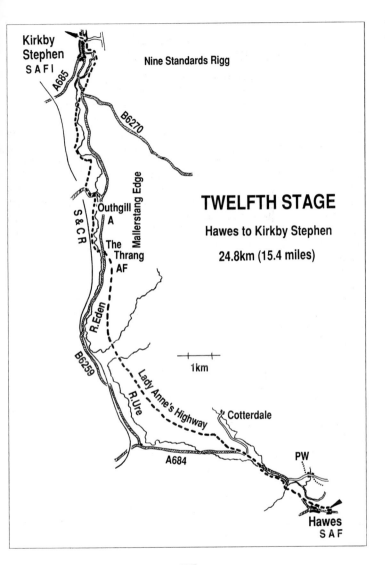

Kirkby
Stephen
S A F I

A685

B6270

Nine Standards Rigg

S & C R

Outhgill
A

The
Thrang
AF

Mallerstang Edge

R. Eden

B6259

R. Ure

TWELFTH STAGE

Hawes to Kirkby Stephen

24.8km (15.4 miles)

1km

Lady Anne's Highway

Cotterdale

A684

PW

Hawes
S A F

Near Hawes

The High Way

On leaving Hawes, the APW takes you on a gentle ramble through lush green fields before you join the ancient route from Wensleydale into the Eden Valley. Surviving from the Bronze Age, this route is known as The High Way and it begins at Cotter Bridge, about five kilometres from Hawes, gently ascending through green fields to the crags at Cotter End. Following the ridge above Lunds, The High Way is joined by the Old Corpse Road from the east which was used by the parishioners of Cotterdale carrying their dead to Lunds Church. Crossing over the headwaters of the River Eden at Hell Gill (be sure to look over the bridge parapet into the deep ravine), The High Way continues northwards and descends the slopes of Mallerstang Edge to join the Hawes to Kirkby Stephen road at The Thrang, near Pendragon Castle, before continuing on its way in the valley bottom to Kirkby Stephen. This prehistoric and medieval route became an important packhorse way before the building of the turnpike. High Paddock, one of several ruined farms on 'the tops', is thought to have been a rudimentary inn for the use of the packhorse men and their animals. However, it was Lady Anne Clifford who really magnified the importance of this old route,

158

A. Emerge from the wood and follow the path to the track. Turn right to get to the bridge and the A684.

B. Left at A684 and walk along this for about 0.75 kilometre.

C. Right through the gate into the Cotterdale Road, then left to ascend the spur parallel to the A684. Path undefined.

D. Path undefined, but way obvious. Ascend spur with wall on left. This is The High Way.

E. Through the gate, then climb the track/path steeply to the top of Cotter End and turn W. Way obvious.

F. Wall on left spoils view over Mossdale to the hills.

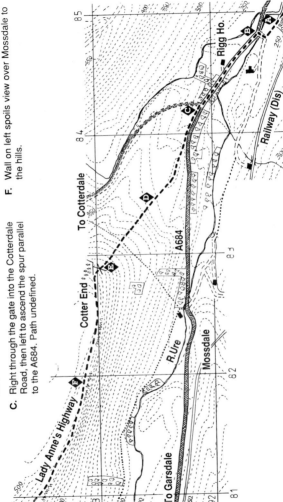

12.1

159

and it became known as Lady Anne Clifford's Way.

Lady Anne Clifford is known for her resolute and tenacious character. Born in 1590, she married into the aristocracy at the age of nineteen and her husband later became the Earl of Dorset. After his death, Lady Anne married the Earl of Pembroke and Montgomery, eventually inheriting vast areas of land. However, due to many protracted lawsuits, she did not gain control of her lands until 1643. A few years later, she came north to visit her numerous castles in Yorkshire and Westmorland. During her early visits she realised that many of her properties were in a sad state of repair, and she introduced an intensive programme of restoration and refurbishment. Being a pious lady, she also built several churches and ensured that she had a preacher in each of her castles. Whilst the work was being carried out on her properties, personal supervision was the order of the day and her slight figure, dressed in black, became a familiar sight around the area. In 26 years, most of the Clifford castles were restored to their original magnificence and Lady Anne, on her many travels between Yorkshire and Westmorland, used The High Way.

The mound on which Pendragon, one of Lady Anne's castles, was built has possible Celtic and Roman origins, but the present castle was built in the twelfth century and legend has it that Uther Pendragon had a son who became King Arthur (the one with the Round Table). The castle has a chequered history, having been burned down at least twice and suffered many attacks from the marauding Scots, even though Baliol, King of the Scots, visited Pendragon in 1333. When Lady Anne began work in 1660, the castle had been roofless for more than 100 years. Travelling from her seat at Skipton she was accompanied by many of her staff, including a 'window carrier' who brought along a glazed window for her draughty bedchamber at Pendragon. Lady Anne died in Brougham Castle, at the age of eighty-six, in 1676 and Pendragon fell into the hands of the Earl of Thanet who allowed it to fall into disrepair, much of the stone being used for buildings in the surrounding area. What little is left is in ruin, but restoration work is again being carried out by a local farmer who bought the Norman ruin for £525 in 1963.

On your journey along The High Way, you may care to ponder; did the legendary King Arthur, as a boy, walk this way? Certainly the indomitable Tudor, Lady Anne Clifford from the House of Lancaster, travelled The High Way in her coach on many occasions, bringing a new look to her properties and helping the poor and needy in the Vale of Eden.

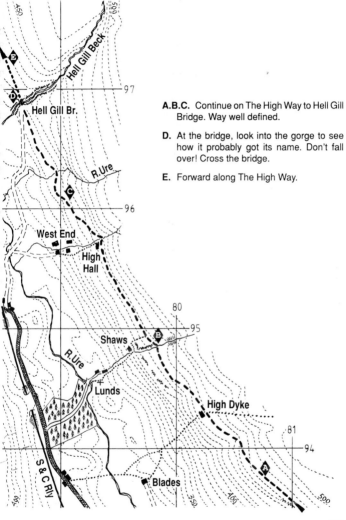

A.B.C. Continue on The High Way to Hell Gill Bridge. Way well defined.

D. At the bridge, look into the gorge to see how it probably got its name. Don't fall over! Cross the bridge.

E. Forward along The High Way.

12.2

The Settle and Carlisle Railway

With the building of St Pancras Station in London in 1868, the Midland Railway Company was very keen to extend its network from the industrial Midlands to Scotland, and although the Parliamentary Act for the construction of this new line had been granted in 1866 the cost was almost prohibitive and the engineering difficulties were considerable. However the Midland overcame its fears, work started in 1869 and the line was completed for goods and passenger travel seven years later, in 1876.

In the feature "M62-Motorway Across The Pennines", we described the engineering feat as "of gigantic proportions". Those words are hardly adequate to describe the feat of building the Settle and Carlisle line, as this was built across similar wild and inhospitable countryside, but by manual labour only. No excavators, no dump trucks, no vibrating rollers, just navvies with picks, shovels and dynamite. The navvies lived on site in shanty towns and enduring harsh climates, especially in winter, as they pushed the lines ever forward to Carlisle. At perhaps the most difficult and remote part, Ribblehead and Dent, some of the navvies spent their 'leisure time' knitting stockings and caps, as there were woollen mills in the valleys near Sedbergh making knitting yarn. Life during the building of the Settle and Carlisle line must have been challenging to say the least, but the result, a superb railway across almost impossible and yet most beautiful countryside, was without any doubt an engineering triumph.

Starting at Settle, the line wends its way over embankments, through cuttings and tunnels for a few kilometres, and then starts to ascend a 1-in-100 gradient, known as 'the big lump', and on to the famous Ribblehead (or Batty Moss) Viaduct. This is most impressive, being 50 metres at its highest point, just over 400 metres long and built on a curve. North of Ribblehead, the line enters Blea Moor Tunnel, which is 2,410 metres long, and then continues high on the fell side to Dent Station which, with an altitude of 349 metres, is the highest main line station in England. Another long tunnel at Rise Hill carries the line into the head of Garsdale, then several tunnels and viaducts later the Mallerstang valley is reached, with Ais Gill signal box, at 356 metres, being the highest point. Down the narrow Mallerstang valley and across the Vale of Eden, the line advances northwards to Carlisle. The Settle and Carlisle Railway must surely be the ultimate scenic railway in England, if not the British Isles, as it makes its way through the valleys and across the fells amidst breathtaking scenery.

As you walk along The High Way, you may think that your eyes and

A.B.C. Continue descending on The High Way.

D. At the B6259 continue N for a few metres, then pass through the gate on the left to descend to the Eden. Cross via the bridge, then turn right to follow the W bank northerly.

E. Through the farmyard.

Kirkby Stephen

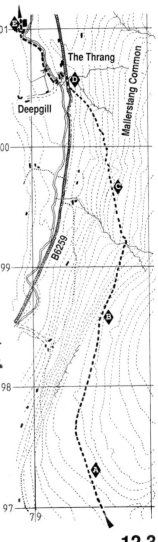

12.3

ears are deceiving you, but no, what you may see and hear may actually be a train (if you're lucky, with a steam engine), descending or ascending the gradient of Mallerstang valley. In 1982, proposals were made to close the Settle and Carlisle, but countrywide opposition, with more than 23,000 formal objections being received, led to a stay of execution and trains still run a very reduced service to this day, with special services for walkers during summer weekends. Ribblehead Viaduct is now only operated single line in order to help alleviate structural problems, in the hope that a few more years' service can be gained without enormous amounts of money being spent on restorative work.

Quite clearly the line is uneconomic and requires a large investment if it is to continue. The debate goes on, but this line is part of our engineering and cultural heritage. British Rail has extolled the virtues of the Settle and Carlisle Railway by promoting it as "England's Greatest Historic Scenic Route", and so it is. Let us hope that it survives.

KIRKBY STEPHEN

The High Way (q.v.) descends the side of Mallerstang valley to continue its journey in the valley bottom. The origin of the name Mallerstang is shrouded in mystery and the place-name experts offer a variety of explanations, none of which is definitive. On arrival at the B6259 road you will find a handily-placed country hotel called The Thrang. A cream tea, or perhaps something less exotic, may be welcome here as the setting is in beautiful surroundings dominated by Wild Boar Fell to the rear, with Mallerstang Edge and High Seat to the front. The Thrang, with its spire, stained glass windows and imposing porch doors, was built in 1838 as a residence for the incumbent of Mallerstang church at Outhgill.

Having crossed the infant River Eden you will walk down the valley towards Kirkby Stephen. Soon, through the trees, you will catch tantalising glimpses of Pendragon Castle (see Feature "The High Way") and a short deviation will enable you to visit this historic site. Nearby Outhgill, apart from being the village associated with Pendragon, has one other claim to fame; the parents of Michael Faraday (who is acclaimed by engineers as the 'Father of Electrical Engineering') lived here before moving to London where Michael was born. There is also Faraday Gill on the slopes of Nine Standards Rigg, but why this is so-called in unknown. Two kilometres to the north of Outhgill, and on the route of the APW, lie the ruins of yet another castle, Lammerside. In the sheep-inhabited ruins, which are not even in as

A. Through the farmyard and then right as if going back to the B6259. A few metres away from the farm, leave the track to cross the field on the left and proceed northerly to the stile in the wall.

B. The way to Shoregill, along the riverside, is straightforward.

C. Through Shoregill and, on leaving northerly, there are three farm gates. Pass through the middle gate and proceed N, keeping the wall on your right. A few metres ahead, it becomes clear that the path really goes between two walls, one of which is derelict.

D. Stiles guide the way.

E. Descend gently towards the river, just E of N, to approach the wall on the right. Keep to the wall (on your right) and, a few metres from the field corner, cross to the other side of the wall through the gate. (Note! OS Pathfinder shows a different route here, and a blocked stile confirms that the route on the ground is intended to be not as OS, official or unofficial?)

F. Now keep the wall on your left. Also keep the out-barn on your left.

G. Cross the beck and ascend, keeping right to go along the edge of the mini escarpment.

H. Through the stile and to the riverside to reach the lane.

I. At the lane, turn left and ascend the hairpin bend.

J. When the lane reaches open land and bends left, leave it northerly on the track.

K. Turn left. Do NOT go ahead.

L. Leave open land through the gate, then right through another gate to leave the track and ascend to Lammerside Castle.

M. Through the gate and ahead for a few metres before bending right to descend to the NE corner of the field.

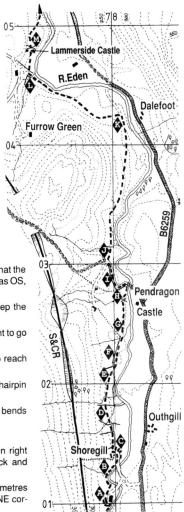

12.4

good a state as Pendragon, can be detected part of a fourteenth-century pele tower and some fine examples of rubble walls.

Before reaching Nateby, you will pass Wharton Hall, a delightful fourteenth-century building with subsequent extensions. Still in a remarkable state of preservation and still inhabited, the hall was built by the Wharton family as is evidenced by the coat-of-arms over the gatehouse. In the village of Nateby, two-and-a-half kilometres from Kirkby Stephen, you can see on the wall of the inn an original, familiar yellow AA sign indicating that you are $1^1/_2$ miles from Kirkby Stephen, $267^1/_4$ miles from London and $9^1/_2$ miles from the Moorcock Inn. The Automobile Association decided on the yellow colour as its 'trade mark' in honour of its president, the Fifth Earl of Lonsdale, elected in 1907. The 'Yellow Earl', as he was known, painted all his private cars and carriages this brilliant yellow colour, which is seen on all AA signs, logos, vans and motorcycles, to this day.

Kirkby Stephen was recorded on early maps as Cherkaby Stephen. Kirkby means 'a village with a church', but Stephen has no connection with Saint Stephen and probably derives from the Celtic words for 'the River Eden'. The town was granted its market charter in 1361, and still has a thriving market each Monday. In the market square, one can see the ancient collar of cobblestones marking out the area used for bull baiting; this being stopped around 1820 when a bull broke lose, much to the consternation of bystanders. Around the town can be seen many fine Georgian buildings and there is a particularly fine unspoilt example of an old English inn, and all the town centre has been designated as a conservation area. On the north side of the market place are the Cloisters, once a butter market, now leading into the churchyard. Through the Cloisters on the right is the old Trupp Stone, where tenants used to pay their tithes. The parish church, known as the 'Cathedral of the Dale' because of the impressive length of its nave, is built on the site of an old Saxon church and dates back to 1220. Containing many features of interest, the church is well worth a visit. There are several ways down to the river taking you through narrow passages, originally designed to make the place easier to defend against the marauding Scots. One of the ways takes you above tunnels, allegedly dug as shelters for women and children during the many Scottish raids between 1250 and 1550.

A. At the time of researching the route, there was no proper stile at the corner of the field, but there was no difficulty in crossing the fence. (Note! This is a bridleway, so horses will have to jump.) Having crossed the fence, ascend gently to the gate opposite.

B. Another gate. Then ahead, keeping the wall on your right all the way to the trees, at which bend left with the field boundary. (Do NOT go through the gate half way along the field - it only gives access to the field beside the river.)

C. Join the track, turn right and follow the concrete track through the farm and past Wharton Hall.

D. Right through the stile and descend to cross the bridge.

E. Left and ascend gently to leave the riverside. Ignore the stile above on your right, remembering that you are on a bridleway.

F. Through the gate and across the field to the B6259.

G. Left at the road for a few metres, then right into the walled path.

H. Keep right.

I. Over the footbridge, then keep left to reach the riverside. Follow the river.

J. Over the footbridge to cross the Eden, and into Kirkby Stephen.

(THE TWELFTH STAGE ENDS IN KIRKBY STEPHEN)

12.5

THIRTEENTH STAGE:
KIRKBY STEPHEN TO APPLEBY-IN-WESTMORLAND
The Vale of Eden
18 kilometres, 10.8 miles

The first few kilometres of the route are westwards out of Kirkby Stephen on minor roads and lanes, after which it takes to the fields and tracks through enclosed farmland and open pasture, across small valleys and through villages; Crosby Garrett, Little Asby, Great Asby and Great Ormside. The Settle and Carlisle Railway is never far away. Finally the entry to Appleby is alongside the River Eden.

In comparison with the previous stage this is relatively low and most of it across cultivated land; even that which is open land is not bleak and hazardous. The scene is quite pastoral and the main hazard may be from frisky young cattle investigating your presence.

It is unwise to recommend not carrying emergency rations, but this stage is one where their necessity is least likely. Don't rely on the villages having shops or even inns, indeed the only inn en route that was discovered was in Great Asby.

Appleby-in-Westmorland is of a similar size to Ashbourne and has plenty of accommodation, shops and other facilities. You could consider having two nights here giving yourself a day's rest and a look round, including a visit to the castle. Alternatively you could spend one night then delay your start for Dufton (the next stage), until after lunch, since it is only a 7.5-kilometre walk. It is a good idea to get your accommodation in Dufton fixed up before setting out from Appleby, as the facilities in the village are not extensive and it is also a stopping place on the Pennine Way.

Signpost in Kirkby Stephen

168

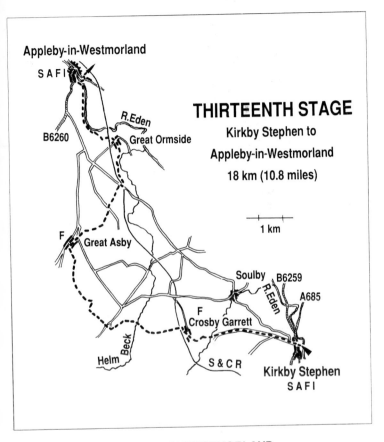

THIRTEENTH STAGE

Kirkby Stephen to
Appleby-in-Westmorland

18 km (10.8 miles)

1 km

APPLEBY-IN-WESTMORLAND

On your journey between Kirkby Stephen and Appleby-in-Westmorland you will pass through Crosby Garrett, Little Asby and Great Asby. Crosby Garrett means 'the settlement with crosses belonging to Garrett (or Gerard)', but no one seems to know who Gerard was, or why the village had crosses. The village nowadays is rather quiet and even the school has closed down, the children being 'bussed' elsewhere, but Crosby Garrett

*The Cathedral of
the Dale
Kirkby Stephen*

has been inhabited since prehistoric times as is evidenced by the burial mounds, or barrows, nearby. Also there are three ancient village settlements with traces of huts and pathways. The church, St Andrew's, dates back to the fifteenth century and is somewhat of a curiosity, as it is built on top of a man-made mound, the purpose of which seems to be unknown. On leaving Crosby Garrett you will cross the Settle and Carlisle Railway (q.v.) using a rather fine Victorian iron bridge.

You will be forgiven if you pass through Little Asby without noticing it, as the only sign of life may be on the farm. The other houses are mainly weekend retreats and the chapel is now a private residence. Asby means 'the settlement with the ash trees'.

There is no inn at Little Asby, but in Great Asby there is an inn with its name represented by statues of three greyhounds outside the main

A. Leave Kirkby Stephen on the Soulby road (opposite the church).

B. Leave the Soulby road and take the lane (NW).

C. Pleasant walk on narrow country lane. Pass Stobars Hall, Moorlands and Stripes.

D. At Smardale Mill Farm, fork right into the farmyard. Proceed straight ahead to leave the yard at the far end into fields. No path.

E. On leaving the farm, bear right to reach Scandale Beck and follow its bank south-westwards for about 100 metres. Cross the beck via the footbridge. (The bridge may be hidden amongst the trees and bushes, so be alert.)

F. After the bridge, enter the fenced path (a bit overgrown). Do NOT be tempted to go over the stile on the right, as this is for the riverside path.

G. Follow the walled/fenced path.

H. Turn right in the lane for Crosby Garrett.

X. Another route to Crosby Garrett.

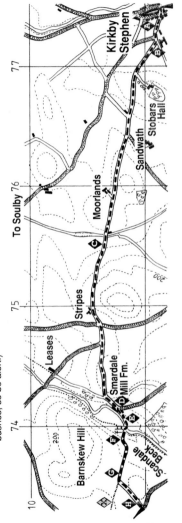

13.1

171

Smardale Mill Farm

entrance. The stream, Asby Gill, is said to originate in Pate Hole, a huge cavern to the west of the village and it is also fed from St Helen's Well near the almshouses. The village has some rather pleasant old cottages and the vicarage is interesting in that the north wing is a pele tower, built in the thirteenth or fourteenth century. There are several pele towers around the Border areas, these being massively built, often with walls two to three metres thick, with the intention of providing a defensible position from which to repel raiders from over the Border. The name pele derives from 'paling', being fences originally used as an outer protection in the motte and bailey style of fortification. The vicarage of Great Asby has an added significance in that it has one of Lady Anne Clifford's locks. Apparently Lady Anne presented these specially designed door locks to people who had done her great favours. This particular lock, dated 1670, was presented to the then vicar, in recognition of his providing shelter to Lady Anne and her entourage during a thunderstorm, which raged whilst she was on one of her journeys between her castles at Appleby and Pendragon (see Feature "The High Way"). There are numerous other grand old houses, including Great Asby Hall, in the village but the church, dedicated to Saint Peter, is fairly modern having been rebuilt in 1866 on the site of the original Norman church. Great Asby is an interesting place and provides a fitting prelude to the town you will visit at the end of this stage.

A. Cross the low bridge over Crosby Garrett Beck. Left for some metres, then right into the lane. Telephone kiosk in lane.

B. Follow the lane past the cottages, parallel with the S&CR.*

C. About 100 metres beyond the cottages, turn left through the stile. Cross the footbridge over the railway and ascend the field ahead.

D. On nearing the wall ahead, bear right to transfer into the field on the right. Use the gaps in the wall, presumably the stile has fallen. A stile is then visible in the wall at the W of this field. Cross.

E. Enter the walled track via stile and proceed W.

F. Immediately after the track turns sharp left (S), go through the gate on the right so as to continue W. Ascend gently.

G. Cross the track (stile then gate) and descend fields. Keep the wall on your left. Path undefined.

H. Transfer to the other side of the wall in field corner. Stile hidden by bushes.

I. About 50 metres before Potts Beck, turn right through gap towards the ruins of Potts (farm).

J. Before the ruins; turn left towards the beck and cross via the footbridge. (THIS BRIDGE IS DANGEROUS! IF IN DOUBT, USE YOUR INITIATIVE.)

K. Fields, stiles and gates. The way ahead is straight forward.

L. In Little Asby, across from the entrance to Chapel Farm Caravan Park, pass through the gate to enter the fields.

M. Turn left at the walled track and follow it to the road.

N. At the road, cross over to re-enter fields.

O. Fields, stiles and gates. Tedious but straightforward. Keep your eyes open to find stiles etc, not always obvious as the path is undefined. At first the wall is on your right, but after about 100 metres transfer to the other side. The wall is now on your left, except for one large field where you cross its centre, descending.

P. On entering the access track to Burtree, between barns, turn right for a few metres then left at the NE end of another barn. Stile gives access to a large field. Descend ahead (path undefined).

X.Y.Z. On this route you see the limestone pavements, but it is not shown on OS as a right of way. However, there appears to be no objection to walking on the open land.

* Settle and Carlisle Railway.

13.2

173

Appleby-in-Westmorland used to be the county town of Westmorland. Unhappily the county of Westmorland no longer exists and Appleby-in-Westmorland is part of Cumbria. Happily, after a great political battle, Appleby has retained the name of its former county so that Westmorland will never be forgotten. Appleby means 'apple tree settlement', so it would seem that Appleby, sheltering in the Vale of Eden between the Pennines to the east and the Cumbrian mountains to the west should be a good place to grow apples, which indeed it is.

You will approach Appleby along the south bank of the River Eden (Eden means 'river') and the nearness of the town will be confirmed when you see the great hall of the castle standing sentinel-like on the skyline before you. The APW crosses the river on the new Jubilee Footbridge, which replaced the old bridge which was washed away in the floods of 1968, and at one time there was a ford here for vehicular traffic and stepping-stones for pedestrians. Whilst crossing the bridge you will see Bongate Mill on the north bank of the river. Dated 1836, the mill once had three enormous water-wheels to power the millstones, some of which can be seen outside the mill, and traces of the mill-race are still evident. Climbing up the hill on the north bank of the river you will arrive in 'old' Appleby, or Bongate as it is known.

The South African War Memorial, at the top of the hill, possibly marks the site of the original village where the Danes settled in the tenth century. Bongate, inhabited by bondsmen in the twelfth century, was considered a separate town even up to the eighteenth century and St Michael's church, disused since 1975, was one of the churches that Lady Anne had pulled down and rebuilt in 1659. There are several hotels in Bongate, but if you decide to stay in Boroughgate, as the new part of Appleby is called, your route is to the left, passing many old cottages and dated houses on your way to the Town Bridge.

Crossing the bridge brings you into Boroughgate and the market square where the whole of the 'new' town is revealed before you. Low Cross and High Cross mark each end of the main thoroughfare and near the seventeenth-century Low Cross, with its three sundials, can be seen a large iron ring used until 1812 to tether bulls during bull baiting sessions. The Cloisters, on the site of the old Market House where the butter market used to be situated, provide an entrance (similar to the one at Kirkby Stephen but more splendid) to the path leading to St Lawrence's church. Lady Anne is buried in this church which she restored in 1655, and her

A. Continue descending NW. Path undefined.

B. Through the gate into the lane. Turn right.

C. The right of way turns left (W) about 200 metres after leaving enclosed land, but is not defined on the ground. However, various green tracks are in evidence - walk westward. From here to Great Asby the route is a bridleway hence there are no stiles, only gates.

D. After crossing this lane, turn NW when a vague track appears.

E. Pass through gate in wire fence.

F. Approach the wall, then keep it on your left.

G. At a group of trees protected by a wall, turn left through a gate, then right to put the wall on your right for a few metres. Then right, through the gate to put the wall on your left again.

H. Gates all the way. Keep walking just E of N. No defined path, so the gates indicate the route.

I. Unfenced track leads into Great Asby.

J. Keep on the road to the SE of Asby Beck.

K. Leave Great Asby on the Appleby road.

L. Fork right, into the lane leading to Goodlie Hill.

The short cut via Asby Grange and Grange Hall is tedious and not recommended.

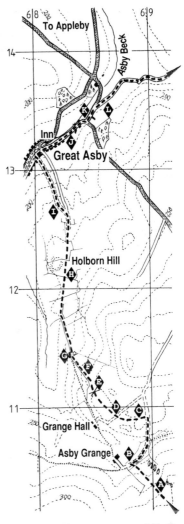

13.3

magnificent tomb bears tribute to her work in Appleby and other areas. If you have an interest in pipe organs, a visit to the church is a must because the organ in St Lawrence's is one of the three oldest organs in the country (although the church claims it is the oldest) and is unusual in that it was originally built for, and installed in Carlisle Cathedral. The organ was presented to the people of Appleby in 1684, the organ case being painted a dark brown colour, but during a complete rebuild in 1976 the paint was stripped off, bringing to light graffiti - clearly not only a modern phenomenon. The restoration revealed a beautiful oak case which now emphasises the beauty of this remarkable and unique instrument.

Back in the market place the black and white Moot Hall, part of which dates back to 1596, is still used for parish council meetings in the upper part, the lower part being occupied by shops and an information centre. Further up Boroughgate, on the left through an archway, are the almshouses of St Anne's Hospital. Founded in 1653 by Lady Anne for the use of "a mother, a reader and twelve sisters forever" the cottages, recently modernised, are still occupied and provide comfortable accommodation for the ladies who live there.

Behind High Cross is the main entrance to Appleby Castle, which is in private ownership and occupies the site of an original Norman motte and bailey style castle. The castle, having been attacked and damaged several times by raiders from the north and besieged and damaged during the Civil War, was restored by Lady Anne in the mid-seventeenth century. The great hall and Norman keep are open to the public and in the grounds is a rare breeds survival centre. Lady Anne spent much of her time here and her influence in Appleby is around for all to see.

In the past, many light industries have prospered in Appleby. These have included a corset factory, the manufacture of nails, the manufacture of carpets, a bobbin mill, breweries (in the mid-nineteenth century there were twenty inns in the town), candle making and lead mining. Nowadays, Appleby's main industrial concern is milk, and reputedly there are two to three thousand tonnes of cheese in store in the town.

Appleby-in-Westmorland is indeed a fascinating place and one can spend hours exploring the many places of historical interest. There is an abundance of hotels, inns, guest-houses, B & Bs, restaurants, shops and banks to ensure a comfortable stay but beware, Appleby Horse Fair (q.v.) is always held on the second Wednesday in June and lodgings will be difficult, if not impossible, to find at this time!

A. Continue the ascent of the lane.

B. Where the lane turns sharp left to go to Goodlie Hill, the APW proceeds ahead through the gate. Keep on the track with the fence on your right.

C. At this gate which gives access to a very large field, turn due N making for the point in the boundary ahead where a wall comes in from the NE (the other side of the boundary). No path.

D. Over the fence at this point, to put the wall on the other side of the fence on your right. (When researched, the stile had not been replaced after repair of the fence and it was necessary to climb over barbed wire.)

E. Keep the wall on your right.

F. Through the gate. The wall is now on your left.

G. Leave the wall and the trees on your left, to make for the gate in the wall ahead. Pass through this and enter the road through another gate.

H. Cross the road and walk up the track, which turns right and then left, to Heights.

I. Where the track turns sharp left again to the farm, keep ahead between farm buildings and on into the fields.

J. Descend through the fields. Gates and stiles lead the way.

K. Enter the road and turn right. Cross the railway and then sharp left through the stile.

L. Keep the railway on your near left.

M. After crossing the watercourse and the fence, leave the railway, walking due N, to cross to the opposite corner of the field. No path.

N. Through the wood. The way is undefined, but keep just W of N.

O. Leave the wood and proceed through the fields. Keep Helm Beck about 50 metres on your right.

P. Keep ahead on the road into Great Ormside.

Q. Just as you enter the village, turn left on to the southern edge of the road triangle. Then right for a few metres. The path to the River Eden and Appleby is then off to the left.

R. Join the walled track, and after a few metres keep left and pass under the railway.

S. The path is well-defined and waymarked.

T. There is only one way - the riverside path.

13.4

Appleby Horse Fair

Markets and fairs have played an important part in the history of some of the villages and towns you have visited thus far, but in Appleby the horse fair has, over the years, achieved a national and possibly an international reputation.

There is some argument amongst historians and commentators as to whether or not the charter granted by King James II, in 1685, actually refers to this fair or to some other now defunct occurrence. The fact remains that Appleby Horse Fair is firmly established, and the whole character of the town and the surrounding areas is completely changed during the fair and the few days preceding and following it.

The fair, originally set up for the "purchase and sale of all manner of goods, cattle, horses, mares and geldings", is always held on the second Wednesday in June and attracts gypsies, traders and travellers from far and wide. Mobile homes, ranging from traditional horse-drawn gypsy vados to Rolls Royce-drawn palatial 'mansions-on-wheels', converge on Appleby several days before the event. Every open space is occupied. Traders set up stalls on Fair Hill. The restaurants are full. Those inns that remain open are full. The shops do a roaring trade and accommodation is booked up months before the event by visitors coming to see the fair.

The fair, said to be the largest of its kind in the world, is now a venue for horse traders to buy, sell and race their animals. It is a venue for them to meet old friends and enemies and a venue for them to make new friends and enemies. Horses are taken to the river to be washed and groomed. Thrilling races take place with bets being placed on winning, and losing, animals. All types of horses, ponies, carriages and equipment are available for sale and throughout, a carnival atmosphere prevails. On Tuesday, harness racing takes place in Holme Meadow and Wednesday is the main trading day with business finishing at about 4.00pm.

It seems as though the fair has changed character over the years and 'things are not what they used to be'. But that applies to many facets of life nowadays. The fair is not run by the town council - it lets the field to the gypsies and the district council provides water, toilet and refuse collecting facilities. The nostalgic remember bygone fairs in a romantic light and are upset by the modern competitiveness and commercialism which surrounds the modern-day events. Maybe in 200 years time, people will be looking back and wishing that Appleby Horse Fair could be as it was in 1990.

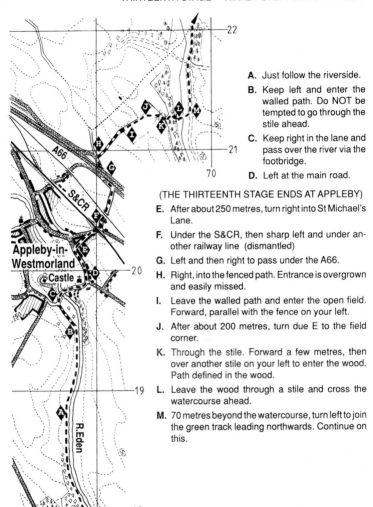

A. Just follow the riverside.

B. Keep left and enter the walled path. Do NOT be tempted to go through the stile ahead.

C. Keep right in the lane and pass over the river via the footbridge.

D. Left at the main road.

(THE THIRTEENTH STAGE ENDS AT APPLEBY)

E. After about 250 metres, turn right into St Michael's Lane.

F. Under the S&CR, then sharp left and under another railway line (dismantled)

G. Left and then right to pass under the A66.

H. Right, into the fenced path. Entrance is overgrown and easily missed.

I. Leave the walled path and enter the open field. Forward, parallel with the fence on your left.

J. After about 200 metres, turn due E to the field corner.

K. Through the stile. Forward a few metres, then over another stile on your left to enter the wood. Path defined in the wood.

L. Leave the wood through a stile and cross the watercourse ahead.

M. 70 metres beyond the watercourse, turn left to join the green track leading northwards. Continue on this.

13.5

In the original plan for the APW this stage was combined with the next, making it a very long one, 35.5 kilometres, over the highest point and out of the valley to the South Tyne and into the valley of the Nent. On reflection, it was decided that the need to reach the destination at Nenthead in a reasonable time would spoil the journey, hence this short stage was created before a strenuous one. Indeed, it is no more than a pleasant stroll through another idyllic part of the Vale of Eden.

It is characterised by fertile farmland all the way, apart from small parts

which pass through woods and plantations. The last kilometre includes a pleasant path beside a beck along a wooded gorge. Most of the paths are undefined on the ground, but the many stiles and gates are the clues to direction. There should be little difficulty underfoot, and even in the worst weather there should be little danger. There is nowhere en route for the purchase of food or drink.

The accommodation in Dufton is limited and it is advisable to arrange lodgings in advance, from Appleby. The Pennine Way also passes through Dufton. There is a small shop/post office and an inn, but the latter did not provide food at the time of research.

St Lawrence's,
Appleby-in-Westmorland

180

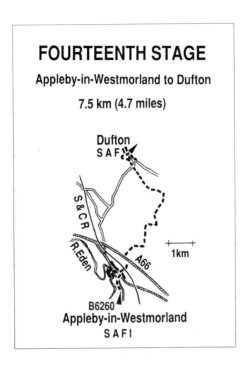

FOURTEENTH STAGE

Appleby-in-Westmorland to Dufton

7.5 km (4.7 miles)

DUFTON

As the journey between Appleby-in-Westmorland and Nenthead may be rather more than you may care to attempt in the space of day, Dufton has been included as a staging-post to break the journey.

Dufton, meaning 'Dove Farm', is a small Cumbrian village situated on the approach to some of the highest fells in England, apart from the Lake District. Mickle Fell, Dufton Fell, Knock Fell and Cross Fell combine to form a superb backdrop that no theatre could match. Cross Fell, due north of Dufton, is the highest of the four at 893 metres (just under 3,000 feet) whilst Mickle Fell, to the east, is 790 metres high. The highest point of the APW is between Knock Fell and Great Dun Fell, at 755 metres.

If you leave Appleby in the early morning you will arrive at Dufton well before lunch, and if you are staying the night at Dufton you may care to visit

High Cup after having confirmed the whereabouts of your lodgings. High Cupgill Head, at the top of High Cup, is about seven kilometres uphill from Dufton, but the climb is very worthwhile as the sight of High Cup in afternoon sunlight is quite spectacular. The famous blue-grey dolerite rock of the Whin Sill (see Feature "Hadrian's Wall") is very apparent in this huge amphitheatre, and the Lakeland hills form a magnificent panorama to the west across the pastoral Vale of Eden. High Cup is often erroneously called High Cup Nick, as the nick is properly a cleft in the rock formation of High Cup. Both Dufton and High Cup are on the PW, so you could use the PW route if you visit this landmark. However, do remember that the round trip is in the order of 14 kilometres and you will have a long walk the next day.

Dufton

A. Follow the track round to enter the forest.

B. At Flakebridge (opposite cottage), turn left up the forest track. Private road, but public footpath.

C. After about 400 metres from Flakebridge, fork right onto the very ill-defined forest track. This point is difficult to locate because of the recent forest harvesting and the consequent damage to the route. As you walk up from Flakebridge, a small deep-cut watercourse is on the right of the track. Your fork right is at the first sensible crossing point. Proceed on 19°.

D. Leave the forest through a gate and continue up the field on 19°. A stile comes into view.

E. Stiles indicate the route. No path.

F. Enter the wood through the stile and cross Burthwaite Beck via the footbridge. Turn N, to follow the contour round to the NW.

G. Keep the wall on your right all the way.

H. At the western end of this very long field proceed towards the left wire fence, ie. left of the wall and oak trees. Through the stile against the wall.

I. Fields with stiles and gates. No difficulty, but no paths.

J. Through the farmyard at Greenhow to its access track. Just beyond the farm, take the stile to cut the corner and reach the road.

K. At the road, left then right for the footpath into Dufton.

L. Follow the well-defined path through the mini wooded gorge.

M. On leaving the gorge, join the track and keep right to ascend into Dufton.

(THE FOURTEENTH STAGE ENDS AT DUFTON)

N. At the road through the village green, turn left (NW) and follow in the direction of Knock.

O. Fork right onto the track to leave the road.

P. Left, to make for the church. (At the time of researching the route, this path was very overgrown but passable.) The fenced path and stiles are easy to follow.

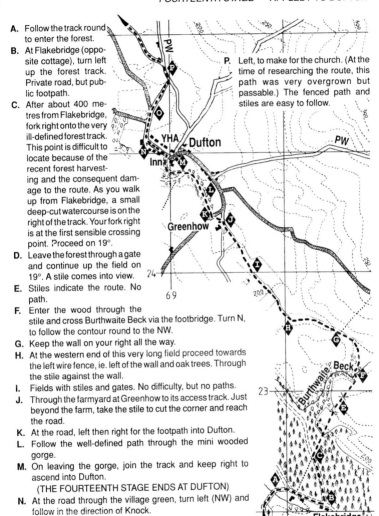

14.1

FIFTEENTH STAGE:
DUFTON TO NENTHEAD
The High Point - Literally
28 kilometres, 17.4 miles

Despite being one of the longest stages which passes over the highest point of the APW, between Knock Fell and Great Dun Fell at 755 metres, this is by no means the most difficult stage. The route leaves Dufton north-westwards to Knock, then ascends the western slopes of the Pennine massif and on to the summit. Instead of going on to Cross Fell, it descends alongside Trout Beck to the River Tees and over Tyne Head into the valley of the River South Tyne. It leaves the valley to enter the gorge at Ashgill and climbs over the moors to Nenthead.

No more idyllic pastoral scenes; it is back to the hills. The highest part of the Pennine chain is near here at Cross Fell (893 metres - just short of 3,000 feet) but, unlike the peat moors of the Dark Peak, these moors seem less menacing. Sheep are rare, but then most of this area is a nature reserve so please keep to the paths and tracks. Throughout the whole journey which is on well-defined paths and tracks, navigation is easy, you will not escape the evidence of lead mining in bygone days.

Since a lot of the route is remote and exposed, it is necessary to take emergency rations and equipment. There is no accommodation en route, nor shops, nor inns. However, if when you get to Ashgill you find that you cannot face the ascent and descent to get to Nenthead, then proceed to Garrigill, but remember that the accommodation is limited and it is on the Pennine Way. It will then be necessary, of course, to retrace your steps to Ashgill.

There is limited accommodation at Nenthead, so advance booking is wise. There is also a small shop.

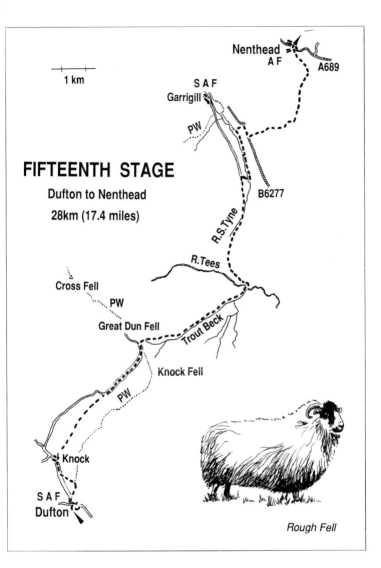

1 km

Nenthead
A F

A689

S A F
Garrigill

PW

FIFTEENTH STAGE

Dufton to Nenthead

28km (17.4 miles)

B6277

R.S.Tyne

R.Tees

△
Cross Fell

PW

Great Dun Fell

Trout Beck

Knock Fell

PW

Knock

S A F
Dufton

Rough Fell

Ashgill Force and Bridge

The Religious Society of Friends

George Fox was born in 1624, and at the age of twenty-two underwent a 'mystical experience' that convinced him that Christianity was the only way of life. He began to preach in 1647 and in 1668 he organised the Religious Society of Friends, or Quakers as they came to be known. Fox believed that a person needed no spiritual mediator, but could find understanding and guidance through an 'inward light' supplied by the Holy Spirit.

In the formative years, many thousands of Friends, including George

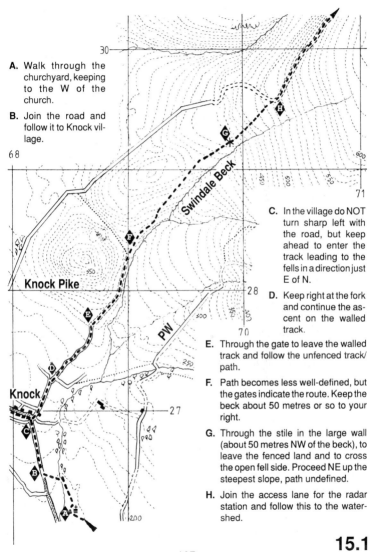

A. Walk through the churchyard, keeping to the W of the church.

B. Join the road and follow it to Knock village.

C. In the village do NOT turn sharp left with the road, but keep ahead to enter the track leading to the fells in a direction just E of N.

D. Keep right at the fork and continue the ascent on the walled track.

E. Through the gate to leave the walled track and follow the unfenced track/path.

F. Path becomes less well-defined, but the gates indicate the route. Keep the beck about 50 metres or so to your right.

G. Through the stile in the large wall (about 50 metres NW of the beck), to leave the fenced land and to cross the open fell side. Proceed NE up the steepest slope, path undefined.

H. Join the access lane for the radar station and follow this to the watershed.

15.1

Fox, were persecuted for their beliefs. Their refusal to take the oath and to remove their hats in the presence of magistrates led Quakers to be imprisoned for disloyalty and contempt of court. Many had distraints imposed upon them which often resulted in property, worth far more than the imposed fine, being removed and sold. Quakers suffered beatings, whippings, stoning and being put in the stocks for being 'rogues and vagabonds'. Because of their faith, they were excluded from the professions and positions of high office, but, by adopting an attitude of 'we'll succeed despite you', they later achieved commercial and industrial independence. Quite clearly the life of the early Quaker was not an easy one, but their faith enabled them to overcome all the hardships and deprivations.

They had their own schools and specialised in science teaching, a rarity in the country at large. The whole Quaker Society was literate, an unusual phenomenon for the late seventeenth century. This helped businesses to flourish, as communication at all levels was possible, and the fundamental belief of equality and brotherhood led to easy exchanges of ideas between employers and employees. In the early years the Quakers formed many small businesses and, whilst the people with whom they dealt were initially suspicious of the Quaker way of life, it was soon realised that to do business with someone whose 'word was his bond' was indeed good business. Quaker merchants and traders became known for their honesty and the quality of their goods, and it was not long before they started to branch out into bigger things.

In the Feature "NENTHEAD" (q.v.), mention is made of the influence of the London Lead Company, or the Quaker Lead Company, on the mining and the social affairs of the Alston Moor communities. In the first half of the eighteenth century, the company took up leases on several mines in Derbyshire, near Ashover, and of particular note is the work it did in driving drainage levels, which enabled miners to work safely at much deeper levels without the danger of flooding. The company also built a canal from Chesterfield to join the River Trent near Stockwith in Nottinghamshire, and a turnpike road from Ashover to join the Mansfield and Chesterfield turnpike. Mining interests in north Wales were developed in the eighteenth century, and here again, as elsewhere, there was guaranteed security of employment for the workers who were considered to be well paid. Also the company was concerned for the well-being of the employees and made sure that houses and adequate supplies of food, at affordable prices, were available.

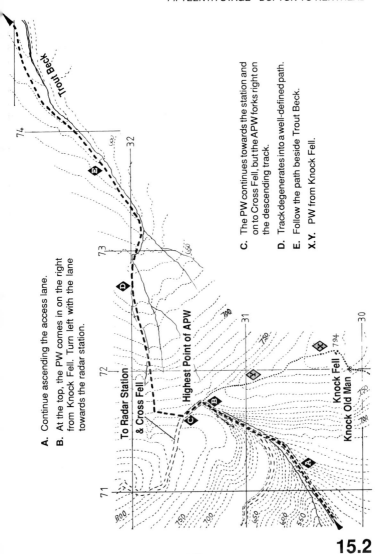

A. Continue ascending the access lane.

B. At the top, the PW comes in on the right from Knock Fell. Turn left with the lane towards the radar station.

C. The PW continues towards the station and on to Cross Fell, but the APW forks right on the descending track.

D. Track degenerates into a well-defined path.

E. Follow the path beside Trout Beck.

X.Y. PW from Knock Fell.

15.2

189

Whenever the Quakers became involved in an industry, they contributed positively to that industry. Not only did they get involved with manufacturing and selling the product, but also they carried out research into ways and means of improving the product and often at the same time improving the lot of their workers. Some examples of such industries are agricultural implements, iron, steel, brass, copper, china, printing and transport to name but a few. Not all Quakers were industrialists, traders and merchants. Indeed, some of them became famous clock-makers, bankers, doctors, botanists and naturalists. They were responsible for many advances in the scientific field, and many Fellows of the Royal Society (FRS), were elected from their ranks.

George Fox died in 1691, and by this time the society had spread to Asia, Africa and America where William Penn started a colony of Quakers in Pennsylvania in 1682. In his journal, published in 1694 with a preface by Penn, Fox wrote that "Justice Bennett of Derby was the first to call us 'Quakers', because I bade him quake and tremble at the word of the Lord."

NENTHEAD

Nenthead, at an average height of 467 metres, claims to be the highest village in England. It also has the highest parish church, the highest occupied house, the highest road crossing and had, at one time, the highest chapel. It is said to have the coldest climate in England. The Co-operative Movement was pioneered here and 'fair wages', medical services,

Overwater, Nenthead

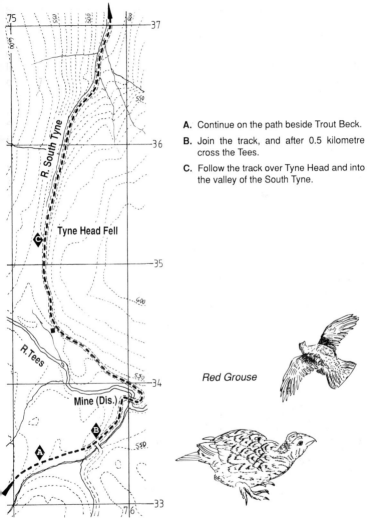

A. Continue on the path beside Trout Beck.

B. Join the track, and after 0.5 kilometre cross the Tees.

C. Follow the track over Tyne Head and into the valley of the South Tyne.

Red Grouse

15.3

pensions and social benefits were the norm in this village, almost from its creation.

Situated amidst the sources of the River Nent, which flows into the River South Tyne at Alston, Nenthead is part of Alston Moor, but there are no records of its existence before the mid-eighteenth century. It is known that Alston Moor was inhabited early in the seventeen century, but prior to that, the history of the moor is somewhat conjectural. Possibly the Picts were the first inhabitants from about the year 270, and the Romans are thought to have worked the mines in this area during their occupation of Britain. In 1131, Edward III granted the mines on Alston Moor to his Belgian queen, Philippa. About 1210, the Alston Moor Estate, which then belonged to William the Lion of Scotland, was granted to William de Vetriponte, a Norman vassal, in whose family the estate remained until the beginning of the seventeenth century. In 1618, the estate was sold for £2,500 to Sir Francis Radcliffe, Earl of Derwentwater. After the death of the earl's son John, in 1729, the Crown took possession before passing on the estate to the Greenwich Hospital for Seamen. The hospital estates owned the farms and mines on Alston Moor until 1964.

In 1750, the London Lead Company (L.L.C.), took over most of the Nent Valley leases from the Greenwich Hospital and, from 1753 the Religious Society of Friends (q.v.), who owned most of the L.L.C., developed Nenthead into a 'model village'. Until this time all the mine workers lived in very poor accommodation in farms in the surrounding area. The Quaker Company, as the L.L.C. was known, extended the smelt mill and built some cottages for the mine workers. They also started a system of 'mine shops', near the mine entrances. These were fitted out to accommodate and feed miners, thus improving their lot in more ways than one.

By 1820, the original cottages had become inadequate and the company embarked on an ambitious scheme to house mine officials and workers. They built more cottages (with gardens), a school, a chapel, a clock tower and a market hall. They also subsidised the Miners' Arms, the village's main inn, when trade was bad due to miners 'preferring books to beer'. In 1850, further improvements to the model village included a post office and a piped public water supply. Then followed a public wash house and baths, all at the company's expense. They also planted 250 hectares of Scots pine and larch trees, not only to supply the mines with timber, but also to improve the appearance of this small village surrounded by desolate moorland.

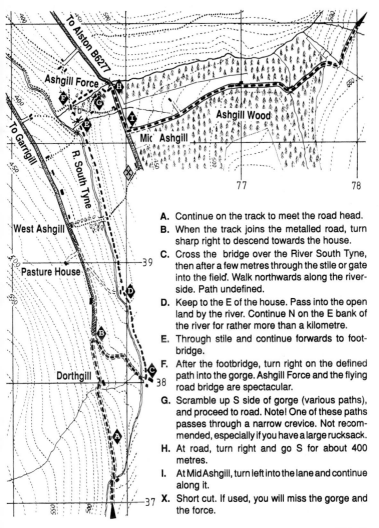

A. Continue on the track to meet the road head.

B. When the track joins the metalled road, turn sharp right to descend towards the house.

C. Cross the bridge over the River South Tyne, then after a few metres through the stile or gate into the field. Walk northwards along the riverside. Path undefined.

D. Keep to the E of the house. Pass into the open land by the river. Continue N on the E bank of the river for rather more than a kilometre.

E. Through stile and continue forwards to footbridge.

F. After the footbridge, turn right on the defined path into the gorge. Ashgill Force and the flying road bridge are spectacular.

G. Scramble up S side of gorge (various paths), and proceed to road. Note! One of these paths passes through a narrow crevice. Not recommended, especially if you have a large rucksack.

H. At road, turn right and go S for about 400 metres.

I. At Mid Ashgill, turn left into the lane and continue along it.

X. Short cut. If used, you will miss the gorge and the force.

15.4

The Quaker Company adopted a benevolent, paternalistic attitude towards its workers. It ensured that the wages paid to the miners were adequate to support families, not in luxurious comfort but at least 'above the breadline', at a time when poverty amongst workers in all trades was the norm. In the 1840s the Corn Association, run by the miners but subsidised by the company, purchased corn in bulk from Newcastle and used the company's wagons to transport it to Nenthead, where it was ground into flour to make bread. Surely, this was the precursor of the Co-operative Movement as we know it today.

Towards the end of the nineteenth century, the mine leases on Alston Moor changed hands. The Vielle Montagne Zinc Company, a Belgian firm, acquired the mines in 1896 and brought workers from many countries to live and work at Nenthead. They mined lead, zinc and silver and, following the example set by the Quaker Company, V.M., as it came to be known, continued improving the village. They installed new equipment above and below ground and installed an electricity supply to power equipment and street lamps. They also bought traction engines and employed men with red flags to walk in front of each, as they transported lead and zinc to Alston railway station where it was loaded into railway wagons for its journey to Belgium by rail and sea.

During the early part of the twenties, and especially immediately after the First World War, the price of lead and zinc plummeted and most of the foreign workers left the district. Various new owners reopened the mines in the 1930s, often only prospecting for ore among the spoil tips. In 1949, Anglo Austral Mines Limited, an Avonmouth firm, took over the leases, its interest being not in lead, zinc or silver, but fluorspar. This mineral is used for several purposes, including the preparation of hydrofluoric acid, as a flux in metallurgy and in making enamel and glass.

Mining in Nenthead ceased in 1968, but the legacy of several hundred years of mining activity remains. Visitors can see the cottages, houses, churches, the reading room and the village hall, all dating back to the mid-nineteenth century and still standing as a tribute to the Religious Society of Friends. Mine workings and buildings are still apparent and it is said that the quickest way to Allendale is underground. However, DO NOT, under any circumstances, enter any of the many mine entrances to be found in this area. They are unsafe and can be very dangerous. You have been warned!

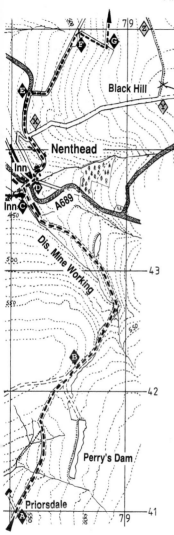

A. At Priorsdale the metalled surface ceases, so the lane becomes a track.

B. Follow the track over the pass.

C. Pass through the car park, then turn right at the road.

(THE FIFTEENTH STAGE ENDS AT NENTHEAD)

D. Leave the A689 up the minor road by the chapel and ascend the winding road. The steepest part of the ascent is cobbled.

E. Turn right into the walled track and ascend.

F. Turn right through the gate and ascend the rough hillside. No path, difficulty walking. (This right turn is about 100 metres before the gate which gives the track access to the open moor.)

G. Left to turn N, then keep the fence on your left.

X.Y.Z. NOT shown on OS as a right of way from Y to Z.

15.5

SIXTEENTH STAGE:
NENTHEAD TO ALLENDALE TOWN

Chimneys and Flues
18 kilometres, 11.2 miles

You leave Nenthead up the steep lane behind the inn and then turn into a track to continue the ascent to The Dodd. Then a long steady descent down Middle Rigg to Hesleywell with breath-taking views down West Allen Dale. A further short descent brings you to a fine footbridge over the River West Allen, followed by a short, steep ascent to the road. After 0.7 kilometre down the road, you continue ascending the valley side and onto Dryburn Moor and the road which links the two Allen dales. After 1.2 kilometres on this road, you arrive at a path leading to the chimneys. A fine path then descends beside the flues, eventually joining a lane leading to Allendale Town.

Most of this stage is over high moorland, but it is broken by the crossing of the cultivated narrow valley of West Allen Dale. The only habitation from start to finish is in the dale near the river.

Although the way over The Dodd and Middle Rigg has no defined path on the higher parts, navigation is not difficult. Most of the remainder of the stage is on defined paths and tracks, or lanes and roads.

There are no facilities for getting provisions en route but, of course, Allendale Town is well provided with all facilities, especially inns.

Lead Mining

The APW passes through several areas where there is abundant evidence of disused and abandoned lead mines. These are the Peak District, Wharfedale, Wensleydale, Nidderdale, Alston Moor and the Allendales. As you will spend some time during the walk negotiating your way through these old workings, it may be of interest for you to know something of the old lead mining techniques.

It was perhaps the Roman occupation of Britain that created a real need for lead, although mining on a relatively small scale had taken place for many years before this. When the Romans arrived, they realised that the mineral was to be found in many areas of Britain and they started up and

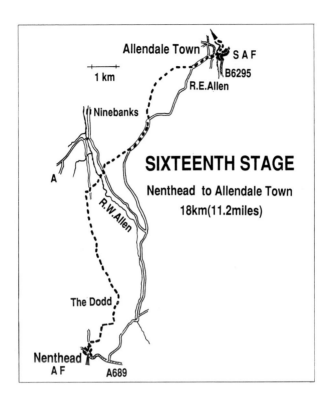

Allendale Town

S A F

1 km

B6295

R.E.Allen

Ninebanks

SIXTEENTH STAGE

Nenthead to Allendale Town
18km(11.2miles)

A

R.W.Allen

The Dodd

Nenthead

A F

A689

worked many mines during their stay. They needed lead in quantity for many purposes, including the manufacture of pipes for water supplies, baths, weights and coffins. After the Romans left this country, early in the fifth century, lead mining declined. A revival occurred late in the Middle Ages, not for ordinary domestic use but for use in the construction of large buildings such as castles, churches, abbeys and monasteries. Lead sheet was used in these structures to provide watertight roofs, also for gutterings and fall-pipes. Silver, a by-product, extracted from lead, was used for minting coins at the various mints around the country.

In order to arrive at the finished products, four main stages were necessary. These were mining the ore, sorting, crushing and smelting. In the early days, mining was simply a matter of digging the ore out of the ground using an opencast trench system. The simplest of tools were used, such as picks, chisels, crow bars, hammers and wedges, and although fire-setting was tried it was not very popular. The technique of fire-setting involved lighting a fire against the rock face to heat the surface, which cracked when quenched with water. The problem with this method was the danger from smoke and fumes in the confined space of a deep trench or pit.

After having been loosened, the ore, together with rock and other debris, was thrown directly to the surface, or wound up in buckets using simple winding systems. It was often necessary to abandon the trench or pit if water could not be removed in sufficient quantities to enable work to continue. Water was always a problem in mines, especially when the only method of remove was by using buckets. Rag-and chain 'pumps' were used at one time, these consisting of an endless chain running through a pipe. Rags were attached at intervals to the chain and as the chain was pulled through the pipe, the rags brought up quantities of water. This, of course, was not very efficient and it was not until the mid-eighteenth century with the onset of the Industrial Revolution that matters improved.

Hushing was another method of gaining ore. At its simplest, a dam was built at the head of a valley and the area behind the dam was allowed to fill with water. When the dam was breached, the water rushed down the valley, removing ore from the surface of the ground. The hushing could be repeated many times and there are reports of permanent dams with sluice gates, thus removing the necessity to constantly rebuild the dam. This simple method was cheap, but obviously had its limitations. It is a matter of conjecture as to whether or not the word 'hush' was meant to be onomatopoeic. Surely, a huge volume of water cascading down a valley, and carrying all before it, would produce a sound which would be the very opposite of 'hush'?

Clearly there was a limit to the amount of ore that could be mined using opencast or hushing methods as it became necessary to mine deeper and deeper. Levels were driven into hillsides (originally using only hand tools) and adits, or water gates, were sometimes driven from a valley side into a mine to allow water to drain away. However, this was very labour and time-consuming, and thus costly.

As can be imagined, the Industrial Revolution brought about many

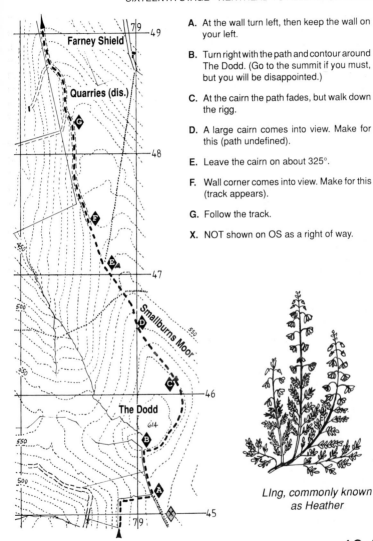

A. At the wall turn left, then keep the wall on your left.

B. Turn right with the path and contour around The Dodd. (Go to the summit if you must, but you will be disappointed.)

C. At the cairn the path fades, but walk down the rigg.

D. A large cairn comes into view. Make for this (path undefined).

E. Leave the cairn on about 325°.

F. Wall corner comes into view. Make for this (track appears).

G. Follow the track.

X. NOT shown on OS as a right of way.

LIng, commonly known as Heather

16.1

changes. The use of steam engines enabled miners to recover ore from even greater depths. The motive power from the engines was used for pumps and winding ore. The primitive railway systems, formerly powered by human effort and then horses, became fully mechanised using engine-driven cable systems. Gunpowder came to be used for blasting rock and ore in the second half of the eighteenth century, and many other techniques were introduced into the industry.

The ore recovered from the mines was, in most cases, mixed with rock and other debris. It was therefore necessary to separate the ore suitable for smelting from the unwanted material and, in the early days, this was simply done by hand sorting. Some large pieces or ore could easily be removed from the rock by using hammers, but in other cases it was necessary to crush the rock and ore into very small pieces (using hand crushers) which were then sorted and washed. Boys and women were often employed on this work. In the sixteenth century, improved methods of separation were introduced. One method consisted of using a sloping wooden trough with water running down it, the idea being that the water would remove the stone and other debris, leaving the ore in the trough. An improvement on this was a sieve in a tub of water. This required fine crushing of the ore/rock mixture, which was then put in the sieves suspended in the tubs. Skilful agitation of the sieve allowed the heavier ore to be separated from the unwanted material.

The Industrial Revolution brought about many developments in the science of hydraulics, and the techniques of separation were considerably improved. The introduction of mechanical rollers for crushing, the rollers being driven by water-wheels and engines, enabled tighter control to be exercised over the size of the crushed material. The resultant fine ore/rock mixture was then separated using mechanically driven sieves and agitators in water troughs. The whole process relied on the relative densities of ore and unwanted material.

Having obtained the wanted ore and discarded the unwanted rock, the final process was smelting. An early and primitive method was the 'bole hill'. This consisted simply of constructing a low, circular stone wall on the brow of a hill facing into the wind. Fuel, generally wood and peat, was used to make a fire behind the wall, and wind blowing though gaps in the wall provided a suitable draught to fan the flames. Ore was thrown onto the fire followed by more fuel and more ore in several layers. The resultant molten lead was run off through a suitable opening in the wall into rough moulds to form pigs of lead. An improvement on this method was to use bellows to provide the draught, the bellows being foot, and later water-wheel, powered.

Purpose-built furnaces, with stone hearths, replaced the bole hills, but it was the introduction of coal-fired reverberatory furnaces in the late seventeenth century that brought about a major improvement in smelting. In this type of furnace, the heat source was separated from the ore, the heat being reflected onto the ore in a second chamber. The draught was created by a tall chimney and did not rely on having a good water supply turning water-wheels to power bellows. This type of (continuous) smelting enabled a more precise temperature control to be obtained and allowed the recovery of larger quantities of lead and silver. The ore hearth continued in many small mining concerns, since it could use any type of fuel, usually cheap or free wood or peat. It could be built near the mines, saving on transport costs and it could deal with small quantities. For the larger mines, or groups of mines, the central mills used reverberatory furnaces.

During your walk, you will see much evidence of the industrial heritage of lead mining. The shape of the countryside changes but slowly and the hushes, spoil heaps and excavations will be there for many years to come. Long gone are most of the water-wheels which dotted the countryside in large numbers (at one time there were as many as seventeen on Grassington Moor alone), although some remain. Long gone also are many of the mills and buildings, but it would indeed be a pity if the historical remains of lead mining were allowed to disappear without trace. However, some of the remains are being renovated so that we may view our industrial heritage in comfort and safety.

B. Where the track turns left, the APW turns right through the gate to enter the cottage yard. Pass between the cottage and the outbuilding, then left, as if to pass in front of the cottage. In the wall, opposite the cottage, a stile gives access to a field.

C. Descend, keeping the wall/fence on your right. Through the gate and continue descending to the stile at the road. Turn left.

D. About 200 metres down the road, pass through the gate on the right and descend in the 'avenue' of trees.

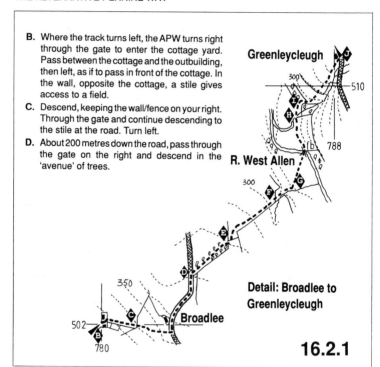

Greenleycleugh

300

510

788

R. West Allen

300

Detail: Broadlee to
Greenleycleugh

350

Broadlee

502

780

16.2.1

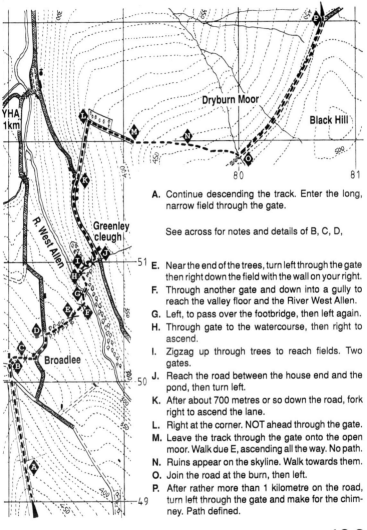

A. Continue descending the track. Enter the long, narrow field through the gate.

See across for notes and details of B, C, D,

E. Near the end of the trees, turn left through the gate then right down the field with the wall on your right.

F. Through another gate and down into a gully to reach the valley floor and the River West Allen.

G. Left, to pass over the footbridge, then left again.

H. Through gate to the watercourse, then right to ascend.

I. Zigzag up through trees to reach fields. Two gates.

J. Reach the road between the house end and the pond, then turn left.

K. After about 700 metres or so down the road, fork right to ascend the lane.

L. Right at the corner. NOT ahead through the gate.

M. Leave the track through the gate onto the open moor. Walk due E, ascending all the way. No path.

N. Ruins appear on the skyline. Walk towards them.

O. Join the road at the burn, then left.

P. After rather more than 1 kilometre on the road, turn left through the gate and make for the chimney. Path defined.

16.2

ALLENDALE TOWN

Assuming that you travel over ground and not underground from Nenthead, you will cross over Allendale Common and down into Allendale Town. During the last few kilometres of this stage you will walk between the remains of two flues, which terminate at the two chimneys (now in a dangerous condition) on the common. At the Allendale Town end, the flues are not apparent, but they used to start at the Allen Mills and Allendale Town was, at one time, an important lead mining area.

Lead was not the only product from the mines to make the owners wealthy. Silver, a by-product from lead mining, was recovered in large quantities from the Allendale mines. It is recorded that in 1869 nearly one-and-a-half tonnes of silver were produced, and in 1851 an ingot weighing 345 kilogrammes was sent to the Crystal Palace in Hyde Park on the occasion of the Great Exhibition.

In 1632 the manor of Hexhamshire, in which Allendale lies, was sold by the Crown to the Fenwick family. They sold it in 1694 to the Blacketts, who also owned mines in Weardale. The estates passed by marriage to the Beaumonts, who managed the mines on similar lines to the London Lead Company (see Feature "Nenthead"). The Blackett-Beaumonts were responsible for many improvements both in social welfare for the mining families and in mining techniques.

The flues, one of which was 4,067 metres long and the other 3,965 metres long, served a dual purpose. Firstly, the flues served to remove the noxious fumes from the area of the smelt mill and secondly, they removed the sublimated lead from the fumes. The long arched flues allowed the sublimate to condense on the brick walls, from where the lead condensate could be periodically removed. The residual, mainly sulphurous, fumes were emitted from the chimneys on the moor and it is still apparent what effect this had on the surrounding flora. The Beaumonts also installed long flues at Allenheads and Rookhope mills, and the total length of all the Beaumont flues exceeded 13 kilometres.

There is an East Allen Dale, a West Allen Dale and an Allen Dale. Allendale Town, often referred to as Allendale, was not always the small quiet country town it is today. In the mid-nineteenth century, when lead mining was at its peak of production, the population stood at 6,400 and Allendale Town had a well-earned reputation for ostentatious living. It was custom and practice in those days for the miners to be paid every six

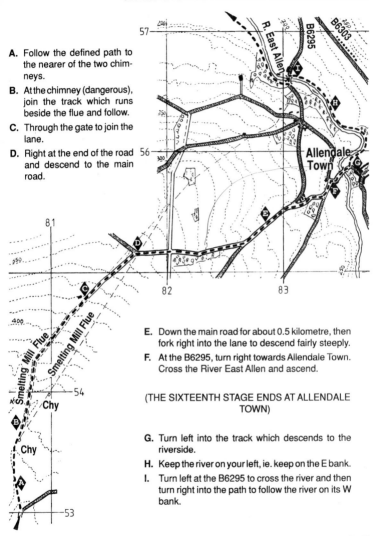

A. Follow the defined path to the nearer of the two chimneys.

B. At the chimney (dangerous), join the track which runs beside the flue and follow.

C. Through the gate to join the lane.

D. Right at the end of the road and descend to the main road.

E. Down the main road for about 0.5 kilometre, then fork right into the lane to descend fairly steeply.

F. At the B6295, turn right towards Allendale Town. Cross the River East Allen and ascend.

(THE SIXTEENTH STAGE ENDS AT ALLENDALE TOWN)

G. Turn left into the track which descends to the riverside.

H. Keep the river on your left, ie. keep on the E bank.

I. Turn left at the B6295 to cross the river and then turn right into the path to follow the river on its W bank.

16.3

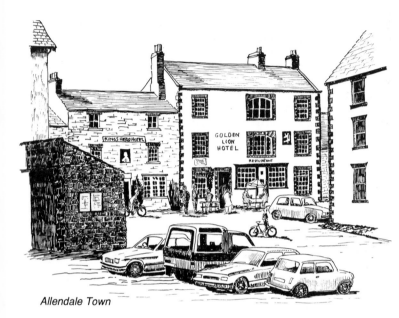

Allendale Town

months. They received an advance of wages every month and that itself led to celebrations taking place. However, the six-monthly pay days or 'The Pays' as they were known, were occasions where everyone 'let down their hair' for several days (and nights) of riotous living. Traders converged on the town from far and wide. Farmers and their wives sold produce. Entertainers amused the crowds, all wearing their 'Sunday best'. Thieves, rogues and vagabonds relieved many a miner of his hard-earned wages. The inns, which were numerous, did a roaring trade and seemed to be open day and night, the consequence of this being many drunken brawls in the town square and surrounding streets.

Allendale Town, the name deriving from Alwentdale or Alwindale meaning 'valley of the River Alwin', claims to be the centre of Great Britain. But then, nearby Hexham also lays claim to that same honour. If it helps you to make up your own mind, the sundial on the church in Allendale Town has an inscription which indicates that it stands at a latitude of 54° 50'. This latitude is allegedly midway between Beachy Head in the sleepy south of England, and Cape Wrath in the wildest of wild places, the north-west coast of Scotland. Allendale Town or Hexham, the choice is yours?

If you stand in the middle of the town square, you are able to see five inns offering accommodation. Whichever you choose for your lodging, or you may prefer a B & B, you will receive a warm welcome. If you care to sample the odd half-pint of Old Peculiar, be careful, it's strong, and if you hear anyone ask for a pint of Scotch don't panic, it's only beer not whisky. You may also notice that ale is, by now, decidedly cheaper than further south.

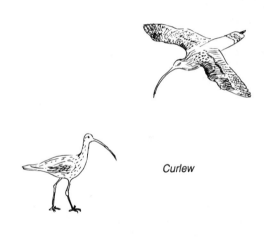

Curlew

SEVENTEENTH STAGE:
ALLENDALE TOWN TO HALTWHISTLE
Riverside and Moorland
17.5 kilometres, 10.9 miles

The route follows the River East Allen until it joins with the West Allen to become the Allen. It continues along the east bank to Plankey Mill and then crosses the river on a pleasant suspension bridge. You then climb out of the dale via Kingswood and Kingswood Rigg to Kingswood Common and on to Plenmeller Common. A long, steady descent then brings you to the River South Tyne (again). A bridge takes you over the river and into Haltwhistle.

The route beside the West Allen is mostly along riverside meadows with occasional woods. The route beside the Allen is mostly dense woodland, indeed the river is only visible in a few places. The ascent out of the dale through Kingswood is on good agricultural land, but on Kingswood Common and beyond to the side of the South Tyne the landscape is rough grazing land.

Suspension Bridge, Plankey Mill

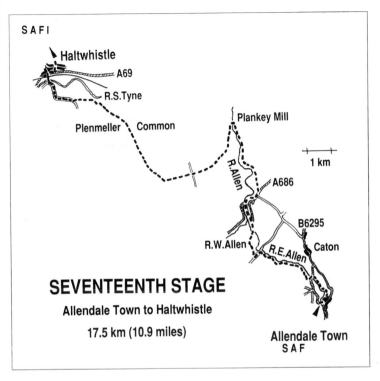

SAFI

Haltwhistle

A69

R.S.Tyne

Plenmeller Common

Plankey Mill

R.Allen

1 km

A686

B6295

R.W.Allen

R.E.Allen

Caton

SEVENTEENTH STAGE

Allendale Town to Haltwhistle

17.5 km (10.9 miles)

Allendale Town
S A F

The crossing from Kingswood to Plenmeller, outside Haltwhistle, could be hazardous in bad weather so emergency rations and gear should be with you. Here the paths are not defined and a compass is advisable. Elsewhere the paths and tracks are well-defined and should give no difficulty.

There is a campsite at Plankey Mill so at certain times there may be limited supplies available, otherwise there is nothing en route.

Haltwhistle is a thriving town with all the facilities you should need.

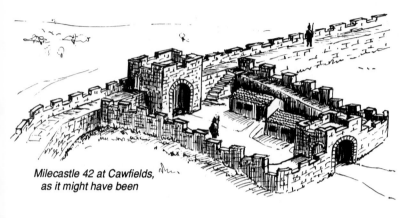

*Milecastle 42 at Cawfields,
as it might have been*

MILECASTLE 42

The APW crosses Hadrian's Wall at milecastle 42 at Cawfields. Here, the remains of the wall are quite dramatic as they climb up the crags of the Whin Sill and continue eastwards for two-thirds of a Roman mile. The Vallum is quite apparent in this area, but the quarry which cuts through the wall here is modern, having been excavated only 150 years ago.

As you proceed on your journey towards Wark Forest, take an occasional look back and imagine the scene, so different 1,850 years ago: the massive wall, four-and-a-half metres high, striding over the horizon from east to west as far as the eye could see; milecastles and turrets standing proud and foreboding; Roman soldiers stationed at the gates and around the wall. Surely this presented an impenetrable barrier. It would have been a magnificent sight if you were a friend, but a formidable deterrent if you were an enemy. (See p216 for more about Hadrian's Wall.)

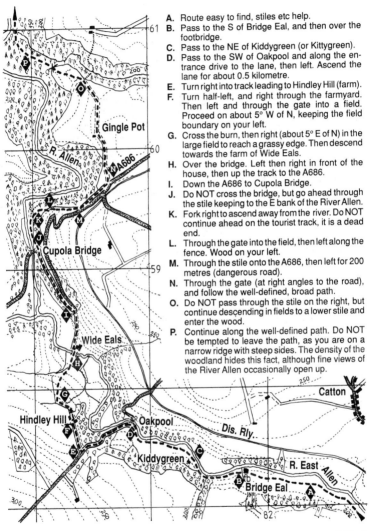

A. Route easy to find, stiles etc help.

B. Pass to the S of Bridge Eal, and then over the footbridge.

C. Pass to the NE of Kiddygreen (or Kittygreen).

D. Pass to the SW of Oakpool and along the entrance drive to the lane, then left. Ascend the lane for about 0.5 kilometre.

E. Turn right into track leading to Hindley Hill (farm).

F. Turn half-left, and right through the farmyard. Then left and through the gate into a field. Proceed on about 5° W of N, keeping the field boundary on your left.

G. Cross the burn, then right (about 5° E of N) in the large field to reach a grassy edge. Then descend towards the farm of Wide Eals.

H. Over the bridge. Left then right in front of the house, then up the track to the A686.

I. Down the A686 to Cupola Bridge.

J. Do NOT cross the bridge, but go ahead through the stile keeping to the E bank of the River Allen.

K. Fork right to ascend away from the river. Do NOT continue ahead on the tourist track, it is a dead end.

L. Through the gate into the field, then left along the fence. Wood on your left.

M. Through the stile onto the A686, then left for 200 metres (dangerous road).

N. Through the gate (at right angles to the road), and follow the well-defined, broad path.

O. Do NOT pass through the stile on the right, but continue descending in fields to a lower stile and enter the wood.

P. Continue along the well-defined path. Do NOT be tempted to leave the path, as you are on a narrow ridge with steep sides. The density of the woodland hides this fact, although fine views of the River Allen occasionally open up.

17.1

HALTWHISTLE

If you study the map of the area surrounding Haltwhistle, you will discover several rather curious place-names, such as Ding Bell Hill, Slaggyford, Mumps Ha', Cupola Bridge and Unthank. The definitive APW route between Allendale and Haltwhistle passes through the last two places.

A cupola was a reverberatory furnace used for smelting metals, smelting being a process whereby metal is extracted from ore by melting. Cupola Bridge, built in 1778 carries the Haydon Bridge to Alston road (A686) over the River Allen, and is so called because lead smelting used to be carried out nearby.

The name Unthank is found in several places in the north of England, and seems to indicate inferior land which 'does not appreciate all the hard work put into it'. Bishop Ridley, who was burned at the stake in Oxford in 1555, is supposed to have lived in a pele tower on the site of the present Unthank Hall, built in the 1860s. Nothing is left of the pele, but a room in the oldest part of the hall was traditionally called the Bishop's Room.

If you descend Plenmeller Common when the visibility is reasonable, you will see on the skyline before you the distinctive feature of the Whin Sill, a bold, craggy escarpment facing north. The dolerite rock forming this scarp varies in colour but is mostly blue-grey. The sill has an average thickness of 30 metres, and was formed about 295 million years ago by molten lava being injected in between rock beds. The sill is apparent in many other places, the most northerly being the Kyloe Hills. It also forms the crags of the well-known High Cup, near Dufton.

Haltwhistle itself is curiously named, and the origin of the place-name is uncertain. In earlier times, various spellings have appeared in historical documents, including Haltwesel, Haltwezel, Hartwhistle, Hautwyssel and Hautwessel. The latter two are possibly combinations of the French 'haut' (high), and the Scandinavian 'wiscle' (river bend). Another reference defines Haltwhistle as being 'the hill at the twisla', twisla being Old English for 'land in the fork of the river'. Whatever the meaning, there is evidence of early settlers in the Haltwhistle area and, as Hadrian's Wall is only two-and-a-half kilometres to the north, there is no doubt that during the Roman occupation, Haltwhistle would have been quite a busy place.

Haltwhistle today, is described as 'a pleasant, delightful, unspoiled market town' and, whilst there are no buildings of outstanding architectural merit, the parish church may be worth a visit. The Church of the Holy Cross, built in the mid-thirteenth century, is considered to be a fine example of an

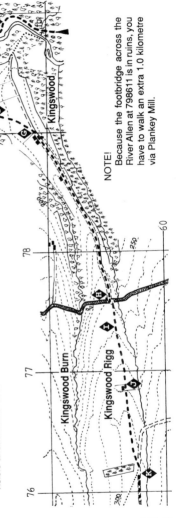

A. Keep to the well-defined path. In places it could be defined as a track.

B. Leave the wood through the stile and follow the E bank of the River Allen.

C. Cross the suspension bridge, then right followed by left at the fork. Do NOT cross the footbridge below you to the right.

D. Ascend steeply on the well-defined path through the wood and enter the field through the stile.

E. Continue ascending (on a bearing of about 197°). No path.

F. Through the gate to enter a very large field. The farm, Kingswood, is visible ahead. Make direct for this.

G. At Kingswood, join the track and pass through the farmyard. Continue along the access lane.

H. Turn left at the road for a few metres, then enter the fields through the gate on your right.

I. Ascend the field (no path), towards the ruins of Kingswood Rigg.

J. Pass to the S of the ruins and enter open, rough fields through the gate. Continue ahead.

K. Join the track and proceed due W.

NOTE!
Because the footbridge across the River Allen at 798611 is in ruins, you have to walk an extra 1.0 kilometre via Plankey Mill.

17.2

213

Early English church. As it does not have a tower, the church is somewhat hidden behind the market place. It is thought that many pele towers would have been built in the Haltwhistle area, but there are remains of only one and these are embodied in the Red Lion Hotel in Westgate.

Perhaps Haltwhistle's main claim to fame is that it was once a railway junction. In the 1830s, the road between Newcastle and Carlisle was so congested with traffic that an alternative means of transporting goods was considered. The idea of building a canal was abandoned in favour of a railway and the line was completed in 1839, having taken nine years to build.

In the mid-nineteenth century, lead mining in the Alston, Nenthead (q.v.) and Allendale (q.v.) areas was at peak production. A Parliamentary Act of 1846 permitted a railway to be built between Haltwhistle and Alston, the 21-kilometre line being completed in 1851. However, the extension to Nenthead was never built. By the mid-twentieth century, due to the decline of lead mining and the fact that the line was never a commercial success, the closure of the line was contemplated. Despite moves by railway enthusiasts to keep the line open, it was closed in 1976. However, that was not quite 'the end of the line', as part of the track from Alston northwards has been relaid as a two-foot (61-centimetre), narrow gauge railway.

A line from Hexham to Allendale, opened in 1869, was kept open for passengers until 1930, although it was used for freight until 1950. A short branch line ran from Haltwhistle up the Butstone Valley, providing a connection to the main line for several industries, including two woollen mills, a tile works, a colliery, a gas works, a corn-mill, a brewery and coke ovens. The industries are no longer there, and neither is the branch line. Nowadays, trains run every two hours or so on the Newcastle to Carlisle line, with extra trains at peak travelling times.

Tawny Owl

Crossbill

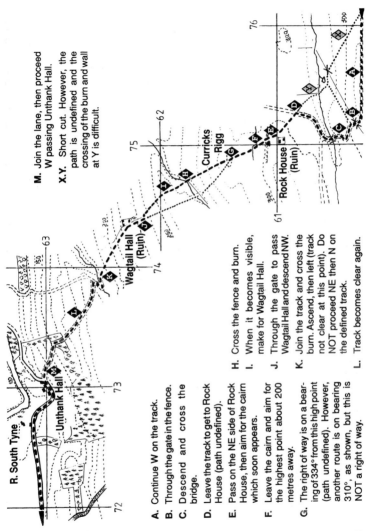

M. Join the lane, then proceed W passing Unthank Hall.

X.Y. Short cut. However, the path is undefined and the crossing of the burn and wall at Y is difficult.

A. Continue W on the track.

B. Through the gate in the fence.

C. Descend and cross the bridge.

D. Leave the track to get to Rock House (path undefined).

E. Pass on the NE side of Rock House, then aim for the cairn which soon appears.

F. Leave the cairn and aim for the highest point about 200 metres away.

G. The right of way is on a bearing of 334° from this high point (path undefined). However, another route is on bearing 310°, as shown, but this is NOT a right of way.

H. Cross the fence and burn.

I. When it becomes visible, make for Wagtail Hall.

J. Through the gate to pass Wagtail Hall and descend NW.

K. Join the track and cross the burn. Ascend, then left (track not clear at this point). Do NOT proceed NE then N on the defined track.

L. Track becomes clear again.

215

17.3

Hadrian's Wall

Publius Aelius Hadranius, born in 74 AD, was the ward of the Roman emperor Trajan and, having demonstrated his abilities as an administrator and commander, Hadrian was chosen to succeed Trajan, following his death in 117 AD. Hadrian was a forceful but prudent emperor and he abandoned the aggressive policies of Trajan in favour of more relaxed, but firm policies. He travelled extensively in the Roman Empire, strengthening his governing bodies and improving his cities. He built many protective walls in Germany, but he will be remembered in Britain for what was perhaps his greatest achievement, the best known frontier in the Roman Empire, Hadrian's Wall.

The well-known emperor Julius Caesar, first visited Britain in 55 BC, but it was not until 43 AD that Emperor Claudius attempted to take over the whole country. Forty years elapsed before the Romans managed to defeat the Caledonians at the battle of Mons Graupius. However, this was not the hoped-for conquest, as troops had to be withdrawn from Britain to attend to some trouble on the River Danube. The most northerly troops left in Britain were stationed south of a line between the River Tyne and the Solway Firth. It was along this line that Hadrian built his wall. Hadrian came to Britain in 122 AD to see the start of building, and he appointed Platorius Nepos as governor-in-charge of the construction.

Hadrian's Wall ran from Wallsend-on-Tyne to Bowness-on-Solway, a distance of 118.3 kilometres, and it was intended to mark the northern boundary and defence line of Roman Britain. The wall, about three metres thick and four-and-a-half metres high was not, as some people think, built by slave labour, but was built by Roman soldiers. Within the legions' ranks were engineer-architects, surveyors and all the tradesmen necessary to carry out the construction of any building, including the wall. Materials were obtained locally and some of the local inhabitants assisted in the preparation of timber and stone. The wall took only six years to build, some sections being of turf blocks and others of stone.

North of the wall a ditch was built, except at places where crags, such as the Whin Sill, made this unnecessary. South of the wall a ditch called the Vallum was built. This probably served as a defence to deter the local inhabitants from attacking from the south, and also it defined the rear of the military zone. Every Roman mile (1,481 metres), there were gates defended by a milecastle and between each pair of milecastles were two observation turrets. (continued on p220)

A. Turn right at the road and pass through the straggling village of Plenmeller.

B. Continue on the minor road towards Haltwhistle.

C. Turn right and cross the River South Tyne.

D. Left at the A69 for 50 metres or so, then right into Haltwhistle.

E. Continue on the main street of the town.

(THE SEVENTEENTH STAGE ENDS AT HALTWHISTLE)

F. Leave the main street up the steps at the W end of the Grey Bull Hotel. Turn right in the road for a few metres, then left to enter the footpath.

G. Descend the steps and cross Haltwhistle Burn by the footbridge.

H. Left to cross the waste ground and join the track (used by heavy vehicles).

I. Keep the old factory on your right, then enter the path through the stile. Continue on the E side of the burn.

J. Cross to the W side of the burn via the footbridge and continue on the path, keeping the burn on your right. Do NOT be tempted to take paths leading away from the burn.

K. Recross the burn to its E side via the footbridge.

L. Cross, yet again, back to the W side of the burn, then ascend the fields to join the B6318.

M. E for 250 metres to the cross-roads at the Milecastle Inn.

N. Left, northwards to Hadrian's Wall.

O. Through the stile into the field and on to the wall.

P. Through the gate in the Whin Sill (and the wall) to the track. Then NE to Cawfields, keeping it on your left.

17.4

EIGHTEENTH STAGE:
HALTWHISTLE TO FALSTONE

Forests
28 kilometres, 17.4 miles

About two-thirds of this stage is through the Kielder Forest. The subject of forests and walking in them seems to evoke emotions, as do hanging, flogging and car parking. Surely this is a fruitless attitude; like it or not, man-made forests exist, so why not view them as another part of the environment to be explored and enjoyed? In the last decade of the twentieth century it is part of the walking scene to visit industrial sites, whereas a couple of decades ago, one would have been 'laughed out of the walking club' if one had suggested an industrial walk. Why are forests derided similarly? Most of Britain was covered in forests at one time anyway and it was man's activity that removed them, so arguments about his spoiling open landscape can be rather hollow. Certain landscapes can be enhanced by sensitive afforestation, as they can be with man-made lakes. To claim that there is an untouched landscape anywhere in Britain is dubious, for as soon as a few sheep or managed deer or grouse have been on it, man has interfered.

The challenge of navigating through a forest is itself a rewarding experience, not to mention looking out for secretive wildlife, or suddenly finding a surprise view.

The route leaves Haltwhistle by following the Haltwhistle burn upstream until it emerges at the B6318, the road which now runs alongside Hadrian's Wall. It then crosses the wall, and the Pennine Way, to enter farm land. After the farm land is a couple of kilometres of open, rough pasture before entering the forest. The way through the forest is on paths, tracks, rides and forest roads, but half way through there is a band of open rough pasture about one kilometre wide with the ruins of a farm beside a burn. Also the last three and a half kilometres of the route, whilst in the forest precinct, are in open countryside.

By and large the ground is firm with little bog, albeit very rough in one or two places. Most of the route is on well-defined tracks or forest roads, but when using the rides it is imperative that extreme care is taken in navigation and that a constant check on position and direction is maintained.

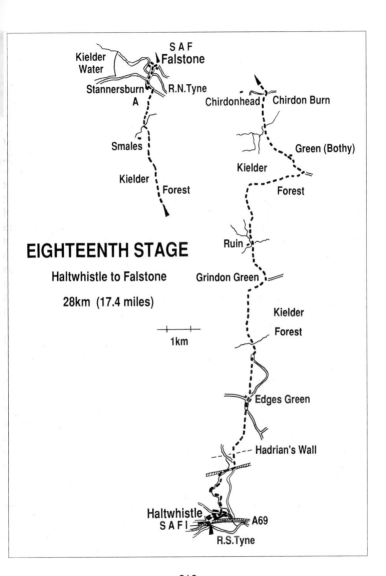

EIGHTEENTH STAGE

Haltwhistle to Falstone

28km (17.4 miles)

1km

For the latter a compass is essential (indeed, when researching the route, the authors used compasses more in Kielder Forest than anywhere else on the whole route).

After leaving Edges Green, there is no habitation whatsoever until reaching Smales; there is nowhere to get provisions between Haltwhistle and Falstone, so be prepared. Emergency rations are essential.

There is limited accommodation at Falstone, Stannersburn and at Yarrow (one and a quarter kilometres off route). However, you can break the journey at Green, where there is a bothy but, of course, all you get is shelter; even water has to be obtained from a nearby burn. There is a small shop in Falstone, a tea room, as well as a single hotel.

Hadrian's Wall (continued from p216)

Every 14 Roman miles or about (about a day's march), were forts manned by regiments of soldiers. The wall was a line of demarcation between the Roman Empire and the 'Barbarians', who were allowed to pass through the wall to trade, as long as they were unarmed and accompanied by guards. The legions were ever ready to put down any insurrections, with all the force at their disposal. However, such was the strength of Roman diplomacy that, towards the year 200, they formed treaties with many Caledonian tribes, up to 160 kilometres beyond the wall.

The soldiers who manned the wall did not, as is popularly supposed, come from Rome, or even Italy. They were, in fact, from the north-western provinces of the Roman Empire. And, although the wall was built by legionaries, it was manned by auxiliaries, who were assistants to the legionaries. The Roman soldiers were not allowed to marry, but that did not prevent them from forming liaisons with women, and these 'common-law' marriages were recognised by the authorities when the soldier retired, thus legitimising the children. Relatively well paid, the soldiers were often the target of wine, food and clothing merchants, who prospered as a result of their trading.

The settlements outside the forts grew in size as the solders' families, merchants and farmers gathered in these areas, and it is thought that the local youths were attracted into the army as recruits. Farmland was, in many cases, affected by the building of the wall in much the same way as farmland today is affected by the building of a modern motorway, although of course, in the days of the Romans, there were no compulsory purchase

A. Pass Cawfields and on to E Cawfields on the track.

B. Through the gate into the field, then diagonally on a bearing of 18° to the footbridge.

C. On to the ruins of Low Close a Burns, then ascend the field side keeping the wall on your right.

D. Through the gate and bend right, to keep the wall on your right, to High Close a Burns.

E. Pass in front of High Close a Burns, then immediately after the gate turn due N across open land. Over the low rise.

F. Down to the stile and into the road. (This stile is hardly visible. It is only projecting stones in the wall.)

G. Follow the road.

H. After the cattle grid at Edges Green, leave the road to keep to the E bank of the burn.

I. Cross the burn and ascend the steep bank, keeping the wall close to your left.

J. Over the wall (no stile) and enter open land.

K. No path. Walk on a bearing of about 5° over the rise.

L. After the dip, ascend on a bearing of about 10°.

M. Join the road and follow it northerly into Wark Forest.

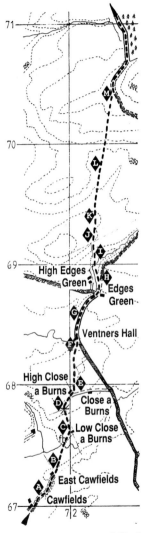

18.1

or appeals procedures. Also, the nature of farming changed in the vicinity of the wall, with more cereal crops being planted to accommodate the needs of the Romans.

Hadrian died in 138 AD and his successor, Antonius Pius, surprisingly decided to abandon the wall. He built a new turf wall, 160 kilometres to the north, across the 60-kilometres length of a line joining the Clyde and the Forth. However, a new emperor, Marcus Aurelius, who was appointed in 161 AD, decided to abandon the Antonine Wall and he ordered his troops to return to, and to re-instate, Hadrian's Wall.

During its occupation, the wall survived many changes of emperor and many attacks. In 407, when the troops discovered that they were not being paid, they gradually dispersed and turned to other activities, such as farming and even brigandage.

Little is known about life on and around Hadrian's Wall since the Romans left but, as it fell into disrepair, much of the stonework was removed and used to build churches, houses and walls. The statues and inscriptions were 'liberated' to decorate the houses of the wealthy. In many places, the ditches have been obliterated by agricultural activities. However, during the last 200 years or so, archaeological excavations have taken place though it was not until the end of the nineteenth century that co-ordinated excavations were started, and the wall's history began to be revealed. Nowadays, the remains of the wall are in the care of responsible organisations such as English Heritage and the State.

Roman Engineering

Anyone who has visited Rome cannot fail to have been impressed by the many buildings, bridges and other structures which are still standing, having been built around 2,000 years ago. The Colosseum, or Flavian Amphitheatre, is perhaps the best known example of Roman architecture. Built between 75 AD and 80 AD, much of the four-storied building is still standing. The 188 by 156-metre oval amphitheatre was built to accommodate an audience of about 45,000 seated on marble seats, and it is perhaps best remembered for its gladiatorial combats.

In Great Britain, the city of Bath-in-Avon is well-known for its elaborate bath houses fed by natural hot springs, built by the Romans during the first century AD. Hadrian's Wall (q.v.), is another fine example of the amazing versatility of the Roman engineers.

A glance at a dictionary will reveal that the word 'engineer' is a Middle

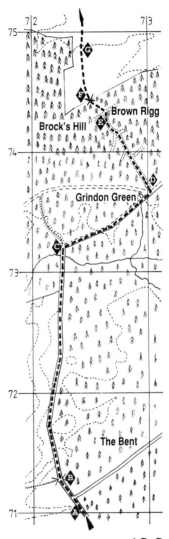

A. Continue on the road, which degenerates to a track at the gate.

B. Through the gate, and ahead on the rough track.

C. Right with the track.

D. At Grindon Green, into the forest NNW along the ride.

E. Where the curved ride joins the transverse ride, enter the trees ahead going generally NW. The lower branches of the trees have been removed to make the passage easy.

F. Leave the forest at the gate and proceed northwards, keeping the forest fence about 200 metres away to the W.

G. Keep N. A drainage ditch helps to keep direction.

18.2

English word from the Old French 'engigneor', derived from the Medieval Latin word 'ingenitor', which means 'with a natural clever talent'. 'Engineering' means "a profession devoted to designing, constructing and operating the structures, machines and other devices of industry and everyday life". Nowadays, because the increase in total knowledge requires some specialisation, engineering is divided into electrical, mechanical, civil, chemical, and so on. However modern approaches are attempting to reunify the profession and engineers are, once again, developing a good working knowledge of disciplines other than their own. It is known that before the Industrial Revolution (1750-1850), most engineering work was undertaken by military engineers who built fortifications and weapons, and civil engineers who built roads, bridges, harbours, aqueducts and other structures.

In the days of the Roman Empire, each engineer dealt with many aspects of engineering. It would have been common for the engineer to deal with everything necessary to ensure satisfactory completion of the structure, whether it was a road, aqueduct, bridge, harbour or building. All this was done, of course, without the benefit of modern instruments, transport, communications or materials. The Romans built their structures of wood and stone using the simplest of equipment, usually made from wood and rope. But it was the adaptability of the talented, inventive and ingenious engineers that saw each job through to a satisfactory conclusion.

Probably the most common structures built by the Romans were roads. Originally built for military purposes, the roads had a significant effect on the civilian population, and the Roman trunk road system at the height of the empire covered some 90,000 kilometres. Roman roads were not straight throughout their length, but consisted of a series of straight sections which deviated to avoid obstructions. The road, many still in use today, usually consisted of four layers to ensure adequate drainage and stability. The surface was paved and cambered, so that the surface water would run off to be collected on each side in ditches. A question that perplexes many historians is how the Romans managed to survey long stretches of road, bearing in mind that there were no detailed maps. One theory is that beacons were used, possibly at dusk or dawn, in hilly or wooded areas and aligned to provide a straight line.

The Romans were particularly good at building aqueducts. Aqueducts should, of course, leak as little as possible and the Romans became adept at building these structures with watertight joins. It was probably the need

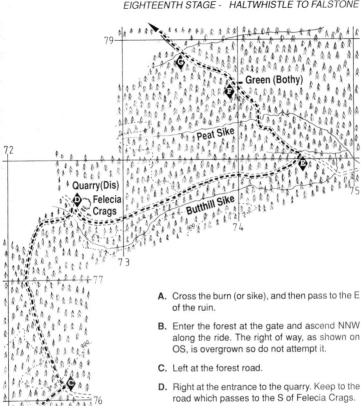

A. Cross the burn (or sike), and then pass to the E of the ruin.

B. Enter the forest at the gate and ascend NNW along the ride. The right of way, as shown on OS, is overgrown so do not attempt it.

C. Left at the forest road.

D. Right at the entrance to the quarry. Keep to the road which passes to the S of Felecia Crags.

E. Left at the junction.

F. You could break this stage here at Green, which is a bothy. If you do, please observe the 'rules of the house'.

G. Continue on the forest road.

18.3

for aqueducts to supply Rome with water that led to the development, first of the pointed arch (two slabs in an inverted 'V'), then of the half-round arch. Several of the aqueducts around Rome were in excess of 60 kilometres long, and water flowed downhill along the whole length, with a typical fall of 1:280. Before the empire, aqueducts in the countryside were built underground to avoid the possibility of sabotage. This necessitated diverting the aqueduct around the contours of the hillsides so that water pressure did not burst the walls. Near Rome, the aqueducts emerged from below ground and were carried on arches to the city. The Aqua Claudia, sweeping grandly across the plain to Rome, is an example of this. Built in about 47 AD, the Aqua Claudia viaduct is about ten kilometres long and five to twenty-five metres high. With over a thousand arches it was a splendid sight. In the building of aqueducts, the Romans used the most primitive tools, such as hammers, chisels, gouges and saws. The surveying instruments consisted of plumb lines, the dioptra (a primitive device used for levelling) and the chorabates, which was a long (six metres), narrow table for checking levels and slopes.

Roman bridges, carrying roads or aqueducts, are particularly noteworthy because of the development of the arch, which the Roman engineers brought to perfection. An essential factor in the building of arched bridges is that the arch must have adequate side supports, either from piers or walls. The Romans not only perfected the skill of building stable foundations, but they ensured that the supports (abutments) were strong enough to support the arches. The one remaining arch of the Pons Aemilius, across the River Tiber in Rome, was built 2,000 years ago and stands as a tribute to the skill of the Roman engineers.

Most of the early structures were built from dry stone, relying on the skills of quarrying, shaping and careful use by the builders to provide a structure that would not collapse with use. To some extent, the gradual development of mortar meant that the masons required less skill, as they no longer had to cut and shape stones precisely. From mortar came the fortuitous discovery of concrete. This was developed during the building of walls with rubble cores, as the addition of mortar to the core was found to produce a stronger wall. In due course, the production of high quality concrete became standardised and this versatile building material was put to good use.

The development of bricks by the Romans was really an extension of the use of roof tiles. Earlier civilisations had used sun-baked clay bricks for

A. Continue on the forest road.

B. Continue on the forest road.

C. Right then left, and continue on the forest road.

D. Leave the road and enter the ride to continue the descent. ENSURE that you enter the ride leading due N. (*)

E. Turn to a bearing of 335° down the ride.

F. At the lowest point, there are the remains of a small tower-hide. Here, turn to 19° and ascend the ride.

* It is important, when walking along forest rides, to use your compass to get the correct bearing. The choice of an incorrect route can be disastrous.

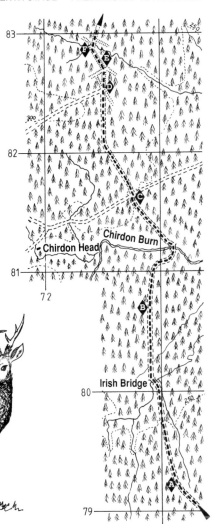

Roe Deer

227

18.4

Ruin near Grindon Green

thousands of years. However these tended to be unsuitable for use as roof tiles since they did not stand up well to the effects of rain. To overcome this problem, roof tiles were given a durable surface by firing them in kilns. The Romans discovered that these tiles made excellent building bricks and were also a decorative feature, so they began to incorporate them into wall construction. Some walls were built entirely of bricks, but in the main stone was used sometimes with large flat bricks inserted as bonding courses. These extended the width and length of the wall and were placed at intervals in the height of the wall. Examples of the use of these (tile) bricks can be seen in the remains of many Roman walls, and particularly good examples are to be found at St Albans in Hertfordshire.

An engineer is sometimes described as 'someone who can first of all determine the nature of the problem, and then can go on to provide a solution to that problem.' The Roman engineers certainly came across many problems, and solved them. Roads, bridges and buildings remain to this day as a historic record of their magnificent achievements.

A. Difficult walking along the ride, gentle ascent. Keep using your compass to monitor your direction.

B. Join the forest road. Turn right, then leave the road after a few metres in a direction of 354°.

C. Leave the forest via the gate and proceed on 10°.

D. Through the gate, then keep the wall on your left.

E. Re-enter the forest through the gate in the corner of the rough field.

F. Follow the ride downwards.

G. Join the forest road and turn left, keeping the quarry on your right.

H. Turn right and over the bridge, then right to leave the forest road. No path.

I. Continue over the spur. Rough underfoot. No path.

J. Keep Smales Burn just to your right. Then pass through the gate and jump over the tributary burn to reach open, very rough pasture.

K. Boggy in places, with transverse watercourses. Ascend.

L. Pass through the gate to join the forest road. Follow this to Stannersburn.

M. Left at the road and pass through the hamlet.

N. Join the main road, then turn right to Falstone.

X. Route to be taken if you find it too difficult between B and C, due to brash.

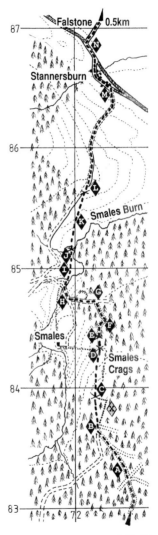

18.5

NINETEENTH STAGE:
FALSTONE TO BYRNESS

More Forest

17 kilometres, 10.5 miles

The route leaves Falstone northerly, to depart from the valley of the North Tyne and to climb through the forest on paths, rides and roads. It traverses the Highfield Burn, and eventually emerges into the open beside Smallhope Burn. A steady climb takes it past the farm at Emblehope and ascends onto Emblehope Moor alongside Long Sike. On the watershed, near Blackman's Law, it re-enters the forest and descends therein to Blackblakehope, traverses the forest drive and then rounds the spur of Raw Hill before descending into Redesdale and Byrness. The view west, south and east from Blackman's Law is superb, and one really gets an impression of the vastness of the forest.

Except for the ascent onto Emblehope Moor the route is on firm ground, apart from one or two boggy bits in the rides. The ascent onto the moor is very boggy, and many minor detours may be necessary to get around the worst parts. Very careful navigation will be required between Highfield Burn and Smallhope Burn, as most of the way is along rides (see comment in eighteenth stage notes).

The only habitation along the route is at Emblehope Farm and there are no facilities for obtaining food, so the day's supplies will have to be carried. Full emergency rations are essential.

The facilities at Byrness are limited, there being only one hotel, a youth hostel, and B & Bs about one kilometre south-eastwards along the A68 towards Redesdale Camp. There is no shop, although the filling station provides limited things such as crisps and biscuits, but it does have a small cafe. The hotel will provide meals for non-residents as well as residents.

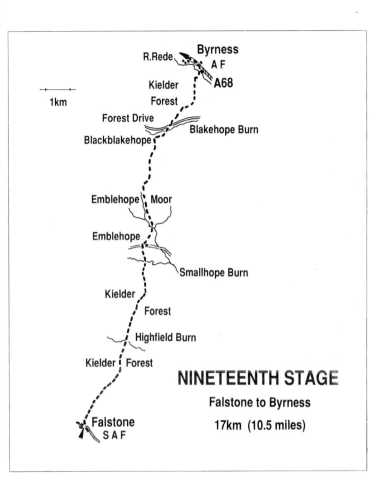

R.Rede

Byrness
A F
A68

Kielder

Forest

Forest Drive

Blackblakehope

Blakehope Burn

Emblehope Moor

Emblehope

Smallhope Burn

Kielder

Forest

Highfield Burn

Kielder Forest

Falstone
S A F

1km

NINETEENTH STAGE

Falstone to Byrness

17km (10.5 miles)

FALSTONE

In earlier days Falstone looked much the same as it does today, with a church, an inn and a shop surrounded by a few houses. There was, however, one important difference; in those days of yore Kielder Reservoir (q.v.) did not exist. We are quite confident that the presence of Kielder Reservoir enhances the beauty of the North Tyne Valley, which was a dull, uninteresting place before the construction of the reservoir.

Falstone - the name allegedly derived from Anglo-Saxon and meaning 'stronghold' - is described as 'the capital of the Upper North Tyne' and, until 1357 the whole of the North Tyne was part of Scotland. In those days the inhabitants tended towards insurgency, which the chiefs of the local clans (the Charltons, Dodds, Milburns and Robsons) did their best to keep in check. However, towards the end of the eighteenth century things calmed down and the commissioners of the Greenwich Hospital (who also managed farms and mines on Alston Moor) built five churches in the area. The Presbyterian Kirk in Falstone, dating back to 1807, is one of the oldest south of the Border.

In the North Tyne Valley there exist several examples of bastle houses - yes, it's like castle, with a 'b' instead of a 'c'. These houses were defensible barn like structures dating from 1520-1640, and some are still occupied today. They were simple rectangular structures, about twelve metres by seven metres, with walls one metre thick. The basement was the storage area with a door in the gable end, whilst access to the first-floor living area was gained by an external stone stair on one of the side walls. The stone stair was not bonded to the wall, as it replaced the original retractable wooden ladders.

Six or seven kilometres to the north-west of Falstone lie the foundations of Plashetts, a long-gone but not forgotten village. Plashetts was unique in the North Tyne Valley in that not only was it a mining village, but also it had a railway. The presence of coal in this area had been known by the valley folk for centuries, and they simply dug it up from primitive opencast workings to supplement their domestic peat fires. In 1851 two gamekeepers were given permission to re-open a small drift mine, on condition that they supplied coal for the fires in Kielder Castle. At the time, it was thought that the coal deposit was rich and extensive. As there was no way of transporting the coal to sell it on Tyneside, a company was formed to build a railway, but progress was slow and it was not completed until 1862. The village expanded, but within a few years the Plashetts Coal Company was in

A. Follow the road into Falstone.
(THE EIGHTEENTH STAGE ENDS AT FALSTONE)

B. Leave the village, passing to the N of the church on the road. Go under the bridge, which used to carry the railway, then sharp left and up the access road to the houses.

C. Behind (E of) the houses, and ascend on the forest access road.

D. Enter the forest, but turn right (NNE) after a few metres. Follow the forest road.

E. Where the road swings right on a sharp curve, keep ahead into the ride. Ascend NE; very rough.

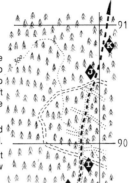

F. Cross the forest road and continue up the ride. Very rough again.

G. A forest road enters from the left and turns NE. Follow this north-eastwards.

H. Continue on the road over the summit. Fire observation tower 250 metres to the right.

I. At the T-junction in the roads (main road turns left), keep ahead into the ride and descend - difficult but passable.

J. Rejoin the forest road, turning right for a few metres. Then leave the road to enter what s now a new plantation, where the road bends right.

K. Follow the cleared way.

19.1

Falstone

financial trouble as the coal was poor and working conditions difficult. The company had two or three different owners until, in 1889, a group led by a John Slater took over and made the company successful, opening several new mines. All the untidy paraphernalia of mining was to be seen, including steam engines, winding gear, screens, railway lines, wagons and tips. Also a brickworks was built nearby. All that industry, in such a tiny, remote and wild place, must have had an enormous visual impact on the itinerant visitor. It looked as though Plashetts was there to stay, but that was not to be the case. The 1926 strike dealt a severe blow. The workings flooded and were never fully re-opened. Many families left the village to seek work elsewhere, and although an attempt was made to re-open the mines in the early 1930s, the whole area declined and was abandoned. The village was submerged with the flooding of Kielder Water.

A few kilometres north-west of the old village of Plashetts lies Kielder Castle (now the Forestry Commission's Visitor Centre for the Border Forest Park) built by Earl Percy, Duke of Northumberland, as a hunting lodge and completed in 1755. In it was installed the first Border gamekeeper and the lodge was used regularly for grouse and blackcock shooting. The Blackcock

Inn at Falstone perpetuates this sporting association.

Falstone, being in the middle of Kielder Forest (q.v.), has a strong association with forestry. The Forestry Commission has built several houses for its workers in the village and a cold store is maintained for the storage of young trees prior to planting.

On your way from Haltwhistle, you will pass an inn providing accommodation at Stannersburn, which is about half a kilometre before you reach Falstone. The only available accommodation in Falstone is at the Blackcock, which describes itself as 'The Last Inn in England'. If that be the case, then presumably it is also the first inn in England?

Kielder Forest

The Forestry Commission's (FC) Kielder Forest District encompasses the former forests of Kielder, Falstone, Redesdale, Wark, Kershope and Spadeadam. The forest straddles the Northumbria/Cumbria border and occupies a large part of the upper North Tyne Valley. The total area is about

60,000 hectares, of which some 50,000 hectares have been planted and the remainder consists of let farms, short-term agricultural lets and land managed for agricultural purposes. This qualifies it as the largest man-made forest in northern Europe today.

Planting began in 1926 and large areas of land were acquired in the 1930s and 1940s from, among others, the Duke of Northumberland and the Church Commissioners. Almost half of the forest was planted between 1945 and 1960. Sitka spruce is

Norway Spruce (Christmas Tree)

235

the principal species; three-quarters of the area is planted with these trees. Other species include Norway spruce, Lodgepole pine, Scots pine, Larch and broad-leaved trees. At the time of writing, broad-leaves form only 1 percent of the planted trees, but this will increase to 10 percent thereby decreasing the area of spruce.

In the early phase of afforestation in the Borders it was quickly discovered that the infant trees did not thrive when planted directly into the cold, wet soil. A new method, turf planting, proved more encouraging, but this demanded much effort being very labour intensive. The new method required the cutting of shallow drains at four-and-a-half metre intervals, and the spreading of the resulting square turves between them, three rows of turves at roughly one-and-a-half metre spacing. All this work was done by hand using a large turfing spade known as a 'rutter'. The turves, wet and weighty, were dragged out and spread using a two-pronged 'hack'. Only when the turves were spread, the drains running, the rides and roads laid out and the area fenced against livestock and rabbits, could planting begin.

The saplings were planted into the turves, either by cutting a slit through the turf to soil level, or by taking out a 'plug' to the same depth with a semi-circular spade. In either case, the roots rested at soil level and the rotting 'sandwich' of vegetation nourished them until they recovered from the shock of planting and were able to spread outwards and downwards (to a limited extent). In the early days the foresters walked to work, sometimes many kilometres over open moorland, carrying their tools and all they needed for the day. Fencing materials and plants from nurseries were taken as far as possible by horse-drawn carts or sledges to shallow storage pits or 'sheughs' on the planting site. Then, as now, every tree was individually planted by hand. In establishing the forest some 200 million trees were planted in this way, and millions more have been planted since. Afforestation is minimal at the present day, but nowadays trees are planted into simple slits, cut into the ground with a spade.

It became obvious that if the forest were to expand more rapidly, then more than manpower and muscle was required. Early trials with farm tractors and agricultural ploughs soon showed that they were not suitable. Purpose-built moorland ploughs drawn by one, or even two, powerful caterpillar tractors were introduced in the late forties, and these formed the backbone of the large planting programme for the next two decades.

Various forms of plough have been used, but all turn out ribbons of turf on one or both sides of the furrow. The furrow then acts as a drain and is

A. Cross the forest road and through the stile. Turn left and descend to the burn. Over the burn, ascend to the gate and into another forest road. Cross this to go NNE into a branch road.

B. The forest road ends. Follow the ride NE, then NNE.

C. Cross the forest road and continue on the ride NNE. For the next 1.5 kilometres the going is not difficult, but it is in dense forest along rides so carefully monitor your position frequently.

D. Remains of farmstead almost buried in vegetation.

E. Emerge from the forest through the gate and cross the burn. If the footbridge is still broken, then you will have to ford the burn.

F. Path undefined, but make for a small ruin and a second bridge which is well maintained.

G. N to the gate in the fence. Through the gate and make for the next gate, just visible, to the left (W) of the wall. Path undefined.

H. Through the gate (path just visible), and up to the road. Keep to the left of the trees. (The right of way actually goes through a gate into the trees, but is impassable.)

I. Right at the road, then left before Emblehope Farm. Through the gate into the very wide ride.

J. Ahead (NE) into open land.

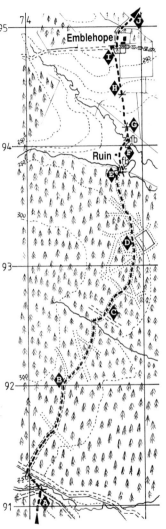

19.2

linked into the main drainage system. The turf ribbons function in exactly the same way as the hand-cut turves, planting became easier in these uninterrupted ribbons and production rose enormously. Roads built throughout the forest to facilitate future harvesting also gave access to new planting areas, and vehicles could be used to transport men and materials.

In creating the plantations, the principles of north European silviculture were followed. These involved planting the trees relatively close together so that they would first grow up providing mutual shelter. They would then develop into a 'thicket' stage, where competition would begin and the lower branches would gradually die. At an age of between twenty and thirty years the trees would grow to a usable size - the 'pole' stage and the 'stand' would then be 'brashed', the lower branches being removed to head height. This made selective thinning possible at intervals of three to five years, the better stems being gradually spaced out to develop into timber trees, finally to be felled at the age of sixty to eighty years. The first thinnings took place in 1948 using handsaws and axes. The trimmed poles were dragged to the nearest ride or road and then cut up by handsaw. The main produce was wood for use in mines.

However, experience showed that thinning was, after all, not a good idea. The remaining trees began to be blown down by the winds, as they could no longer support each other at root level. In the mid- 1960s, thinning was almost at a standstill and after a period of intensive research and reappraisal, the decision was taken to abandon thinning in most areas. In Kielder, most crops over 250 metres altitude (about 84 percent of the forest) are now considered as unfit to thin. The average tree at harvest is therefore small, with a high proportion of pulpwood. However, the yields are high, and the trees can be harvested mechanically when forty to fifty years old, this being less than the biologically mature age.

Harvesting began in the early 1970s and the current programme is 270,000 cubic metres annually, a figure which will rise to around 400,000 cubic metres in the next ten to fifteen years. Around one third of the timber is sold standing, one third is worked by direct contract and one third is worked by FC employees. The produce from the harvest is mainly pulpwood (or chipwood) and sawlogs. The pulpwood may go to make paper or packaging materials and various forms of reconstituted wood, mainly chipboard. The logs go mainly for construction timbers, pallets and packaging. The debris from the harvesting operation is left to rot on the ground and, after a couple of years or so, the decaying remains are utilised

Harvesting Machine

as a nutrient for new trees which are planted close to the stumps of the felled trees. Surely, this is a fine example of recycling and furthermore the use of fertilisers is virtually nil!

Kielder is typical of an upland spruce forest established in the post-war period. Only with the advent of felling and restocking has the FC been able to redesign or 'restructure' the forest. An ambitious programme is now under way, with the aim of changing the even-aged blanket plantations into a mosaic of 'stands' of different ages. These 'stands' will be interspersed with open spaces and corridors of broad-leaved woodland located along the major watercourses. Some 500 kilometres of watercourse have been identified for such treatment and no timber production is expected from these areas, which are intended to become permanent features of landscape and wildlife interest. Broad-leaved species such as the Sessile Oak, Ash, Alder, Willow and Rowan are all adding structure and colour to the forest as well as supporting a rich wildlife.

Whilst researching this walk the authors spent many days in Kielder Forest. Without exception, they were met with kindness and understanding from the foresters who, whilst going about their business, were always willing to stop and help with advice about the best route to take. Quite clearly the FC wishes to foster good relations with visitors and the foresters go out of their way to do so. The Commission is keen to improve the landscape and encourage visitors to share and understand the beauty and interest of the forest.

A wide range of outdoor activities is available in Kielder and the FC's Visitor Centre, the eighteenth-century Kielder Castle, provides up-to-the-minute information about recreation in the forest. Public access on foot is unrestricted except in fenced areas of new planting and, of course, in times of extreme fire danger; but remember, that at any time you are in the forest, responsible behaviour is imperative as it is a workshop as well as a leisure area.

The maturing forest is becoming increasingly attractive and the addition of the beautiful expanse of Kielder Water (q.v.) has added a new dimension to recreation in this area.

Kielder Water

There has never been any shortage of water around the Kielder area, the average annual rainfall being some 1,200 millimetres. The forest trees, which thrive in the moist climate, catch some of the rain before it reaches

Sitka Spruce   *Scots Pine*

A. Continue NE, keeping the plantation on your left.

B. On leaving the corner of the plantation, turn to 10° towards the brow. Path undefined.

C. Over the brow. The walled enclosure and the rusty roof of Reedswood Fold comes into view. Make for this.

D. Over the footbridge and up towards the enclosure, then NNW to follow Long Sike. Path undefined, except in a few places. Do not be confused with sheep trods.

E. Very boggy in places. Large detours may be necessary to make progress.

F. Aim for the W end of the outcrop of Reedswood Crag.

G. Follow the broad, grassy gully up to the plateau.

H. Path undefined, but aim for a point in the forest fence about 250 metres E of Blackman's Law.

I. A simple stile gives access to the forest ride. This stile may not be recognised when approached at right angles to the fence. It is easily seen from any point along the fence, so if you reach the fence not at the stile, look along the fence to determine the correct crossing point.

DO NOT ENTER THE FOREST AT ANY OTHER POINT THAN THIS STILE

IF YOU FAIL TO HEED THIS WARNING YOU COULD GET COMPLETELY LOST!

J. Follow the ride downwards, monitoring your position all the time.

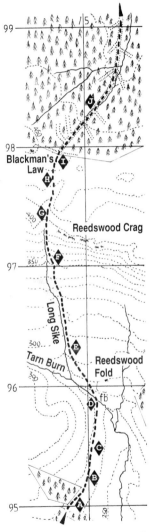

19.3

the ground. However, plenty of water remains to fill the peat bogs (known locally as 'mires' and 'mosses'), swell the streams and eventually form the main rivers - the North Tyne, the Rede, the Irthing and Liddel Water. Many place-names hereabouts owe their origin to associations with water. 'Burn', 'sike' and 'cleugh' are all names for streams or valleys containing them. 'Well' usually means a spring, 'linn' is a waterfall and 'haugh' refers to the better land along a riverside, whilst 'lough' is the Northumbrian equivalent of loch or lake. The old mining village of Plashetts (see Feature "Falstone") meant 'watterlogged-ground' and Kielder means 'violent stream', referring to the lively Kielder Burn.

Whilst there is ample water in the Kielder area there is not enough in the Newcastle, Sunderland and Middlesbrough areas to meet industrial requirements. Although this demand has decreased since the early 1980s, the level of domestic water consumption is rising, largely due to the increasing use of showers, washing machines, dishwashers and other water-using devices.

Kielder Water, besides enhancing the beauty of the North Tyne Valley, ensures that the industrial and domestic water requirements of the north-east of England will be met well into the next century. The reservoir controls the flow of the River North Tyne by storing water when there is a surplus, and releasing it into the river when required. Water drawn from the reservoir through the 69-metre-high valve tower passes through pipes and valves in the base of the dam and back into the River North Tyne. Water for Tyneside is pumped from the river in the Wylam/Ovingham area and other water, as required, is drawn from the river through a large pumping station below Riding Mill near Hexham and distributed through 32 kilometres of tunnels to the rivers Wear and Tees.

Kielder Dam holds back 200,000 million litres of water in Europe's largest man-made lake, covering an area of 1,086 hectares within a shoreline of 44 kilometres and with a reservoir length of 13 kilometres. The dam is 1,045 metres long and nearly 52 metres high. It is built of clay, river sand and gravel, and rock taken from the floor of the valley and contains nearly 4.4 million cubic metres of material. There are more than 700 instruments (is this more than Scammonden Dam? q.v.) located within the dam to measure pressure, internal movements and flows through the drainage layers. All these readings are recorded and monitored in two instrument centres downstream of the dam. When the reservoir becomes full to capacity, flood-water is discharged across the overflow weir and into

Blackman's Law

the spillway at the north end of the dam. From here the water runs into the stilling basin at the base of the dam, achieving speeds of up to 110 kilometres per hour on its way down.

The upper end of Kielder Water, near Kielder Village, is very shallow and, to overcome unsightly mud flats, a secondary dam built at Bakethin ensures that this upper end will always be submerged. Bakethin Dam is 137 metres long and 12.5 metres high, and its apex is normally under water. The lake is a designated nature conservation area and many species of flora and fauna thrive here.

Works started on the Kielder scheme in February 1975 with the building of the superb North Tyne road up the valley, a road which affords magnificent views over Kielder Water. Kielder Dam was started in April 1976 and flooding started in winter 1980, the reservoir taking two winters to fill. The scheme was officially opened by the Queen on May 26 1982. During the height of construction work in 1979, some 750 men and women were employed, about two-thirds of them travelling each day from the surrounding areas of north-east and north-west England and from southern Scotland.

In 1982, following an approach from Northumbrian Water, the Central

Electricity Generating Board agreed on a joint venture to create a hydroelectric power station utilising water released from Kielder Water. Two hydroelectric generators were installed in the dam to produce electricity for the national grid. One is a 4.4 megawatt turbo-alternator, powered by the operational water releases for regulation of the main rivers. The other, a 500 kilowatt turbo-alternator, takes advantage of the releases of compensation water (the minimum daily flow from the reservoir into the River North Tyne). With water releases ranging from between 57 and 900 million litres per day, the total power produced can vary from between 200 kilowatts and 6 megawatts - enough to supply power to a town of 10,000 inhabitants. The power station is designed for unattended operation and is controlled from Howden, Northumbrian Water's control centre 80 kilometre away on Tyneside. It can also be controlled locally at Kielder. In order to preserve the beauty of the countryside, the 33,000 volt power transmission line is laid underground for the first 4.8 kilometres from the power station.

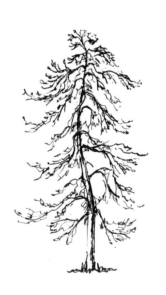

Kielder Water, surrounded by the trees of Kielder Forest, as well as providing water for industrial and domestic use and a contribution to the nation's power grid system, is a place of outstanding beauty. Recreational and leisure facilities have been developed, but so large is the area that, even on a busy bank holiday weekend, it does not seem over-populated. However, the Tower Knowe Visitor Centre and some of the recreation areas will no doubt be very busy. Whether you like cruising, canoeing, caravanning or camping, backpacking or birdwatching, sailing or sub aqua, there is always plenty to see and do. Kielder Water can provide something for everyone, in a spectacular setting.

Larch

244

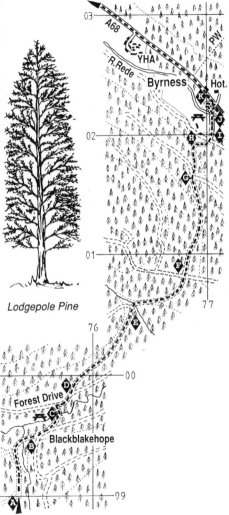

Lodgepole Pine

A. The ride runs straight into the forest road head. Continue descending on the forest road.

B. Another road comes in from the right. Keep ahead for a few metres before forking left to descend to Blakehope Burn.

C. Cross the burn and then turn right at the forest drive.

D. After 200 metres or so, fork left to leave the drive.

E. Follow the road steadily upwards.

F. Cross another forest road.

G. Having descended to a forest road, cross into what was once a forest road but is now no more than an overgrown ride.

H. Boggy.

I. Cross the road and emerge from the forest.

J. Cross the River Rede via the footbridge and continue through the picnic site up to the A68.

(THE NINETEENTH STAGE ENDS AT BYRNESS)

K. Left at the A68, walking towards Scotland.

19.4

TWENTIETH (LAST) STAGE:
BYRNESS TO JEDBURGH

Roads - Roman and Modern
31 kilometres, 19.3 miles

This is the longest (just) of the twenty stages, but it is not the most difficult. Sadly, in the part of Scotland hereabouts, there is not the proliferation of footpaths through agricultural land that there is in England. The consequence is that there is a higher proportion of the route on metalled lanes and roads than was hoped. However, there is negligible traffic and the countryside is pleasant enough.

Leaving the A68, the route enters the forest, yet again, to ascend onto the Cheviots; however, the forest walk is only a couple of kilometres. On emerging from the forest, an outcrop of rocks is at hand from which there are fine views. Indeed, the route onto Hungry Law is high and the skyline westwards is many kilometres away. At Hungry Law, the fence crossing takes you into Scotland and keeps high with the forest on your right and a vast panorama to your left (northwards) over the foothills. In the opinion of one author, the view from Hungry Law shares the honour of being the most spectacular point of the APW with the walk from Cotter End to the descent to The Thrang (see Twelfth Stage Notes). At the end of the forest fence, the route joins the Pennine Way for about half a kilometre before descending into the valley of Kale Water. The valley is followed northwards until Dere Street is met, where the course of the Roman road is followed on lane and track until four kilometres from Jedburgh. A lane is followed until Jedburgh is overlooked, then the final descent is on a path after which Jed Water is crossed by the old bridge. A few hundred metres takes you into the town and the APW is completed.

There are few problems underfoot and few problems in navigation. However, there are no facilities en route so the day's provisions must be carried. Habitation en route is sparse but having descended into farm land it is never far away. Emergency rations must be carried as the high part of the route could be problematic in bad weather.

Of course, there is every facility required in Jedburgh.

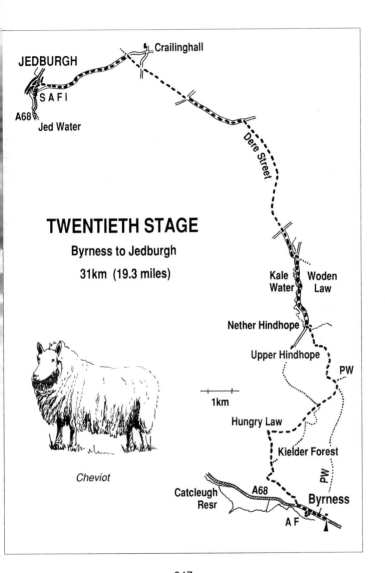

Crailinghall

JEDBURGH

S A F I

A68

Jed Water

Dere Street

TWENTIETH STAGE

Byrness to Jedburgh

31km (19.3 miles)

Kale
Water

Woden
Law

Nether Hindhope

Upper Hindhope

PW

1km

Hungry Law

Kielder Forest

PW

Cheviot

Catcleugh
Resr

A68

Byrness

A F

Byrness

BYRNESS

Byrness is an important end-of-stage for walkers of the APW. It marks the end of the last stage in England and the start of the stage which takes you to your final destination at Jedburgh in Scotland. Byrness is a small village in Redesdale on the A68, which runs from Darlington in the south to Edinburgh in the north.

In the 1950s, three forest villages were built to house the labour force necessary to create the forests. They were Kielder, where there was already a very small forestry and farming community, Stonehaugh, in what was Wark Forest, and Byrness in Redesdale Forest. At each site, sufficient houses were built (about fifty in Byrness) for immediate needs, the intention being to add more houses as the work programme developed. There was no shortage of applicants for the new jobs and the new houses. Many came from urban and industrial backgrounds but, as they found the work and the life in these remote areas demanding and unfamiliar, turnover was high in the early years. Gradually a more stable population was achieved, and in many cases a second generation now works alongside the first, with a number of houses now occupied by retired staff. Increases in mechanisation and productivity have resulted in a smaller than anticipated workforce, and

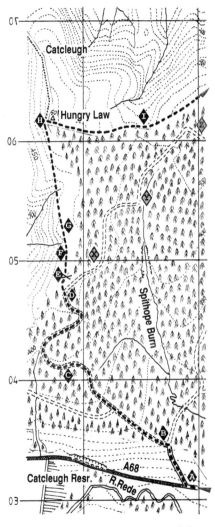

A. Leave the A68 and ascend the track to the forest.

B. Just after entering the forest, turn left and continue on the forest road.

C. Keep ascending on the forest road.

D. When the forest road levels and turns NE, leave it along the ride. A fence is visible 100 metres ahead.

E. On reaching the fence, turn right (NE) along the fence to the gate. Through the gate and onto the open moor.

F. Make for the cairns on the outcrop.

G. Off the end of the outcrop, a path becomes visible. Follow this to the trig point at Hungry Law.

H. Over the fence at the trig point and into Scotland.

I. Follow the fence, keep the forest and England on your right. A well-walked path is defined on the ground, although this is not marked as a path on OS.

XYZ. Short cut but no views

20.1

houses in the villages are now being sold.

Byrness has a hotel, a youth hostel, a church, a filling-station-cum-cafe-cum-shop, and as well as the forestry houses there are two or three private houses. Nearby, just a kilometre to the north-west on the A68, is Catcleugh Reservoir which was the biggest reservoir in the Tyne river basin prior to the construction of Kielder Reservoir (q.v.).

Work started on Catcleugh Reservoir in 1890 and continued until 1905. From the dam, a pipeline was laid down the valley of the River Rede to an existing aqueduct serving Hallinton Reservoir. To assist construction, 3-foot (91.5-centimetre) gauge railways were constructed from the North British Railway at Woodburn, and from a claypit at Yatesfield, to Catcleugh. At the height of the construction, about 500 workmen and their wives and children lived on each side of the river at Catcleugh in two camps known as 'Newcastle' and 'Gateshead'. During the period of construction some sixty men, women and children died, and they are remembered in the little Byrness Church by a stained glass window and brass plaque given by their fellow workmen, families and friends. Some of those who died of cholera are buried in an unmarked grave on the edge of a public park opposite St Oswald's Church in Bellingham. The building of the dam at Catcleugh entailed a great deal of manual labour, assisted by steam power, the clay core of the dam being puddled by men's bare feet. The reservoir yields four-and-a-half million litres a day, this being a very small proportion of the region's water supplies, and a still smaller proportion when compared with the projected future needs.

As accommodation at Byrness is limited, it would be wise to book ahead before leaving Falstone.

Midges, Clegs and Things

The enjoyment of the wild magnificent area of the Scottish Highlands has been marred to some extent by the presence of the famous Scottish midges, and to a lesser extent by clegs. To those who have not met these particular species of fauna the dubious 'pleasure' of being 'eaten alive' can also be experienced in the Kielder area during the summer months.

Not all midges bite, but the females of some species do so ferociously. Although tiny, with a wing-span of less than one millimetre, they can make dusk and dawn or a hot summer day in the shelter of trees or by the waterside a real misery. The midges that feed on humans should not be confused with the dancing swarms of gnats, which rise and fall on the

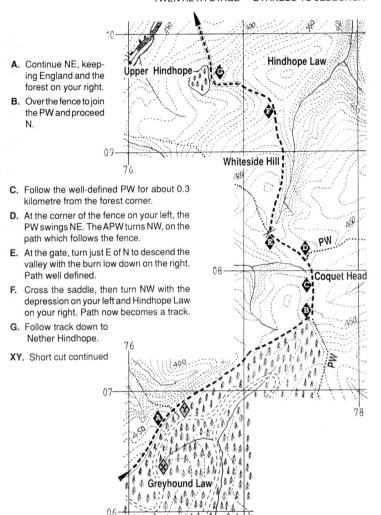

A. Continue NE, keeping England and the forest on your right.

B. Over the fence to join the PW and proceed N.

C. Follow the well-defined PW for about 0.3 kilometre from the forest corner.

D. At the corner of the fence on your left, the PW swings NE. The APW turns NW, on the path which follows the fence.

E. At the gate, turn just E of N to descend the valley with the burn low down on the right. Path well defined.

F. Cross the saddle, then turn NW with the depression on your left and Hindhope Law on your right. Path now becomes a track.

G. Follow track down to Nether Hindhope.

XY. Short cut continued

evening air. These are harmless non-biting midges which are only looking for mates. The swarms nearly always appear when there is a definite although very light wind, and they often keep station above conspicuous trees, bushes or other markers risen above the surrounding ground or vegetation.

Do not think that you can escape the midges; you cannot. You may be walking through an apparently midge-free part of the forest and decide to 'take five' and enjoy the view and peace and tranquillity. Having chosen your spot, you will seat yourself and make yourself comfortable. Then, as if commanded by an invisible authority, a million midges will land on your exposed 'surfaces' and they will tuck in to enjoy a meal of human blood. The bites are not serious, but the constant irritation is quite exasperating. Brush them off, thousands more take their place. Try moving left or right, they follow. Try covering all exposed parts, it will be to no avail, they will get inside any cover. There seems to be only one way to escape from this malignant presence, and that is to stand up, carry on walking and hopefully find a breeze.

Applications of insect repellent seem to work sometimes and this may help in Kielder, but we have never found anything which will deal effectively with the fearsome Scottish midge. If it is of any consolation to you whilst under attack, you may care to know that for every species which feeds on you, there are many more that suck the blood of birds, animals and other insects.

Forest Gate above Byrness

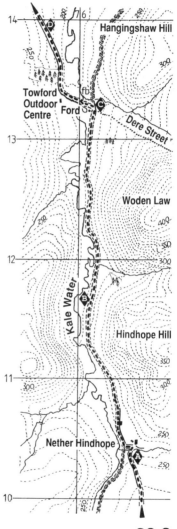

A. At Nether Hindhope cross the burn via the bridge, then turn left and, after 50 metres, turn right at the lane.

B. 3 kilometres on the lane.

C. Turn left at junction beyond the cattle grid and cross Kale Water by the ford or the footbridge.

D. Continue on the road.

20.3

The cleg, a type of horsefly, is a different beast altogether. They have dull ash-grey or brown speckled wings, which they fold roof-like over their back. They have brilliantly coloured banded eyes, commonly green, gold and red. They are about one centimetre long from the biting end to the tail end, and usually attack from the waist downwards. That is not all. There is another type of horsefly, called deerflies in America, with boldly banded wings and brilliant spotted eyes. They are to be found in the forest clearings and along the forest rides. These flies usually bite the upper arms and head. Both these flies are particularly nasty in that they inject the unfortunate human with an anti-coagulant, in order to ensure a steady flow of blood. They can also 'operate' through light clothing. The horsefly is not as numerous as the midge, by any means, but they can nevertheless be a nuisance.

On a warm summer day the plantation will be filled with sound. An all-pervading hum (not to be confused with the distant hum of chain-saws) is produced by countless flies, including headflies which are similar to houseflies. Whilst the swarms which will surround you are annoying, they do not bite. It is the midges and the clegs that you should be on the lookout for.

Having warned you about the 'nasties', it must be said that there are many varieties of fauna which serve only to enhance your enjoyment of the forest, and will cause you no problems whatsoever. Rodents of many varieties and birds (including birds of prey) are to be seen, as indeed are roe deer and foxes. The Forestry Commission has an ambitious management plan to redesign or 'restructure' the forest, introducing open spaces and corridors of broad-leaved woodland located around the major watercourses (see Feature "Kielder Forest"). There is no doubt that when this is developed, the numbers and varieties of woodland creatures will be even more delightful to the keen-eyed observer.

The Cheviot and Dere Street

After leaving Byrness on the last stage of your walk you will climb steadily through the forest to arrive at Hungry Law, which is situated on the Scottish border at a height of 500 metres. Hungry Law (law meaning 'conical hill'), in the Cheviot Hills, provides an excellent viewpoint and the Cheviot itself, at 816 metres, can, on a clear day, be seen towards the north-east. The Cheviots, formed of great masses of volcanic rock of Old Red Sandstone age, include no really impressive hills but are nevertheless quite fascinating.

A. At the road junction, proceed ahead through the stile to open land. Playing fields on your left, at Pennymuir.

B. Continue on the well-defined path, which is Dere Street, keeping the wall/fence on your left.

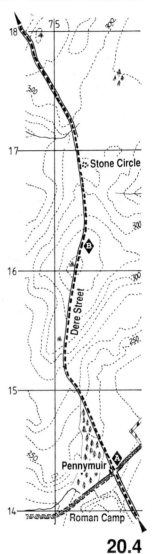

20.4

What catches the eye is the large number of hills, stretching from south-west to north-east. Rounded, peat-covered shapes are typical of much of the area. They are quite distinctive, and there are few rocky outcrops. The smooth dome-shaped Cheviot is covered with thick peat, and anyone who has climbed to the summit (perhaps whilst walking the PW), will be aware that it can be difficult to reach the OS triangulation column, surrounded as it is by a morass of thick, wet, black peat.

Continuing your journey, you will eventually walk along the line of the old Roman road, Dere Street. As is well known, the Romans built many roads during their occupation of Britain (see Feature "Roman Engineering"), some of the better known being Watling Street, Fosse Way and Ermine Street. The latter is the road which ran from London, via Lincoln, to York. Dere Street is the Saxon name for the Roman road which was a continuation of Ermine Street, and it ran from York, via Aldborough and Catterick, to Corbridge and then on north past High Rochester. A glance at the map will show that this, an inland route between the River Tees and the River Forth, was the eastern of the two major roads into Scotland.

In 80 AD the Roman governor of Britain, Gnaeus Julius Agricola, advanced through the lowlands of Scotland. Agricola constructed a network of forts and fortlets, connected together by roads, so that he could maintain his positions against the local tribes. Historians are of the opinion that during this conquest, after which southern Scotland became a part of the Roman empire, the Roman army may have been divided to form two fronts. One moved in the west through Annandale and the upper Clyde Valley, with the other advancing in the east along the line of Dere Street.

On the Borders, two native forts were taken over by the Romans and used for training purposes. One of these, Woden Law, is situated where Dere Street leaves the Cheviots and comes down to Kale Water, a tributary of the River Tweed. You will walk along the banks of Kale Water for a time with Woden Law to your right. The presence of earthworks enclosing this Iron Age native fort, is a result of the Romans training their legionaries in the construction of siege works and the use of siege engines. It is thought that the presence of troops undergoing training on such a prominent site must have had a depressing effect on local morale.

The position of native forts along Dere Street has led to suggestions that the line of Dere Street may have existed long before the Roman occupation, as indeed did other routes such as Icknield Street (or Way), in the Home Counties.

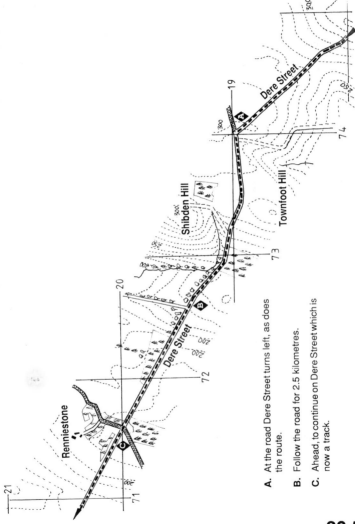

A. At the road Dere Street turns left, as does the route.

B. Follow the road for 2.5 kilometres.

C. Ahead, to continue on Dere Street which is now a track.

20.5

Cannongate Bridge, Jedburgh

JEDBURGH

As you walk down the hill into Jedburgh, you may notice a monument on a hill to the north. This is the Waterloo Monument on Penielheugh Hill, 226 metres, and it was erected by the Marquis of Lothian and his tenants shortly after the main victory at Waterloo.

It is appropriate that you should enter Jedburgh over Cannongate Bridge, as this splendid fifteenth-century medieval bridge crossing the Jed Water was at one time the main approach to this ancient town. On crossing the bridge you will be a few hundred metres from the end of the APW at Jedburgh Abbey, which is a magnificent example of a twelfth-century monastery.

It is known that more than 3,000 years ago there was a community at Jedburgh living and working along the banks of Jed Water, a tributary of the Teviot and, according to the Lindisfarne annals, a church was first built at Jedburgh in the ninth century. Fragments of stonework found during restoration indicate that Jedburgh Abbey stands on the site of the former church and in 1138 a priory, dedicated to Saint Mary, was founded on the site by King David I. The priory was inhabited by Augustinian canons (known as 'black canons' because of the colour of their habits), from St.

258

A. Continue along Dere Street.

B. Cross the road and take the path which descends to Oxnam Water. Cross via the footbridge, which is a few metres upstream and not apparent at first sight.

C. Leave Dere Street, by turning left at the road.

D. March along the road.

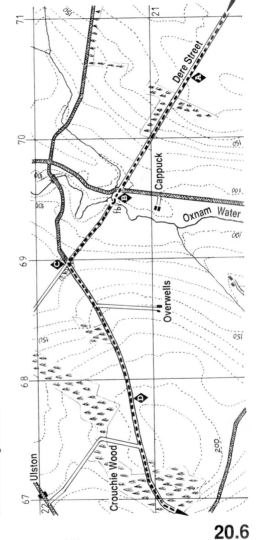

20.6

Quentin Abbey in northern France. In 1147 the priory was elevated to abbey status and the incumbent, Prior Osbert, became its first abbot. Being in the Border area, the abbey suffered on many occasions from English attacks. About 1305, the English removed part of the lead roofing and further damage was sustained in 1410, 1416 and 1464. In 1523, the Earl of Surrey's troops attacked and the men of Jedburgh, though all accomplished fighters and each armed with a 'Jethart staff', were unable to repel the devastating attacks on the abbey. 'Jethart' was the local name for Jedburgh and the staff was two-and-a-half metres long with a hook or axe head on the end. In the winter of 1545-6, the Earl of Hertford completed the destruction and during the Reformation of 1560 the abbey ceased to exist. The church, however, continued to be used as a parish kirk until April 4th, 1875, and this helped to ensure that the abbey church at Jedburgh still stands as the best preserved of the four Border abbeys.

Jedburgh Castle, built at about the same time as the abbey, also suffered many times from attacks by the English. It was one of the fortresses surrendered to the English under the Treaty of Falaise in 1174 as surety for the ransom of William the Lion, King of Scotland, after his

Queen Mary's House

260

A. Continue descending on the road.

B. At the point where the road bends left and leaves the boundary of the industrial estate, enter the fenced path to continue the descent.

C. Cross the road and Jed Water is ahead. Cross the Water via the ancient bridge and then pass under the A68 to emerge into Jedburgh.

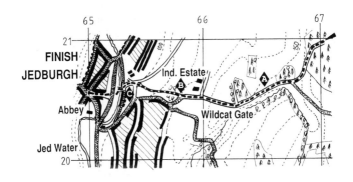

YOU HAVE COMPLETED THE ALTERNATIVE PENNINE WAY

CONGRATULATIONS!

THERE WILL BE NO RECEPTION BY THE PROVOST AND NO BANDS PLAYING TO CELEBRATE

20.7

defeat and capture at Alnwick. The castle later became a favourite royal residence, but such was its attraction to the English attackers that the Scots demolished it in 1409, at national expense, to avoid the embarrassment of its frequent occupation by enemy forces. In 1823, a county gaol was erected on the site and remains to this day, known as the Castle Gaol and serving as a museum of social history.

On October 9, 1566, Mary Queen of Scots visited Jedburgh to preside over the Circuit Court. Whilst in Jedburgh she stayed at a bastle house (see Feature "Falstone"), allegedly because it was the only house in Jedburgh with indoor sanitation. During her stay Mary, then only twenty-three years old, heard that the Earl of Bothwell had been wounded in a Border skirmish and was lying ill in Hermitage Castle, some 32 kilometres away. The Queen set out to visit the earl but the weather was appalling and, having completed the return journey in one day, the Queen fell ill with a fever. She lay "sick unto death" for nearly a month and left Jedburgh on November 9 with her retinue, which included the now recovered Bothwell. The bastle house still stands, but now as a museum, and as you admire the exhibits you may well wonder what intrigue caused Mary to make the near fatal visit to Hermitage, especially as she was married to Lord Darnley at the time.

Each year, on the first Saturday in July, a festival is held in Jedburgh. The festival lasts for two weeks and consists, amongst other events, of several 'rides' (originally horse rides but nowadays usually coach rides). The main and longest ride is to Reidswire, on the Border at Carter Bar, to celebrate the Raid of Reidswire in 1575. There are also speeches, races, dances and many displays of pageantry and ceremony, and the festival ends with the traditional Jedburgh Games on the last Saturday.

If you cast your mind back to Ashbourne, you may recollect that a curious ball game called the Ashbourne Royal Shrovetide Football Match is held annually (see Feature "Ashbourne"). A traditional ball game, with few rules and lasting many hours, is also played at Jedburgh. Known as Handba', it is played at Candlemas and Easter E'en between the 'Uppies' and the 'Doonies', all over the town. The game is reputed to originate from before the Reformation when the Scots allegedly played with the severed heads of their enemies.

Well, you've made it! Jedburgh at long last. With many kilometres behind you Jedburgh is a delightful place in which to relax and rest your weary limbs at the end of your great adventure.

Jedburgh Abbey

ADDENDUM STAGE:
JEDBURGH TO MELROSE
22 kilometres, 13.6 miles

A. Get to Sharplaw Road, at the north end of Jedburgh, on the west side of Jed Water. Ascend the steep part, about 150 metres, and near the top turn into Ladylands Drive, which is the access road for a small housing development.

B. After 10 or 20 metres, fork right, up what appears to be a private drive. Keep the garage on your left, so as to enter the fenced path which becomes overgrown in places and is clearly not often used. It bends left.

C. Turn right. The fenced path is heavily overgrown with bushes. (You will have to use your initiative.)

D. Gate; forward, bending left steadily, another gate, gentle ascent. Diagonally across the field (NW).

E. Gate, but track beyond is overgrown. Use your initiative again!

F. Well-defined track into plantation.

G. Continue NW through plantation.

H. Leave the plantation and descend the track, keeping the fence on your right.

I. Left then right, to continue the descent to the A698.

J. Right at the A698.

K. Left at the A68, and over the River Teviot.

L. Left into the B6400, to Ancrum.

M. Right and left to pass through the village, keeping to the B6400.

N. About 0.7 kilometre clear of Ancrum, turn right to descend the lane to the cemetery.

O. Over the bridge by the ruined kirk, then left (N) beside Ale Water. Through the gate.

P. Cross the meadow and through the gate into the wood.

Q. Emerge from the wood and turn to the NE.

R. Left at the lane and march 4.5 kilometres to Long Newton.

S. Through Long Newton and leave in the direction of Bewlie and Lilliesleaf.

T. Fork right into the track to Birselees.

U. Beyond Birselees, the track degenerates to a path.

V. Cross the lane and continue ahead.

W. Cross the A699 and into the lane to Bowden.

X. Right and left at the B6398 in Bowden.

Y. Follow the tourist path between the two main cones of the Eildon Hills.

Z. Descend the tourist path to the B6359, then right and into Melrose.

The Southern Upland Way crosses the River Tweed via the Chain Bridge, which is easily found from the centre of Melrose.

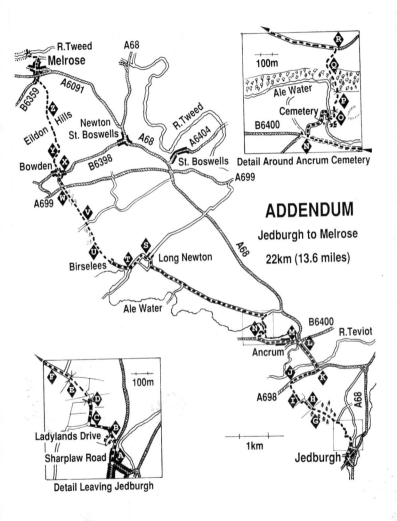

Detail Around Ancrum Cemetery

ADDENDUM

Jedburgh to Melrose

22km (13.6 miles)

Detail Leaving Jedburgh

If you want to continue walking after completing the APW, you can continue to Melrose and join the Southern Upland Way. You can either turn eastwards at Melrose and walk on to Cockburnspath on the east coast, or turn westwards and walk to Portpatrick in Galloway on the west coast. This addendum is the link between the two long distance paths.

It passes through mainly agricultural land and it is pleasant but not spectacular, except for the Eildon Hills; which is fine, but even these are small fry in comparison with what you have been over. Because of the dearth of footpaths, unfortunately, about a third of the distance is on roads, mostly minor ones, however.

MELROSE

If you decide to walk to Melrose to join the Southern Upland Way, or just to enjoy the walk, you will approach the town by way of the Eildon Hills which are of volcanic origin. The distinctive features of the three hills, Wester Hill, Mid Hill and Hill North, can be seen during the journey from Jedburgh even though the highest, Mid Hill, is only 420 metres. According to legend, King Arthur is buried in these hills, but then it seems that King Arthur is buried in many places around Britain. What is not legend is the fact that the Roman governor Agricola established a fortress at Trimontium, at the base of the Eildons, east of Melrose. It is thought that the Romans built a bridge here to carry Dere Street (see Feature "The Cheviot and Dere Street") over the River Tweed and on to Edinburgh. Newstead, a village built partly on the site of the fort, of which nothing remains, claims to be Scotland's oldest continuously inhabited village, going back to the time of the Roman occupation.

Abbotsford stands just outside Melrose to the west, and it was here that Sir Walter Scott spent the last twenty years of his life. He bought the old farm in 1811 and renamed it Abbotsford, because the monks of Melrose Abbey used to ford the river at this point. Scott added an armoury, dining room, study, conservatory and several bedrooms, and in 1822 he demolished the old farmhouse and built what is now the main block of the house. On Scott's death, Abbotsford remained in the family and although still inhabited by his descendants the house may be visited by those interested in the life and times of this notable author.

The central attraction of Melrose is, of course, its abbey, one of four famous Border abbeys, the others being Jedburgh, Kelso and Dryburgh. Early records show that there was a monastery in Old Melrose in the seventh century inhabited by monks who came from Iona via Lindisfarne. The present abbey, said by some to be the most impressive of the Border abbeys, was founded by David I in 1136 for monks from the Cistercian abbey of Rievaulx. Historians suggest that not only did the monks come from Yorkshire, but also the master mason responsible for much of the work at Melrose was a Yorkshire craftsman. In common with the other Border Abbeys, Melrose suffered repeatedly from English attacks. Edward II burnt the abbey in 1322 and Robert the Bruce, whose heart is buried in the abbey, paid for the rebuilding. Richard II virtually destroyed the abbey in 1388 but, as at Jedburgh, it was the infamous Earl of Hertford who in 1545 pillaged and desecrated the abbey to such an extent that it became uninhabitable. By 1570, the ruins had become a handy source of stone for local builders.

Just to the north of the abbey is the Chain Bridge which links Melrose with Gattonside. The bridge, opened in 1826 over the River Tweed, was one of the first suspension bridges in Scotland. Near the bridge is displayed a notice warning that the maximum load on the bridge is eight persons, and that they should refrain from causing the bridge to 'swing'.

Like Jedburgh, Melrose has its festival and 'rides', starting in mid-June. Melrose also has its famous seven-a-side Rugby Football Tournament, held in April each year. Unlike Jedburgh, Melrose no longer plays Handba', but this game (descriptions make it seem more like a war) used to be played here until the town council banned it in 1901.

There are many features of interest for visitors to Melrose, and a walk around the small town is very worthwhile. If you pass the parish kirk take out your compass and compare the cardinal points with the weather-vane on top of the church tower. You will discover that west is opposite north, and south is opposite east. Having navigated all the way from Ashbourne to Melrose, you may have thought that Melrose was in the south-east of Scotland. The people of Melrose know differently, as their weather-vane shows quite plainly that Melrose is in 'west-south' Scotland.

The railway station at Melrose is a grade one listed building, and nowadays serves as a cafe and museum. The tracks are gone and a modern by-pass road has been built where once railway engines used to run. Melrose is a small town, but has a range of accommodation, including a youth hostel. There are shops and banks to replenish your supplies and cash if required. If you are going to proceed on the Southern Upland Way, you will need to make a decision whether to go eastwards to Cockburnspath or westwards to Portpatrick.

Appendix 1: Accommodation

The use of the words "Hotel", "Guest House", "Inn" and "Bed & Breakfast" is not consistent in the various publications. In order to help you ,the authors give below their own definitions so that you can use the Accommodation List wisely.

HOTEL - Accommodation provided with various facilities, which could include en suite toilet/bath/shower, telephone, radio and television etc.
- Will usually have liquor licence and bar(s).
- Breakfast, lunch and dinner available with full restaurant facilities.

AA and RAC hotels have star ratings (maximum five), indicating the level of facilities and services provided - the higher the number of stars, the better the facilities and services. Most hotels will also have an English or Scottish Tourist Board crown classification (maximum six), indicating the level of facilities provided - the higher the number of crowns, the better the facilities.

GUEST HOUSE - Accommodation as hotels. May have 'crown rating'.
- May have liquor licence, (could be for residents only).
- Will serve breakfast but may provide dinner, usually in dining room.

INN - Accommodation as hotels. May have 'star' and/or 'crown' rating.
- Will definitely have liquor licence and bar(s).
- Will serve breakfast and usually lunch/dinner in bar or separate dining area/restaurant.

NOTE! "INN", as shown on the route map, is used generically and does not necessarily imply that accommodation is available.

BED & BREAKFAST - Accommodation usually in a private house and can be quite basic, sharing facilities with other occupants.
- Will not have a liquor licence.
- Will serve breakfast and usually dinner (by arrangement)in domestic dining area, or sometimes in separate guest dining area.

YOUTH HOSTELS - Vary widely from quite basic to almost sumptuous.

INDEPENDENT HOSTELS - Privately run on YHA lines, but with fewer restrictions. Some provide meals.

CAMPING BARN, NATIONAL PARK CAMPING BARN, BUNKHOUSE BARN AND BUNKHOUSE.
All converted buildings. Usually with limited facilities and little or no privacy. The camping barn is often compared to a 'stone tent', but the bunkhouse should be furnished and provide cooking facilities, showers and drying rooms.
NOTE! Some guest houses, B & Bs and bunkhouses may not be open all the year round.

Notes on Accommodation List

The Accommodation List, which does not set out to be comprehensive, comprises towns and villages where accommodation on the route of the APW was known to exist at the time of writing. 'Stage' accommodation is shown in **bold** capitals, whereas 'intermediate' accommodation is shown inset. Some off route accommodation is included and this is show further inset.

Where there was only one example of a particular category of accommodation, this is indicated by the figure '1'. If more than one was known, this is indicated by a tick '√'. (See "Accommodation" for definitions of categories of accommodation.) It should be remembered that some accommodation (for instance B & B), may not be open all the year round.

Walkers of the APW are advised to make use of the many publications listing accommodation in England and Scotland. Tourist Information Centres (TICs) are also a good source of information, and some of them operate a 'Book-A-Bed-Ahead' scheme. TICs, where known, are shown on the list.

ACCOMODATION LIST

	Hotel	Guest house	Inn	B & B	Youth Hostel	Other bunkhouse etc	TIC
ASHBOURNE	√	1	√	√	-	-	1
Dovedale	√	-	-	-	-	-	-
Biggin	-	-	-	1	-	-	-
Middleton	-	-	-	1	-	-	-
YOULGREAVE	1	1	1	√	1	-	-
Bakewell	√	√	√	√	1	-	1
BASLOW	√	-	-	-	-	-	-
Hathersage	√	√	√	√	1	-	-
BAMFORD	√	-	-	√	-	-	-
DUNFORD BRIDGE	1	-	-	-	-	-	-
Holme	1	-	-	-	-	-	-
MARSDEN**	-	1	-	-	-	1	-
(Marsden)	1	-	-	-	-	-	-
Baitings	-	-	1	-	-	-	-
HEBDEN BRIDGE	√	√	√	√	-	-	1
HOWARTH	√	√	√	√	1	-	1
Bingley	-	-	√	-	-	-	-
ILKLEY	√	√	√	√	-	-	1
Bolton Park Farm	-	-	-	1	-	-	-
Barden Tower	-	-	-	-	-	1	-
Appletreewick	-	-	-	√	-	-	-
PATELEY BRIDGE	1	√	1	√	-	-	1
Wath	1	-	-	-	-	-	-
Ramsgill	1	-	-	1	-	-	-
Longside House	-	-	-	1	-	-	-
Lofthouse	-	-	1	-	-	-	-
CARLTON	-	-	1	√	-	-	-

	Hotel	Guest house	Inn	B & B	Youth Hostel	Other bunkhouse etc	TIC
Aysgarth	√	-	-	√	1	-	-
Askrigg	-	-	1	-	-	-	-
Helm	-	-	-	1	-	-	-
HAWES	√	√	√	√	1	-	1*
Thrang	-	1	-	-	-	-	-
Outhgill	-	1	-	-	-	-	-
KIRKBY STEPHEN	√	1	√	√	1	-	1*
Asby Grange Farm	-	-	-	1	-	-	-
APPLEBY	√	√	√	√	-	-	1
DUFTON	-	-	-	√	1	-	-
Garrigill	-	-	1	√	-	-	-
NENTHEAD	-	-	√	-	-	-	-
Ninebanks	-	-	-	-	1	-	-
ALLENDALE TOWN	√	√	√	√	-	-	-
HALTWHISTLE	√	1	√	√	-	-	1*
Green	-	-	-	-	-	1	-
Stannersburn	-	-	1	-	-	-	-
FALSTONE	-	-	1	-	-	-	-
Yarrow	-	-	-	1	-	-	-
BYRNESS	1	-	-	-	1	-	-
2km SE	-	-	-	1	-	-	-
JEDBURGH	√	√	√	√	-	-	1
MELROSE	√	√	√	√	1	-	1*

*Not open all year round

MARSDEN ** The guesthouse/bunkhouse are on the same premises at 041103. The hotel is at 031128.

Appendix 2: Rights of Way

All walkers will be familiar with the term 'rights of way', but how often have you found that a right of way indicated on an Ordnance Survey map does not actually exist on the ground? That, of course, could be due to the path being little used, or never used until you came along. More importantly, how often have you found a right of way obstructed? - many times we suspect.

England and Wales have 174,000 kilometres of public footpaths and 43,500 kilometres of bridleways and unsurfaced roads. On footpaths there is a right of passage on foot only, whereas on bridleways there is right of passage on foot, horseback and pedal cycle. A recent study, carried out by the Countryside Commission, discovered that 60 percent of paths were not signposted but, even if you did manage to find the path, there is a 60 percent chance of it being obstructed by difficult-to-use or closed stiles, for instance. If you negotiate these obstructions, then there is a 70 percent chance of finding the path closed due to 'agriculture'.

So, what are the laws relating to rights of way? Well, a public right of way is a way over which the public has a right to pass and repass. Rights of way usually refer to unsurfaced tracks or paths and both are highways, just like the A5 or the M1. Local authorities have a duty to prepare definitive maps of all rights of way within their boundaries and, if a right of way is shown on a definitive map, then the public has a right to walk on it. Ordnance Survey maps also show rights of way but remember that, even though OS does its best, the map may be inaccurate or simply out of date. All rights of way must be signposted where they meet metalled roads, and local authorities have powers to waymark paths along their route. Local authorities are responsible for maintaining the surface of paths (including bridges), but stiles and gates are the landowner's or farmer's responsibility.

It is illegal for anyone to obstruct a right of way, for example with barbed wire, and it is the duty of the landowner or farmer to see that any such obstruction is removed. If a highway you are using properly is obstructed, you may remove just enough of the obstruction to allow you to pass. But you must be careful and do the minimum of damage to the obstruction. If the path really is impassable, you are entitled to pass around the obstruction and deviate from the highway. However, if your deviation takes you onto land belonging to someone other than the person responsible for the obstruction, you may be trespassing.

A farmer may plough across a field path but should make good its surface within two weeks, and paths running around the edges of fields should never be ploughed. Legally, by the way, if a right of way is shown across a cultivated field, then you have the right to walk through whatever crop is planted. That, of course, has its problems, as anyone who has tried to walk through a crop of wheat, barley, or worse still oilseed rape, will know. If a crop itself constitutes an impenetrable obstruction, you will have no option but to try to (legally) walk around it.

Another sort of path, not found on older OS maps, is the permissive path. On more recent OS publications, some of these are marked and coloured orange. In England, Scotland and Wales, permissive paths are linear routes which do not have the same legal status as rights of way, but the landowners have agreed to allow the public to use the paths, whilst not allowing them to become formal rights of way.

The laws regarding rights of way in Scotland are different from those in England. The OS shows no rights of way on maps in Scotland, but there is a de facto right to wander in the hills and mountains at will. You are, of course, prohibited from entering certain areas for security or safety reasons, and these reasons must be respected. It is rare for Scottish landowners to have confrontations with hill walkers, but siting caravans or camping without permission may constitute an offence. There are, however, increasing threats to the de facto access that is enjoyed by walkers in the Scottish hills. More and more estates are being bought by incomers, as financial investments. The access rights of ordinary people may, in some circumstances, be threatened, but let us hope that in the main we may continue to wander the hills of Scotland with the freedom that we have enjoyed for many years.

During the course of our walking life, we have come across all the problems mentioned above and many more: stiles obstructed by barbed wire, or removed altogether, paths not restored across cultivated fields, paths not signed at the roadside and certainly not waymarked in fields and farmyards etc. On this walk we have done our best to avoid all obstructed rights of way and we have sometimes used permissive paths. We feel that this approach makes for easier walking and, after all, who wants to climb over a barbed wire obstruction or negotiate a dry stone wall with the stile stones removed, when one is carrying a rucksack, it's raining and it's getting to the end of an arduous day? - we don't.

Appendix 3: Useful Addresses

Backpackers Club,
PO Box 381,
7/10 Friar Street,
Reading,
Berks RG3 4RL
(04917 739)

British Tourist Authority,
12 Regent Street,
London SW1Y
(071 730 3400)

Camping & Caravan Club,
Greenfields House,
Westwood Way,
Coventry CV4 8JH
(0203 694995)

English Heritage,
Fortress House,
23 Saville Row,
London W1X
(071 973 3000)

English Tourist Board,
Thames Tower,
Black's Road,
Hammersmith,
London W6 9EL
(081 846 9000)

Farm Holiday Bureau,
National Agricultural Centre,
Stoneleigh,
Kenilworth,
Warwickshire CV8 2LZ
(0203 696969)

Forestry Commission,
Corstophine Road,
Edinburgh EH12 7AT
(031 334 0303)

F,C, Kielder Forest District,
Eals Burn,
Bellingham,
Hexham,
Northumberland NE8 2AJ
(0434 220242)

National Trust
36 Queen Anne's Gate,
London SW1H 9AS
(071 222 9251)

National Trust Scotland,
5 Charlotte Square,
Edinburgh EH2 4DU
(031 226 5922)

North York Moors National Park,
The Old Vicarage,
Bondgate, Helmsley,
N Yorks YO6 5BP
(0439 70657)

Northumberland National Park,
Eastburn,
South Park, Hexham,
Northumberland NE46 1BS
(0434 605555)

Ordnance Survey,
Romsey Road,
Maybush,
Southampton,
Hants SO9 4DH
(0703 792000)

Peak District National Park,
National Park Office,
Baslow Road,
Bakewell,
Derbyshire DE4 1AE
(0629 814321)

Ramblers' Association,
1/5 Wandsworth Road,
London SW8 2XX
(071 582 6878)

Scottish Tourist Board,
23 Ravelston Terrace,
Edinburgh EH4 3EU
(031 332 2433)

Scottish YHA,
7 Glebe Crescent,
Stirling FK8 2JA
(0786 51181)

YHA,
Trevelyan House,
St Albans,
Herts AL1 2DY
(0727 55215)

Yorkshire Dales National Park,
Colvend,
Hebden Road,
Grassington,
Skipton,
N Yorks BD23 5LB
(0756 752748)

Melrose Abbey

Appendix 4: Relevant OS Maps

Landranger (1:50,000)

119	-	Buxton, Matlock & Dovedale Area
110	-	Sheffield and Huddersfield
104	-	Leeds and Bradford
99	-	Northallerton and Surrounding Area
98	-	Wensleydale and Upper Wharfedale
91	-	Appleby-in-Westmorland
87	-	Hexham, Haltwhistle and Surrounding Area
80	-	Cheviot Hills and the Kielder Forest Area
74	-	Kelso and Surrounding Area

Outdoor Leisure (1:25,000)

24	-	The Peak District (White Peak Area)
1	-	The Peak District (Dark Peak Area)
21	-	South Pennines
30	-	Yorkshire Dales (North and Central Area)

Bibliography

From the many reference and other books constantly used during the preparation of this publication, the authors would, in particular, like to record the following:-

Bolton G.D. *Yorkshire Revealed* Oliver and Boyd. 1955

Breeze D.J. *Hadrian's Wall* English Heritage. 1989

Christian R. *The Peak District* David & Charles Inc. 1976

Ffinch M. *Portrait of the Howgills and the Upper Eden Valley* Rober Hale Ltd. 1982

Hadfield J. (Ed) *The Shell Book of English Villages* Michael Joseph Ltd. 1980

Hamey L.J. & J.A. *The Roman Engineers* Cambridge University Press. 1990

Harrington E. *The Meaning of English Place Names* The Blackstaff Press Ltd. 1984

Hartley M. & Ingilby J. *Life and Tradition in the Yorkshire Dales* J.M.Dent & Sons Ltd. 1968

Hartley M. & Ingilby J. *Life and Tradition in West Yorkshire* J.M.Dent & Sons Ltd. 1976

Hartley M. & Ingilby J. *The Yorkshire Dales* J.M.Dent & Sons Ltd. 1963

Holt G.O. *A Regional History of the Railways of Great Britain Vol 10* David & Charles Plc. 1986

Macnie D.L. (Ed) *The New Shell Guide to Scotland* Ebury Press. 1977

Mantell K.H. et al. *Illustrated Survey and Guide Hadrian's Wall* English Life Publications Ltd. 1964

Merrill J.N. *Peak District A to Z* Dalesman Books. 1976

Raistrick A. *The Pennine Dales* Eyre & Spottiswood. 1968

Raistrick A. *Old Yorkshire Dales* Pan Books. 1967

Raistrick A. *Quakers in Science and Industry* The Bannisdale Press. 1950

Raistrick A. & Jennings B. *A History of Lead Mining in the Pennines*
    Longmans. 1965

Reaney P.H. *The Origin of English Place Names* Routledge & Kegan Paul
    Ltd. 1977

Rolt L.T.C. *The Inland Waterways of England* George Allen & Unwin Ltd.
    1979

Russell R. *Lost Canals & Waterways of Britain* David & Charles. 1982

Smith R. *A Visitors Guide to the Scottish Borders and Edinburgh*
    Moorland Publishing. 1983

Speakman C. *The Dales Way* Dalesman Publishing Co Ltd. 1970

Speakman C. *Transport in Yorkshire* Dalesman Publishing Co Ltd. 1969

Thomas L. *The Hidden Places of Britain* Arlington Books. 1981

Tomes J. *Blue Guide to Scotland* A & G Black. 1980

Trueman A.E. *Geology and Scenery in England and Wales* Penguin Books.
    1949

Wainwright A. *A Coast to Coast Walk* Westmorland Gazette. 1972

Wainwright A. *A Pennine Way Companion* Westmorland Gazette. 1968

Whitehead L.B. *Bygone Marsden* Privately Published. 1942

Wilson K. & Leathart S. (Ed) *The Kielder Forests* Forestry Commission. 1982

Wood C.H. (Ed) *Chatsworth* Derbyshire Countryside Ltd. 1975

Woodhead T.W. *A History of the Huddersfield Water Supplies*
    Tolson Memorial Museum. 1939

In addition, many town guides, tourist guides and brochures were read. Our appreciation goes to all the (often anonymous) authors and publishers who compiled them.

* * *

CICERONE GUIDES

Cicerone publish a wide range of reliable guides to walking and climbing in Britain - and other general interest books

LAKE DISTRICT - General Books
LAKELAND VILLAGES
WORDSWORTH'S DUDDON REVISITED
THE REGATTA MEN
REFLECTIONS ON THE LAKES
OUR CUMBRIA
PETTIE
THE HIGH FELLS OF LAKELAND
CONISTON COPPER A History
LAKELAND - A taste to remember (Recipes)
THE LOST RESORT?
CHRONICLES OF MILNTHORPE
LOST LANCASHIRE

LAKE DISTRICT - Guide Books
CASTLES IN CUMBRIA
WESTMORLAND HERITAGE WALK
IN SEARCH OF WESTMORLAND
CONISTON COPPER MINES
SCRAMBLES IN THE LAKE DISTRICT
MORE SCRAMBLES IN THE LAKE DISTRICT
WINTER CLIMBS IN THE LAKE DISTRICT
WALKS IN SILVERDALE/ARNSIDE
BIRDS OF MORECAMBE BAY
THE EDEN WAY

NORTHERN ENGLAND (outside the Lakes
THE YORKSHIRE DALES A walker's guide
WALKING IN THE SOUTH PENNINES
LAUGHS ALONG THE PENNINE WAY
WALKS IN THE YORKSHIRE DALES (3 VOL)
WALKS TO YORKSHIRE WATERFALLS
NORTH YORK MOORS Walks
THE CLEVELAND WAY & MISSING LINK
DOUGLAS VALLEY WAY
THE RIBBLE WAY
WALKING NORTHERN RAILWAYS EAST
WALKING NORTHERN RAILWAYS WEST
HERITAGE TRAILS IN NW ENGLAND
BIRDWATCHING ON MERSEYSIDE
THE LANCASTER CANAL
FIELD EXCURSIONS IN NW ENGLAND
ROCK CLIMBS LANCASHIRE & NW
THE ISLE OF MAN COASTAL PATH

DERBYSHIRE & EAST MIDLANDS
WHITE PEAK WALKS - 2 Vols
HIGH PEAK WALKS
WHITE PEAK WAY
KINDER LOG
THE VIKING WAY
THE DEVIL'S MILL (Novel)
WHISTLING CLOUGH (Novel)
WALES & WEST MIDLANDS
THE RIDGES OF SNOWDONIA
HILLWALKING IN SNOWDONIA
ASCENT OF SNOWDON
WELSH WINTER CLIMBS
SNOWDONIA WHITE WATER SEA & SURF
SCRAMBLES IN SNOWDONIA
ROCK CLIMBS IN WEST MIDLANDS
THE SHROPSHIRE HILLS A Walker's Guide

SOUTH & SOUTH WEST ENGLAND
WALKS IN KENT
THE WEALDWAY & VANGUARD WAY
SOUTH DOWNS WAY & DOWNS LINK
COTSWOLD WAY
WALKING ON DARTMOOR
SOUTH WEST WAY - 2 Vol

SCOTLAND
SCRAMBLES IN LOCHABER
SCRAMBLES IN SKYE
THE ISLAND OF RHUM
CAIRNGORMS WINTER CLIMBS
WINTER CLIMBS BEN NEVIS & GLENCOE
SCOTTISH RAILWAY WALKS
TORRIDON A Walker's Guide
SKI TOURING IN SCOTLAND

THE MOUNTAINS OF ENGLAND & WALES
VOL 1 WALES
VOL 2 ENGLAND

*Also a full range of guidebooks
to walking, scrambling, ice-climbing,
rock climbing, and other adventurous
pursuits in Europe*

---

*Other guides are constantly being added to the Cicerone List.
Available from bookshops, outdoor equipment shops or direct (send for price list)
from CICERONE, 2 POLICE SQUARE, MILNTHORPE, CUMBRIA, LA7 7PY*

MOUNTAIN

Still the Definitive International Magazine for Mountaineers and Rock Climbers.

Mountain is published six times a year: January, March, May, July, September, and November and is available from specialist retailers throughout Britain and the world. Subscriptions and back issues are available from Mountain Magazine Limited, Globe Works, Penistone Rd., Sheffield, S6 3AE. Tel: 0742-922340 Fax: 0742-820016

Maps based on Ordnance Survey maps with the permission of the Controller of Her Majesty's Stationery Office Crown copyright reserved

Front cover: Descending Rombald's Moor to White Wells and Ilkley Photo: Walt Unsworth

IF YOU LIKE ADVENTUROUS ACTIVITIES ON MOUNTAINS OR HILLS YOU WILL ENJOY READING:

CLIMBER
AND HILLWALKER

MOUNTAINEERING/HILLWALKING/TREKKING ROCK CLIMBING/SCRAMBLING IN BRITAIN AND ABROAD

AVAILABLE FROM NEWSAGENTS, OUTDOOR EQUIPMENT SHOPS, OR BY SUBSCRIPTION (6-12 MONTHS) FROM OUTRAM MAGAZINES, THE PLAZA TOWER, EAST KILBRIDE, GLASGOW G74 1LW

THE WALKERS' MAGAZINE

the great OUTDOORS

COMPULSIVE MONTHLY READING FOR ANYONE INTERESTED IN WALKING

AVAILABLE FROM NEWSAGENTS, OUTDOOR EQUIPMENT SHOPS, OR BY SUBSCRIPTION (6-12 MONTHS) FROM OUTRAM MAGAZINES, THE PLAZA TOWER, EAST KILBRIDE, GLASGOW G74 1LW

Printed by
Carnmor Print & Design, London Road, Preston